CROSSING CALIFORNIA

A Cultural Topography of a Land of Wonder and Weirdness

Sam McManis

CRAVEN STREET

B O O K S

Fresno, California

These stories originally appeared, in different forms,
in the *Sacramento Bee*.

All photos by Sam McManis. All photos originally appeared in the
Sacramento Bee and appear here courtesy of the *Sacramento Bee,*

Cover design by Dominic Grijalva

Published by Craven Street Books
An imprint of Linden Publishing
2006 South Mary Street, Fresno, California 93721
(559) 233-6633 / (800) 345-4447
CravenStreetBooks.com

Craven Street Books and Colophon are trademarks of
Linden Publishing, Inc.

ISBN 978-1-61035-313-7

135798642
Printed in the United States of America
on acid-free paper.

Library of Congress Cataloging-in-Publication Data on file.

For Beth, and for my mother

Contents

Introduction

I was tired, bone tired. Not the kind of tired that is of the Man-I-Really-Worked-My-Tush-Off-Punching-the-Clock variety, or even the soporific blahs that come from sheer unadulterated boredom, and certainly not the type of tired that involves actual physical exertion of, say, a running a marathon or scaling Half Dome.

No, this was a specific kind of tired known, at least to me, as California Freeway Ennui. I had just concluded yet another weeklong sortie into the wilds of California. I'd visited deserts high and low, a traffic-choked metropolis, a few one-pump-of-the-brake-pedal towns, a mountain retreat and a seaside highway. I'd even traversed a dusty trail to the summit of Mount Wilson, where, if you squinted real hard and engaged in selective observation, you might forget you're still in Los Angeles, where even after all these years the air is opaque and palpable.

Weary as I may have been, longing to just set cruise control and zone out on Interstate 5 back to my Northern California home, I had one last mission to complete: to stand in the center, the dead geographic center, of the state. It was stupid and sentimental and probably would be a colossal disappointment, but so be it. I had seemingly been everywhere else in California, all four corners and many pit stops in between, but had always put off this side trip, mostly because it was so far afield—about 7 miles south of North Fork in the Sierra Nevada foothills, where pine and oak battle for arboristic supremacy and where a gas station is as hard to find as an extinct grizzly—and I had always quasi-scheduled it on the return trip from a Southern California sojourn. Something always came up. I'd be barreling down the Grapevine, that asphalt DMZ that separates SoCal from the Central Valley, where you can view miles of flat agriculture land straight ahead on I-5 and look east and see the Sierra range from the Highway 99 route. Inevitably, I'd think up excuses not to veer right. It was either the wrong time of year and snow would be obscuring the center-of-California marker said to be put there by proud Sierra dwellers, or ominous summer thunder clouds would loom over the range, or I was losing the light and the prudent thing would be to put it off to another time.

This time, I remained vigilant and veered right onto 99. No more excuses. The center of California, and the enlightenment that I surely thought would come to me there, awaited. I followed the GPS (which, in the foothills, I like to think stands for Giving Poor Service) directions exactly as plotted. Naturally, I got lost. I had gone 7.1 miles beyond North Fork, as directed. I had seen that the highway, which changed names several times, had turned into Italian Bar Road, which was right on course. I had passed the U.S. Forest Service office, another marker. But now I found myself whizzing by a sign welcoming me to Fresno County—decidedly not my destination.

Lost, I tell you. Hopelessly lost. Donner Party lost.

As I pulled over to the soft shoulder to regain my bearings—and fret about the mere quarter tank of gas I had remaining—my smartphone was dumbstruck: "No service." I put my head against the steering wheel, ready to bag the whole idea, which was flawed from the start, anyway.

Then it hit me: How futile even to try to get to the center of California, either literally or figuratively. It may exist on some brass marker set in stone on some nondescript hillside, but what does that have to do with trying to find the real heart of the state, to understand the inner core of California's being, to, in the callow words of the New Agey folks I encountered so many times in my travels, center one's self?

Enough. I turned the car around and headed back.

So, sorry to disappoint those who embrace cliché, those who find comfort in easy categorization and a sense of order in the reinforcement of hoary stereotypes, but there is no one California. No such thing as a typical Californian, either. Nope. Nada. Doesn't exist.

My fellow media mavens lie—or maybe just lazily exaggerate to avoid diligent sussing out such inconvenient things as facts or nuanced stories—when defining California as "where all the fruits and nuts are on the Left Coast." Many a comedian, lo these many years at your local Laff Factory, has made a decent living skewering wacky Left Coasters. They do it because that's what people want or expect to hear; that's where the punch lines reside. Whether it be from jealousy (the mild weather, the gorgeous terrain) or insecurity (those Hollywood elite "Beautiful People," with their hard bodies and smooth Botoxed visages, and those equally hardy, healthy NorCal outdoorsy types), they want to believe that Californians just aren't authentically American, that they do not possess values of the heartland, that they will not let pass through their artificially plumped lips anything foodstuff not organic, vegan, macrobiotic, locavore and artisan crafted, that they would, as with their extreme opposites in Texas, secede from the Union in a heartbeat if they could.

But I'm here to tell you that it's just not so. Some of the most conservative, antigovernment, scarlet-necked shit kickers I've encountered reside along the Interstate 5 corridor north of Sacramento and on up to the state line. And, by contrast, some of the crunchiest, patchouli-scented neo-hippie slackers call Austin, Texas, home, even after the South by Southwest carnival packs its tents and moves on. So, like, go figure.

True story, one that says it all about the hearts, minds and lower intestines of a bifurcated (or maybe just bipolar) Californian: In late 2015, I saw an SUV—do note, a hybrid SUV—careening down Interstate 5 in the San Fernando Valley with an "I'm Ready for Hillary" sticker on the left back bumper and a "TrustTed" sticker, as in Texas Sen. Ted Cruz, on the right bumper. As if that wasn't confusing enough, a window sticker proclaimed, "Deer: The Other Red Meat," contrasted with the license-plate holder boasting, "This Car Stops for Broccoli." I sped up, changed lanes like a madman, to catch a glimpse of the driver, but he or she hit the gas and took off before the inevitable freeway gridlock near Burbank.

Little matter, nothing surprises me anymore. It could've been an Asian American skinhead with septum piercings listening to Joni Mitchell while sipping boba tea, or a trustafarian white girl whose vaping mist enveloped her Native American dream catcher dangling from the rearview mirror while cranking up the Toby Keith on the radio.

Believe me, I've been up and down California, traversed much of its 163,696 square miles by car, foot, train, bike, bladder-jarring jeep, Greyhound and recalcitrant horse. I've roamed from the pine-scented forests of Del Norte County to the fragrant sage scrub of Imperial County; from the otherworldly starkness of Mono Lake to the crashing waves along the Lost Coast. I've stalked the tony aisles of the newly minted Broad Museum in gentrified downtown Los Angeles, and quick-footed it through the International Banana Museum along the desiccated shores of the moonscaped Salton Sea. I've inadvertently gotten my car stuck in a tree at a cheesy "drive-thru" giant sequoia roadside attraction along the hemp highway between Mendocino and Humboldt, and witnessed, with both fascination and can't-look-away horror, grown men and women, sans children and sans inhibitions, belt out full-throated versions of "Let It Go" at a Disneyland sing-along.

As Neil Young warbled, "I've been to Hollywood, I've been to Redwood." He, of course, was seeking a heart of gold; I merely sought to make sense of my home state, its quirks and contradictions, its character and characters, its inner core and surface facade, the "there" that crabby old Gertrude Stein insisted wasn't there when she ventured back to her native Oakland from her Paris salon.

California contains multitudes, all right, and that's not just a reference to the 38.8 million calling the state home. Its strength, and intrigue, lie in its diversity. Not just a diversity categorized by race or ethnicity or even bank balance. At first blush, you may think otherwise, but there is a slippery but tenable commonality between the rancher in Fresno and the surfer in Hermosa; the bearded-hipster techie in San Francisco's scruffily fancy Mission District and the fresh-faced Knott's Berry Farm "team member" in sanitized Orange County; the creationist zealot awaiting the rapture on the parched plains of inland San Diego County and the neo-hippie nudist awaiting enlightenment through chakra clearing in the lush hills of Mendocino County.

It is a testament to the geographic and cultural ties that bind the state that these disparate spirits can live in (relative) harmony or, at least, without killing each other—yet.

In my five years on the road, I met a Kerouacian cast of characters that could serve you well if you ever decided that famous book needed a sequel.

I think of Monty Patterson, the adrenaline-junkie mountain biker-slash-shuttle driver with the backward Pabst Blue Ribbon ball cap, who entertained a van full of hikers, runners and mountain bikers with tales of derring-do on Tahoe's famous and infamously narrow Flume Trail.

I think of the wry and sly presentation of Liz Michaud, a guide for an outfit that provides Segway tours of the touristy Fisherman's Wharf, completely composed weaving in and out of San Francisco noonday traffic.

Or astronomer Dennis Mammana, geeking out to the max while jabbing a laser pointer at the inky darkness of Anza-Borrego Desert State Park and nattering on about the Double Cluster of Perseus or something while we craned our necks and gawked and coyotes yipped in the distance.

Or the three old-timers I shared a Sunday brunch with at the Samoa Cookhouse, a 119-year-old former logging cafeteria hugging the shore west of Arcata in the far north-west of the state. These guys, septuagenarians all, regaled outsiders at the family-style restaurant by tossing around stories about the old days while tossing back stack-after-stack of flapjacks and mounds of scrambled eggs, their ethos being, "Eat and eat and keep eating until you can't do it anymore."

Oh, the strange and ineffable things I have seen. They have run the gamut of sensory experiences. I have taken a vow of silence at a meditation retreat in the foothills north of Nevada City, and laughed on command as part of a studio audience at a TV sitcom taping. I've snowshoed under a full moon in Lake Tahoe, communed with cacti at Joshua Tree. I have stalked celebrities on a TMZ tour of Hollywood, dropped faux "acid" on the Magic Bus tour of Haight-Ashbury, nursed my inner guitar hero at the Fender factory tour in Corona, lurked during a tarantula peep show during mating season on Mount Diablo.

To truly be a Californian, rather than just being a resident, is to recognize the state's ambiguities and inherent contradictions. It's best if you can get out and explore beyond the confines of your personal fiefdom, embed yourself among the state's many warring factions: West LAers versus San Fernando Valleyites; San Franciscans versus Silicon Valleyites; Humboldt growers versus Central Valley farmers; Telecaster-wielding Bakersfield country dandies in nudie suits with whiskey-soaked croaks versus post-punk nihilists in Oakland to whom harmony and melody are anathema and attitude is everything.

Consider me, then, the village explainer. Like most people in the state, I'm not a native Californian. Everyone has come from somewhere else, eternal Gold Rushers. But that, in a way, makes me typical and, perhaps, perfectly suited to the task. I arrived here early enough—preschool years—not to have been exposed to another milieu outside the Golden State. And, since my father was a salesman who, like a minor chess piece, was always being moved from one "regional office" to another, I was peripatetic enough to live in many different Californias. I "graduated" from kindergarten in Danville, the monied Bay Area suburb in the shadow of Mount Diablo, came of age in the suburban sprawl of inland Orange County, inland San Diego County and inland Ventura County—"inland" being something of a code word for lower-rent districts—escaped to Los Angeles County's gloriously briny ocean-aired South Bay as a young adult, then migrated northward to the Bay Area and Sacramento (with a two-year interregnum in Washington state; long story, don't ask) to rear my brood.

I might have been yet another well-traveled Californian who dwelt only among my immediate geographic tribe had it not been for an editor whose ulterior motivation (or so I expect, though to this day she denies it) was to get me as far away from the *Sacramento Bee* office that the travel budget allowed. This redheaded demon, in cahoots with the Richard Lewis-lookalike managing editor, hatched a newspaper section called "California Traveler" and armed me with a corporate credit card, the company's hybrid Honda Civic and a rather too-hard slap on the back before sending me careening down the road for five years, the sole mandate being to scope out interesting people and places and "fer Gawd's sake make it interesting, will ya?" Another mandate, which extends to this book, is that its examination of California is entirely anecdotal. You won't be getting much, if any, census data thrown at you, no learned, chin-pulling analysis from sociologists, sure as heck no blatant political rants or dogmatic agenda-setting. Leave that for the pundits.

A friend, sensing the vastness and vagueness of my undertaking, gave me as a parting gift what used to be called by old fogeys a "mixtape" but now is perhaps a "personalized playlist" or "Spotify channel," featuring songs about California. I'm not sure of the parameters for inclusion, but it seemed that either California had to be in the song's title or its cities, towns or geographic features had to play a significant part in the lyrical narrative.

It was the perfect road-trip present, at once evoking that Kerouacian mood, a John Muirish sense of time and place, a Twain-like Gold Rush feeling and a gritty NWA street vibe. Plus, so many California musical paeans have been penned that a complete playlist, I shit you not, easily could last the entire 796.4 miles from the Oregon border to the Mexican border.

Wikipedia tells me that there are 96 different songs named, simply, "California," from such diverse artists as Lenny Kravitz to Debby Boone. Artists tend to obsess over the weather—"California Rain" (The Rescues), "California Snow" (Tom Russell), "California Sun" (Gin Blossoms), "California Zephyr" (Jay Farrar), "California Sunshine" (The Game)—or the outrageously high cost-of-living—"House in California" (Keb Mo)—or the earthquake threats—"San Andreas Fault" (Natalie Merchant). You'll hear sentimental slop from Al Jolson ("California Here I Come") and barely contained bile from The Presidents of the United States of America ("F*** California").

I thought, maybe every state evokes such passions. Maybe I had overestimated California's fascination among the citizenry, pictured it like that old *New Yorker* magazine cover that showed Manhattan as the center of the universe and New Jersey and the rest of the U.S. as mere specks on the horizon. But when I searched for songs about, oh, I don't know, Ohio, only 31 popped up . . . and several were cover versions of Crosby, Stills, Nash & Young's indictment of the Kent State shootings.

Yes, there was no doubt that something about California inspires—and maybe infuriates. My mission was to find out what that something was. The AUX cable was plugged into my iPhone playlist, the company hybrid Honda had a full tank of gas and I was off. Didn't matter which direction I headed—the mountains, beach, valley, desert or even the exact geographic center—a different California awaited wherever I ended up.

I never did, by the way, make it to the center south of North Fork. If you ever find it, let me know what it's like.

1

Desert Dwellers

"If it gets much hotter," he muttered, wringing the sweat from his thick fell of hair and mustache, "if it gets much hotter, I don't know what I'll do."
—Frank Norris, *McTeague*

Always blame conditions, not men.
—Norris, *The Octopus*

The Center of the World

March 2015
Town: Felicity
County: Imperial
Population: 2
Elevation: 285 feet

Empires rise and fall, whole civilizations flourish and fade, great mountain ranges erode over time, so only a fool deluded by hubris would be presumptuous enough to believe he has created something of permanence.

And Jacques-André Istel may be many things—thinker, autodidactic student of history, mayor-for-life, former stock analyst, parachute designer, recall candidate for governor in 2003, loving husband—but he's certainly no fool. But, for the sake of argument, let's say you wanted to erect an elaborate, lasting monument of and for humankind, firm of foundation and with the solidity and mass to repel the elements. What material would you choose?

Istel's answer: granite.

His art installation-cum-museum, straightforwardly called Museum of History in Granite, lies along a particularly arid stretch of Imperial County, just off Interstate 8.

Imperial may just be the most schizophrenic of California's 52 counties, at once hotter than Hades and Dust Bowl parched, but it also is one of the state's most productive agricultural regions. If you've eaten spinach, most likely it was grown either in Imperial County or in the so-called salad bowl of Salinas in San Luis Obispo County. Salinas makes sense, given its location in the Central Valley's rich ag plains. But Imperial? Well, you think no way even a tumbleweed could grow here—until you venture closer and closer to the Arizona state line. Then, it all makes sense. You hit the Colorado River, which flows by right at the state line, much of its precious water siphoned off to irrigate the alfalfa fields and spinach patches on the California side, though the Arizonan metropolis of Yuma sucks up its share as well.

There really is not much reason for anyone other than farmers and cheap roadside motel and convenience-store operators to set down roots in this southeasternmost sector of the state, though it does get its share of the tourist dollar from the ATV enthusiasts carving up the sublime beauty of the Algodones Dunes with heroin-like tracks.

A more remote place, then, could hardly be found for a dreamer such as Istel to plant his flag and deem the site his life's work in what has been a very full life, the Center of the World. Spread over 2,600 acres, 922 granite panels are set 3 feet into the ground with reinforced concrete and rise about 5 feet in geometric patterns, weighing, by Istel's calculation, 4,865,378 pounds. Engraved on most of the surfaces—the project is ongoing and also includes a pyramid and a church on a man-made hill—is nothing less than the history of the universe, from the Big Bang and Genesis to the invention of the TV remote control, replete with timelines, reproduced etchings of great artworks and what Istel deems epoch-making events.

So, if this was your all-consuming undertaking, wouldn't you, too, opt for a rock of such substance?

"It is intriguing in the digital age, writing in granite," Istel muses in his upstairs office just to the east of the monument. He is in his late 80s but sports the wiry body of the extreme-sport parachutist he was as a younger man and the keen mind of a born promoter. "An atomic explosion can wipe out the (Internet) cloud (storage system) and cause a certain amount of embarrassment. But this'll be here. It'll stay."

Then, he paused and raised an index finger. He acknowledged the museum's impermanence with a sly smile. "I'm asked, 'What about a major earthquake burying it?'" Istel said. "I have a very good answer for them. It's this: Think how happy future archaeologists will be with the rubble!"

Istel refrained from laughing at his own witticism. You can tell, by his smooth delivery, that this is not the first time he's used that line. He's well-accustomed to entertaining the press and telling the story of the museum, the town on which it sits and his adventuresome life and times that, if Hollywood bigwigs had any sense, it would be made into a biopic starring George Clooney or somebody equally as dashing.

Actually, volumes could be written about Istel's life, but since he wants you to focus on the museum, this will have to do in terms of background:

Son of a distinguished financier who was a confidant to Charles de Gaulle, Jacques and his family fled France after the Nazi occupation, arriving in New York in 1940, whereupon he hitchhiked across the country before heading back East to attend Princeton. After an eventual stint in the Marine Corps and a dull stretch as a Wall Street analyst, Istel circumnavigated the earth in a twin-engine plane. He then parlayed his love of flying and skydiving to open three parachuting schools and develop a modern parachute in 1957. *Sports Illustrated* profiled him, and he ended up marrying the writer, Felicia Lee. A few years later, he bought some land in the California desert, which sat fallow for decades.

Then, in the mid-1980s, he turned that parcel of land into a town named for his wife, Felicity, became its mayor in a landslide victory (with both ballots counted) and set about turning the beige landscape into something memorable and, yes, lasting.

At the south end of "town" he built a 20-foot marble-and-glass pyramid that he cheekily called the Center of the World and at the "north" end a church called the Chapel on the Hill, having employed men in bulldozers to move 150,000 tons of dirt to create the hillock. Standing as a sentinel, 25 feet high, at the entrance is part of the original Eiffel Tower, a nod to Istel's Gallic roots.

"Jacques saw they were auctioning it off and wanted it as a souvenir of his childhood," said Felicia, who runs the gift shop, serves as docent and even rents out a few rooms to travelers when she's not using her journalistic background to help her husband methodically etch history in slabs of granite for posterity.

But Istel doesn't like anyone to dwell too much on that whole "Center of the World" hooey, thinking it detracts from the serious work of the granite panels of history. In fact, Istel wrote a scathing letter to the *New York Times Magazine* because, in an otherwise laudatory 4,000-word profile of him in 2014, it detailed the pyramid and, in Istel's estimation, "relegated a fine museum to a roadside attraction."

Istel is serious about his scholarship, all right, and mentions several times that he does not advertise his site, though visitors are welcome. Felicia, it seems, has few qualms about having a little fun with the, in her words, "whimsical" pyramid. She takes you inside the pyramid and stops in front of a circular brass plaque embedded in the marble floor, saying "Official Center of the World." She takes your picture standing on it and then hands you a certificate authenticating that you stood at the "center of the world." Said Felicia: "Really, the center is wherever you are at any time, but we got the (Imperial County) Board of Supervisors to make it official."

But enough about that, for fear of incurring Jacques' written wrath. The historical slabs of granite are what matters, he insists. It's his life's work to chisel history (he actually hires artisans to do the installation and etching), trying to explain the world in all its complexity to future generations. He considers himself a discerning editor and writes the text himself, Felicia doing the proofreading—important to have no typos when putting text into granite. There's a wall dedicated to the state of Arizona, another about California, which was dedicated in March 2016. Istel proudly shows letters of congratulation from dignitaries, including recent missives from Arizona Gov. Doug Ducey and University of California system President Janet Napolitano.

A 60-panel *History of the United States* was dedicated in February 2014 in a ceremony that included a Marine color guard, the U.S. flag arriving by parachutist and the ringing of a half-to-scale copy of the Liberty Bell. As big an accomplishment as that was, it pales compared to the ongoing 461-panel *History of Humanity*, about 30 percent completed, from the dawn of time to the Battle of Hastings in 1066.

Lots of history remains. How does Istel decide what to leave in, what to take out?

"You put your finger on the difficult job we've had," he said. "Remember, I'm not a historian, although modestly speaking, I've now published three books of history. Call me a half-assed historian. When I started *History of Humanity*, we took three immense books, all 1,200 to 1,500 pages, one translated from German, one in French and one in English. I took the number of pages, by average, they allocated to each segment of history and then applied that percentage to my 400 or so panels."

Yes, but by what criteria does he decide an event is worthy enough to be etched in granite?

"The only answer I can give you is, one does the best one can," he said. "Look, when I did the history of the U.S., you have to treat certain subjects whether you want to or not. Watergate. Civil rights. Sports. Food. I got a great quote on the American food and beverage panel. It's from (humorist) James Thurber: 'The most dangerous food is—wedding cake.'"

Istel's wry humor is evident on many panels. In a *History of Humanity* panel titled "Man Evolves: Homo habilis to Homo erectus to Homo sapiens," he had an artist engrave the classic *New Yorker* cartoon of a mother ape complaining to her offspring who stands ramrod straight, "How many times must I tell you, stoop." The next panel over, though, "The Creation of Adam" by Michelangelo is reproduced with loving exactitude.

Not only choosing a mix of world-changing events but sussing out the veracity of events can be a challenge, Istel said.

"It's caused me to lose some sleep," he said. He ran his fingers through his thinning gray hair and emitted a world-weary sigh. "In the U.S. (monument), I really felt I'd bitten off more than I could chew. You see, when you write about what occurred 3,000 years ago, no one really knows what went on. Can you imagine writing about the last 50 years and putting that in granite? Now that was serious."

Though he says he adheres to the facts, there is a point of view expressed in some panels. He mentions on the "Food and Beverage" panel that "soft drinks . . . caused concern about obesity in the 21st" (century). One panel titled "Still Living Above Our Means: 1980 to 2012" features the *Sesame Street* character Elmo standing before a bar chart comparing U.S. debt per capita to income per capita, with the caption: "Elmo asks, 'Can you tell which one is growing faster?'"

Most of the panels, however, are straightforward recitation of events, everything from the 9/11 terrorist attack on the World Trade Center to the moon landing to how the continents formed starting 65 million years ago.

Istel knows he has opened himself up to criticism from "those with an agenda." He does not care. He is a historian. He's on a mission. He could beat the crap out of anyone who'd confront him, believe you me.

"You're talking to an old Marine," he said. "We welcome controversy. Don't put that in. Just say we do the best we can. If you find three people who say you're an idiot, you can find three people who say you're a genius. But I must tell you, when we got done engraving the text (on the U.S. panels) and it couldn't be changed, I sent (photographs of it) to a famous historian, who chaired the Princeton history department, and I got, in writing from him, the only A-plus of my life."

Istel then rose to shake my hand and usher me out of his upstairs office and walked with a slight limp down the hall and haltingly down the stairs, where Felicia waited by the piece of the Eiffel Tower for a goodbye photo op. Jacques had more history to write and wanted me gone, but I could tell something was bothering him. You could sense he was concerned about what I would write about the Center of the World.

"Look, PBS was here for a serious story; so was French TV," he said, then broke into another sly smile. "We've gone from kooks in the desert to partial kooks in the desert."

The Cradle of Civilization

January 2016
Town: Blythe
County: Riverside
Population: 19,832
Elevation: 272 feet

The desert wind howled, and Alfredo Acosta Figueroa moaned. It was a deep, guttural sound rising clear from his diaphragm, anguished and heartsick.

"Ah, *mannnn*," he lamented, voice trailing consonants like kicked-up gravel, evoking the same poignancy as when he once sang *corridos* at 1960s farmworker rallies. "*Ohhhh*. Ridiculous! They're destroying it."

**Alfredo Acosta Figueroa, a one-man activist group, is trying to protect an
ancient Indian holy site, the Blythe Intaglios, a series of geoglyphs,
from development.**

He paused, sighed audibly and seemed to deflate a bit into the passenger's seat. Figueroa, at that moment, looked every bit of his 83 years, face
fissured like the hillsides ringing Blythe and the Palo Verde Valley, his
signature straw fedora falling lower over a furrowed brow.

"Pull over," he said, at last. "Just park right here. Yeah, on that shoulder.
Ah, *mannnn.* Get out. I'll show you. I don't want to show you, after what
they've done. But I show you."

We had been driving for an hour on the back roads north of Interstate
10 near the Arizona border, me at the wheel, Figueroa riding shotgun and
his eldest son, also named Alfredo, mostly silent in the backseat. Plenty
of times on this sunny February afternoon Figueroa had requested we
stop the car on sandy shoulders. Each time, it was to point out features in
the hills and the arid landscape that, he said, supports his fervent, almost
messianic, belief that this is the sacred ground known as Aztlán, the site
that tells the creation story of Figueroa's Chemehuevi ancestors and, pretty
much, those of all Aztecs.

But this was the first time all day he had asked to stop and wander in
the desert to get a close-up look at one of the huge (50 feet wide and 200
feet long) geoglyphs, Native American symbols carved into the rock,

7

desert as canvas. He wanted to show me Kokopilli and Cicimitl, two of the most prominent geoglyphs that constitute the Blythe Intaglios, renderings of Aztec gods and symbols depicted as either human or animal, formed by scraping away the dark, manganese-stained top layer of rock to show pale, powdery caliche soil underneath. He wanted to inspect what's left after, more than a year ago, bulldozers from Blythe Solar and McCoy Solar Power built a road that skirts and somewhat alters the geoglyphs, and to show how close (less than 300 meters) the solar-panel farms come to the "sacred" site.

The geoglyphs that make up the intaglios are, arguably, Blythe's single (or perhaps it's kinder to say "singular") attraction, unless you count the world-class number of fast-food joints and array of gas stations that line the four exits off I-10 leading to the Arizona border. But don't mention the A-word around Figueroa. To him, dismissing the geoglyphs as a mere oddity would be like sloughing off the Wailing Wall as a quirky collection of brick and mortar.

When I first met up with Figueroa and his eldest son at the parking lot of the Denny's on the town's main drag, he almost couldn't bring himself to come and see what he calls a desecration but what the Bureau of Land Management, which manages the public land, and Blythe Solar, which has contracted with the state to build the alternative-energy plant, calls a site capable of "generating enough electricity to power 264,000 homes." Twice, on the drive over, Figueroa demurred, saying "I don't want to go. It hurts me too much. Leave me at the house. You go with him, son." A silence ensued, fraught with tension. "OK," he said at last, "I go. First time I'll see it since the road (was built), you know."

And here we now stood outside the car, wind whipping so hard that the brush was sibilant and animated. A metal BLM sign ("Restoration in Progress") on the barbed-wire fencing paralleling the freshly paved, two-lane road creaked in the gusts. We had to wait to cross the road until a stream of cars, heading southbound toward the freeway, had passed.

"Working on a Saturday," Figueroa's son muttered, referring to the solar-farm construction. "Man, there used to be nobody. No road."

"Ridiculous!" the elder Figueroa growled.

It was only a short walk, maybe 50 feet, from this new road to the *meseta* where the two geoglyphs sit. From the sky, via satellite images or Google maps, the forms are fully shaped and easily discernible. Kokopilli, a massive representation of the Aztec god Quetzalcoatl, shows a round-headed figure either playing a flute or drinking from a straw, five plumes jutting from his head and his body breastplate taking the appearance of an anthropomorphized bee or bird in flight. Cicimitl, farther east on the same *meseta*, is said to be an animist figure aligned at 13 degrees magnetic north with the three peaks of the Mule Mountains. Up close, though, stepping carefully on the jagged, blackened rocks, all I could see is sculpted lines that give only a partial rendering of the work as a whole. In time, Figueroa will explain that significance but, first, he and his son are still trying to process the transformed landscape.

"Ah, *mannnn*, see how they broke it up; it used to be all together before they plowed through," Figueroa said. "The sun and arrow (geoglyphs), they are gone. They really did a job on it. Look at the fancy bridge. And there's a concrete (culvert) and wash over (to the north). Ridiculous!"

Figueroa reached into his satchel and took out a paper with the image of, among others, Gov. Jerry Brown, Secretary of the Interior Ken Salazar and former state assemblyman V. Manuel Perez grasping ceremonial shovels at the 2011 groundbreaking of the solar project, spurred by Assembly Bill 32, a state mandate to reduce carbon emissions. The paper billows in the wind. Figueroa will say later that he tried all avenues to stop the project, appealing to the California Energy Commission, the BLM, the builders of the Blythe Mesa Solar Power Project themselves—all to no avail.

His current effort is more modest: to build fences around these two geoglyphs, in the same manner that, since 1957, fences have protected the other intaglios 13 miles away near the Colorado River. Figueroa says it will take about $50,000 to build and will need the approval of the BLM to construct. But he says his nonprofit, the La Cuna de Aztlán Sacred Sites Protection Circle, has a memorandum of understanding with the BLM to partner in protecting "the cultural resources" of the area.

He took out a signed copy of the memorandum and waved it around, to emphasize the point.

"I get worked up over this," Figueroa said. "But I have to. This is sacred land. Our (Chemehuevi) tribe chairman Charles Woods, he said, 'What would people do if they were plowing through the walls of the Vatican?' People would be going nuts. But I don't like to say this is sacred (just) to Native Americans, because it should be sacred to all humans. *La cuna* means 'the cradle.' And this is the cradle, the umbilical, of civilization in the Northern Hemisphere."

Figueroa's contention that the Palo Verde Valley is where the Aztec gods descended and that these geoglyphs date back to around 8000 B.C. draws arched brows and maybe even a little eye-rolling from academics. Figueroa has tried to interest archaeologists in hearing his theological theories; mostly he's been ignored. Figueroa has, however, been invited to give lectures from his book, *Ancient Footprints of the Colorado River*, at UC Riverside and other institutions with Chicano studies programs.

I later called Tom Jones, the BLM archaeologist in charge of the intaglios—but not the two geoglyphs near the solar farm—and he said, speaking slowly and choosing words carefully, that his agency "recognizes the antiquity of these items. We believe them to be very ancient and important to the tribal entities that live on the river." But he said proving the age of the geoglyphs and determining whether they are the "cradle" of Aztec civilization is impossible.

"I wouldn't necessarily discount Mr. Figueroa's assertion," Jones said, voice lightening in tone and timber. "It's kind of a gray area in terms of archaeology. The prevailing view among archaeologists is that the cradle of the Aztec civilization is probably more appropriately placed in northern Mexico. But, I mean, well, you can kind of extrapolate, people had to get from one place to another, eventually, and if people came across the Bering Strait and down, they had to go through the Southwest (of the United States) to get to northern Mexico. The intaglio process is a removal process, so what you're doing is essentially moving rocks from one place to another. To try to determine at what point a rock moved several thousand years ago is really, really difficult."

The genesis of the geoglyphs, essentially who built them, is a matter more of faith than empirical data. Most historians deem the idea of Aztlán as mythical. Figueroa and an organization called the Inland Mexican Heritage believe early Mojave and Quechan settlers to the Colorado River basin built them nearly 10,000 years ago. Artifacts, such as ceramics, show that native people have been in the desert around Blythe for only 3,000 years.

Figueroa, a sixth-generation Blythe resident, said his ancestors passed down the origin and migration stories over hundreds of years. But the intaglios became widely known—aka "discovered"—only in 1932, when the *London News* published aerial photos of geoglyphs. No such geoglyphs exist in Mexico, where many archaeologists say Aztec civilization first took root hundreds of years before the Spanish conquistadors arrived in 1521.

A set of geoglyphs in Peru, called the Nazca Lines, is the only other similar site in the Americas. A UNESCO World Heritage site, the Nazca Lines have been intensely studied by academics, who have reached no consensus as to their purpose or exact age, but some theorize that ancient people were signaling to their gods in the firmament.

One skeptic-turned-grudging-supporter is Boma Johnson, a retired BLM archaeologist. Writing in the preface of Figueroa's book, Johnson stated he studied evidence Figueroa compiled from Aztecan codices and, "I see many difficulties in his reasoning and lines of evidence, yet I see enough good evidence to intrigue me. . . . (T)he idea of the lower Colorado River being the so-called 'Lost Aztlán' is not that wild of an idea."

Johnson's partial endorsement may be the only outside support Figueroa has for his theory that the geoglyphs were made by the ancient ones before heading south to Mexico City, but he does not care. "They tell us, you cannot prove anything," he said, raising a crooked index finger. "The hell I can't. I have the codices."

When I apparently didn't express enough enthusiasm in his study of 20 volumes of ancient writings he perused in university libraries, he repeated, louder into the wind, "I. Have. The. Codices! These are codices written prior to the invasion of the Spanish (in Mexico). People have no respect for our culture."

Then he smiled, jutting his chin out into a significant headwind.

"Don't use the word 'myth,'" he continued. "It's facts. Like, Blythe originally was an island. It's written in the codices! I'd show it to you, but I can tell from your expression it's too big of a shock right now. The last (journalist) I showed around told me, 'Stop, stop, I can't take anymore, my brains are coming out of my ears.' Facts are facts. But if you have no kind of imagination, then, sorry, you won't see it out here. Might as well take me back home."

Figueroa, father of nine, grandfather of 26, is more lithe than frail and, though partially stooped, strides around the geoglyphs like a man a few decades younger. He is used to a fight, used to people being dismissive. He comes from six generations of miners and agricultural workers in the area around Blythe. He has worked in—literally, *in*—those hills and has long been an advocate for Chicano and Native American rights. In the 1960s, he worked alongside United Farm Workers leaders Cesar Chavez and Bert Corona, brandishing a guitar and singing *corridos* at rallies up and down the state. Once his days working in the nearby mines ended, he became an activist protecting the land, first stopping the proposed Ward Valley nuclear dump and later successfully protesting against the Eagle Mountain landfill.

"I know struggle, and the sites here are very delicate but have little protection, especially Kokopilli and Cicimitl, thanks to those damn solar panels," he said. "They can willfully ignore that this is the sacred *la cuna*, the cradle, but I was a miner and I know these hills. Anglos, they think you gotta go to Babylonia or some place to see the beginning, the Tower of Babel or something. But I show you our towers."

Stops we made around the valley earlier in the afternoon included pop quizzes, something like huge Rorschach tests. He had me point the car toward the Big Maria Mountains north of town, and pressed a finger against the windshield toward a jutting rock. When I failed to identify the telltale beak-like rock formation, he took pity on me.

"That's Huitzilopochtil (Aztec sun god)," he said. "Now look over to the left. See that mountain? Who was the mother of Quetzalcoatl? That's Chimalman. It's spelled C-h-i-m-a-l-m-a-n. I see you struggling. It's important to get the spelling right. That dark peak on the extreme left. See? It's got a face and got her breasts. She's pregnant. That's Chimalman. When the Spanish came, they said, 'Oh, that must be the mother of Jesus Christ,' and they named it the Maria Mountains. But this whole range is where (civilization) got started."

Now we found ourselves walking slowly inside the dark stones that make up the head of Kokopilli, which "represents the creation of the cosmos and mother earth." We stood silently at the mouth, Figueroa's son apologizing when his cellphone rang and respectfully wandered off to answer it.

Then Figueroa led me to the eye. We stood over it, just staring for a few seconds. Someone had put a stone threaded with turquoise in the middle of the eye/cairn.

"New Age–type people," Figueroa said, only somewhat dismissively. "They must've added that. They mostly like to take the (peyote) out here. But at least they've got some feeling for the land."

He paused, bent lower to inspect, but not touch, the turquoise stone.

"This is the center of the universe," he said, with a practiced arm sweep. "You're standing on it."

We stood for a while longer, then headed back to the car. We had to wait for another armada of vehicles to pass before crossing the new two-lane road again.

"Ridiculous!" he spat. Then we headed back to Denny's.

Wintering in Death Valley

February 2015
Area: Death Valley National Park
County: Inyo County
Visitors in July 2015: 729,117
Visitors in January 2015: 71,979
Average temperature in July: 117°F
Average temperature in January: 67°F
Elevation: (at Badwater Basin): –282 feet

High noon at Badwater Basin, and I'm shivering. This is the last place on earth I figured I'd need a coat, for cripe's sake. But here I am wearing a flimsy light fleece jacket and cursing it because, well, it's not my high-end, breathable Gore-Tex raincoat, hanging uselessly back home in the hallway closet.

Yes, it's January and it's raining in Death Valley. This never happens. Oh, all right, they do get a tiny measure of precipitation here in this famously parched desert that spans 5,270 square miles—a whopping 1.9 inches a year. Mostly, whatever falls from the sky is slurped right up by the thirsty soil, making nary a significant puddle, yet, coming in winter like this abbreviated shower, helping the always-iffy prospects for a hearty spring wildflower bloom into being.

But let's not get carried away with this meteorological anomaly: no torrential downpour, no Old Testament gully gusher, only enough to make drivers turn the wipers to "intermittent."

For those who've visited here only at the height of summer—or heck, even as early as April—this January drizzle is such a stark contrast to the kiln that usually is the valley floor, where triple-digit readings are the norm by lunchtime. You'd never think you'd actually need to use a furnace at the Furnace Creek Resort, but the woman in front of me at check-in asked

In the summer, Death Valley's Badwater basin can get up to 129 degrees. But in the winter, when this photo was taken, it was a mild 74 and mostly deserted by tourists.

about central heating on this (*brrrr*) 61-degree day, forecast to drop to an even more bone-chilling 47 overnight.

People were agog and talk was abuzz. There was a giddiness you normally only see in people stocking up at grocery stores in a pre-hurricane tizzy.

"Isn't this amazing?" said Linda Slater, Death Valley's chief interpretive ranger. She hustled over to the information desk at the Furnace Creek visitors' center and looked up this season's rainfall total: a whopping 0.16 inches.

"It seems like a lot out there today, though, huh?" she said. "We did have some rain in the beginning of December, but nothing more until (today)."

For the record, in that 24-hour period, the official weather station at Furnace Creek registered 0.26 inches of rainfall; it was the talk of the visitors center. In fact, in an amusing exhibit at the attached museum, tourists are asked to write on Post-it notes their answers to the question, "Where are you from and how is Death Valley different?" One response, in large letters slanting to the right, as if scribbled in annoyance: "From Seattle—Wasn't raining there when we left. Rained here instead. Oh well."

There are two ways to look at a Death Valley rainy day: the proverbial rain bucket's either half full or half empty. Thinking positively, the land-

14

scape takes on a brooding, almost vulnerable presence, far removed from the fiery malevolence of summer. Up at the geologic paint-swatch that is Artist's Palette, looming above Badwater Basin, the rough volcanic rock and multihued mineral deposits are so slick they look as if someone just slathered on a fresh glossy coat. Below, in the salt-encrusted basin, you can see the drops make dark brown dots in the granular surface before fading, like time-lapse photography, in front of your eyes, and you wonder if the briny earth there remembers that 4,000 years ago—a mere geologic eyeblink, after all—that it was a lake.

Thinking negatively, hitting you like a drop of barometric pressure that led to this rain, you feel the same letdown you might experience when you get to see a handsome actor in person and find his skin is pockmarked by acne scars and discover he's wearing lifts in his shoes. The landscape is not the vivid eye candy you expected to see, in fact, what you did see when Googling "Artist's Palette" before the trip. In the overcast and sprinkles, all seems slightly washed out, the usually rutilant serrated hillsides almost a sickly pastel, the greens and yellow tinge of the deep fissures reduced to varying shades of beige. Nary a glimmer, either, of Badwater's celebrated brilliant winter sunset, the Panamint Mountains in the distance hiding behind thick cloud cover. Hell, if novelist Frank Norris' famous character McTeague had wandered into the desert this time of year, the story would've ended far differently.

Death Valley's visitors on this day—many of whom, I notice with self-laceration, have thought ahead and brought raincoats—seemed a little befuddled but entirely undeterred. Cameras still clicked mightily, no one bemoaning the lack of vivacity in the images before posting to Snapchat. Sturdy hiking poles went right on plunging into the slightly sticky silt and clay on the popular Golden Canyon Trail heading to Red Cathedral, which, though not quite so brilliant as their names imply on this day, were still Crayola-like sharp. Twelve miles up Dante's View, 5,000 feet above the basin, people still gamely got out of their cars and gazed down on the view, however obscured.

I mean, what else can you do? You can't Photoshop nature, can you? Remember this, too: That scrim of moisture on your brow has come from misty rain, not ever-accumulating beads of sweat from baking in the summer heat. Always a good thing, in my book.

There is, after all, a large subset of Death Valley visitors who have a perfectly pleasant time visiting here in winter, the so-called off-peak season. While March and August are reportedly the most popular months among the park's 1 million annual visitors—the first because of spring break ("All the college kids," Slater said) and the second because some off-hinged folks crave intense heat ("Especially the Germans," Slater said)—some make it a point to visit in December, January and February, before the thermometer and tourists rise precipitously.

"Of course, I've always known it gets hot here," said Chris Fitzpatrick, a tourist from Wisconsin, quite comfortable in a cardigan sweater on the observation deck at Badwater. "My husband, Bob, was laughing because he said the name, Death Valley, doesn't really draw you here. This is a good time to come."

"I've been here in May before," Ali Barnes, her friend, interjected. "That's definitely the latest I'd come. It was over 100 then, yeah."

"That is a little scary," Fitzpatrick added. "There was a story, wasn't there, recently about a lady who went through here in summer with her kid, and she didn't have water along and, you know what happened. Oh, it was terrible."

Stories such as that abound. Hey, there's a reason it's called Death Valley. Visitors shouldn't feel as if they'd visited Disneyland and discovered that Space Mountain was closed for repairs. Better to revel in the incongruity.

"It's something different," said Barnes, as we both were getting increasingly soggy. "I've been here five times. First time it's rained. Wintertime, well, today the sun's not really shining, but when we've come out in winter before, the angle of the sunlight, because it's such a low angle, is so much more dramatic than the one time I was here in May. Then, it was hot and little miserable. (In May) you had this real tall, direct sunlight. No thanks. The low angle of the winter sun makes the rocks shimmer, the definition pops out."

The winter visitor does, indeed, have some advantages without having to endure sweat-lodge conditions. Hiking is not limited to mornings. Mid-afternoon saw the parking area near the popular Mosaic Canyon Trail, hard by Stovepipe Wells Village, packed, as was an area dotted with shutterbugs nearby searching for "good light" while training their lenses on the Mesquite Dunes. People looped around the volcanic crater at Ubehebe without feeling the hot breath of phantom eruptions.

You don't have to weigh yourself down with provisions like a survivalist, either, though rangers still recommend bringing plenty of water and maybe some electrolytes, even in cooler weather. Your car's radiator will thank you, as well. It's easier to get a reservation at either the Furnace Creek Inn and Ranch or accommodations at Stovepipe Wells Village or Panamint Springs, but, alas, you'll still pay felonious prices for food (a three-topping pizza for $31; a chicken Caesar salad for $19) and gas ($3.47 a gallon).

It's true that fewer people may visit in winter, but there seems to be more action. Maybe the extreme heat just encourages sloth, making even the 400-yard trek from your room at the Furnace Creek Ranch to the on-site Borax Museum an act of Olympian toil and testament to personal bravery. Not so in milder days. I passed several pelotons of cyclists whirring like a swarm of bees down Highway 190 and along Badwater Road.

On my second day at the park, the rain now a misty memory, I awoke early and saw a bunch of runners wearing bib numbers. I asked around and learned the annual Death Valley Marathon and Half Marathon was about to start. I plopped down $60, grabbed a number and took off with the 100 or so other perfectly sane runners. As I ambled along the roads and trails, admiring a few early blooms, I could not help but think about the crazy participants of the summer madness known as the Badwater Ultramarathon, more than 100 miles from the aptly named Badwater Basin to Mount Whitney. Those hardy souls brave temperatures averaging about 120 in the heat of the day. It's so hot, participants say, that they must wear these silly white heat-resistant suits that cover their entire epidermis and make them appear like aliens just so they aren't grilled to perfection on the roads. Many a Death Valley runner (heck, even hiker) in summer has had their shoe soles melted clear to the insole.

The late January rain also augured a fertile, if still too brief, wildflower season coming very soon, perhaps as early as late February, Slater said. "The flower season here starts earlier than (at) other desert parks," she said. "If it gets real hot in March, then the flowers wilt and droop. That's happened before. It all depends on the weather, of course. If it stays reasonably cool in March, then the flower season will last. Remember, (the flowers) move up in elevation. If you were to go to Telescope Peak (11,049 feet) or Mahogany Flat (8,133 feet) in the summer, you'll still see the flowers up there. This rain (in late January) may even do something by tomorrow. You may see all these little sprouts shoot up, with this rain—maybe."

The only reason flowers can take root and sprout in such a harsh milieu is that they are annuals, meaning they bloom for one growing season, the seeds using the modicum of rainfall to flourish briefly before bowing down. They come in yellow, pink, red and pale blue to purple, everything from the woolly daisy to gravel ghosts to Mojave aster. Death Valley veterans still talk about the so-called Super Bloom of 2005, when above-normal rain brought out scores of photographers, not to mention droves of butterflies, hummingbirds and bees.

I was more interested in the variety of critters hanging out at different elevations and how they deal with such temperature extremes. Snails and cottonball pupfish struggle to survive on the salt flats, snakes and kangaroo rats around the sand dunes and valley floor, desert tortoise, fringe-toed lizards and bobcats at high elevations. No matter the season, you have to go searching for many desert creatures (though doesn't it always seem rattle-snakes will seek you out?), but they can be found if you're willing to stray from the familiar, i.e., paved, path. Slater and others recommend lesser-known trail offshoots for those seeking a wilder, as well as a quieter, nature experience.

"The thing about Death Valley," she said, "is that it's so big that if you want to get away from crowds, you can get away. I've been here on a Presidents Day weekend, and it's been very busy. But I can find another canyon to walk in where I won't see a soul. I did one recently. If you go to the west side of Titus Canyon (northeast, in the Grapevine Mountains, on the way to Scotty's Castle), there's a trailhead for Fall Canyon. Lots of folks hike there. But I went into the next one over (Red Wall Canyon) and there was nobody there. Maybe it's not as pretty as Fall Canyon, but it was very peaceful."

Peace and quiet lured tourists Kathleen and Darryl Toupkin from their Scottsdale, Ariz., home. They are runners and cyclists who use the park as a playground, yet they said they also like to slow down and enjoy the solitude in Death Valley.

"This is one of our favorite places on the planet," Darryl said. "Best way to describe it: It's the closest mankind can get to being on the moon."

"One time we were riding our bikes up Artist's Drive, and it's kind of hard, uphill, you know," Kathleen added. "So we're biking along and there's absolute silence. Just beautiful. Except for this one big old crow just following us and (seemingly) laughing at us. But it's the quiet. That's what I like, the quiet."

So quiet that, on this day, you could hear the rain, faint yet steady, plink against the salty, crusty Badwater soil.

High Art in the Low Desert

February 2015
Town: Death Valley Junction
County: Inyo
Population: 4 (according to city limit sign); 20 (according to locals)
Elevation: 2,041 feet

Incredible what can bloom in the desert, what gems can be unearthed purely by chance—in this instance, stopping at a one-pump-of-the-brake-pedal town to wonder how many more miles a fella had to go before he could gas up his car, which, though a hybrid, was getting as parched as the guy behind the wheel.

Here, amid the flaking adobe ruins of the (still operating, barely) Amargosa Hotel, where only the exceedingly brave or desperate dare spend the night, I stumbled upon the Amargosa Opera House, home for five decades to ballerina Marta Becket, a noted New York expat, and her one-woman show. Nearing 90, Becket is too frail these days to grace the stage she built with her own toil and toe shoes, but into the breach has come Jenna McClintock, best known for her years with the Oakland and Richmond (Va.) ballet companies, to perform Becket's original works, pay homage to her enduring appeal and keep alive a Death Valley tradition.

The only thing that tipped me off was a weathered poster in the window of the hotel, about 20 miles east of the Badwater Basin. Nightlife not being Death Valley's strength—in the winter, even the lone bar at Furnace Creek isn't exactly hopping and the country-music jukebox stays mostly silent—I decided to purchase a ticket. Best 20 bucks I ever spent. This is a must-see show, even if your knowledge of ballet and interpretive dance is so minimal that it can be inscribed with a dull pencil on the narrow shank of a wooden barre.

McClintock is a wonderful dancer, moving with both the geometric precision of a Mondrian painting and the fluidity of a swirling van Gogh. But the show, which has run January to April, begins well before the dancer graces the stage.

The theater itself, and the story behind its founding, are just as much a draw. At 6:45 on a Saturday night, when doors with white peeling paint fling open and the nine patrons holding thumbnail-size generic blue tickets are admitted, a visual, almost visceral, delight awaits.

Floor to ceiling, the walls are covered with Renaissance-meets-Spanish-Colonial murals, deep red and richly ornate in some spots, light blue and ethereal in others, all painted by Becket. Flickering light from flames of the wood stove in the front left corner send shadows off the scuffed and irregularly planked hardwood floor. The stage itself, smooth plywood rubbed bare in spots and cloaked with a red velvet curtain, is lit by overhead spotlights whose shades were made from Folgers coffee cans. The rows of seats, threadbare from years of being exposed to the elements and patrons' ample backsides, creak with complaint.

But it's the figures depicted in the mural—actually, it's one flowing scene, the permanent, if two-dimensional, "audience" at the Opera House—that demand your gaze. There are depictions of Spanish nobility and Louis XIV aristocrats looking down from the gilded balcony in all their finery, the aloof-looking king and queen dead-on center. There are jousters and jesters and bullfighters hoisting goblets, priests and nuns and courtesans, ballerinas milling backstage doing warm-up pliés and tenors dressed as Vikings. From the ceiling, circling a golden dome depicting ladies playing antique instruments, float-dancing cherubs are tossed about by the embodiment of the four winds.

None of the theatergoers on this night could stay seated preshow. They roamed the aisles, taking in the murals.

"Right now," says Kristina Walker of Washington, D.C., who was staying at the hotel with partner Stephen Zippe, "I'm just giggling as I walk here and see all of this. You wouldn't expect it here."

Actually, Randy and Jackie Monge of Orcas Island, Wash., did expect it. They've been to Death Valley several times and bought the DVD of the documentary about Becket. But they'd never been here before when a performance is scheduled.

"Incredible lady," Jackie says. "We have handed the video around to everybody we know, and we have to ask for it back. I've been enamored with it and her ever since I watched it. I hear she still lives here. They say she still goes to some of the shows and signs autographs. It would be great if she came tonight."

With house lights still on, the recorded voice of Becket emits from the speakers, welcoming the crowd and giving the theater's history and the briefest of outlines of her personal story, which was the subject of an Emmy Award–winning documentary in 2000.

Voice faltering a little with age, but augmented by a mournful cello accompaniment, Becket tells that the theater originally was a "social hall" for workers from the mining company that once toiled in the town and that once the company town moved on, circa 1947, the hall, the hotel and assorted other buildings in town were deserted. She glosses over her career—Broadway chorus line appearances, assorted ballerina roles, choreographed one-woman shows—and her avocation as a painter and moves on to her discovery of Amargosa in 1967. She was in her early 40s then, her ballet career seemingly in decline.

The gist: She and her then husband were on vacation in Death Valley's Furnace Creek campground when they had a flat tire. The nearest service was 30 miles east in Death Valley Junction. Nosing about town while the tire was changed, Becket stumbled upon the auditorium, poked her head through the hole in the backdoor and saw her future. She left New York for good and paid the owner $45 a month to rent the theater, as is, sans roof and infested with native kangaroo rats. A year later, she opened the rechristened Amargosa Opera House, where until 2013 she danced en pointe to classical music, weaving stories in movement to entertain the few locals and the curious among Death Valley tourists. On nights when no one showed, she danced to the "audience" in the murals.

Lights dimmed, and McClintock took the stage to recreate a Becket selection. She wore a frilly and frothy white costume and pirouetted and kicked to the fervent strains of violins and cellos, her back arched against the painted backdrop of the Amargosa Hotel's colonnade. After the piece, the curtain fell and it took the audience, from the looks of us not your normal ballet crowd, a beat to commence applauding, but it was prolonged and spirited. Two pieces later, McClintock walked to the foot of the stage to address the audience.

"I discovered ballet from Marta Becket about 33 years ago when I was 6 years old, camping here with my family," McClintock said. "We stumbled upon a sign: 'Performance Tonight.' We came to see her show. Marta put on quite a show that evening. She was dancing en pointe. I'd never forget it. She was in a red tutu, levitating on stage. To my eyes, she was floating on top of the stage. From that night on, I decided I'd be a ballerina. I had a great, long career. I'm retired from company work now, and I've come back . . . to Marta to make sure her work still lives on. Obviously, her murals will live on forever. They keep this theater alive even though this stage has been dormant. Now, I want the stage to be alive as well."

McClintock finished with an excerpt from a ballet she herself is developing, called *Dream Weaving*. To rousing applause from all nine in attendance, she bowed as the curtain closed, and production manager Gregory Perez thanked the audience for attending.

Becket, who lives at the hotel but is having health issues, was a no-show for this performance, but McClintock seemed the next best thing. She, too, has discovered Death Valley Junction late in her ballet career. She says she sought out Becket in 2010 to thank her for inspiring her own career.

"Marta just stared at me and said, 'You can do this, too,'" McClintock said. "And it just stung in my ear. I came back in 2014, and I said, 'Hey my life ain't working out retiring.' I asked, 'What's going on here?' and nothing was. So here we are. And she is just such a soul sister, such a kindred spirit that it wasn't really like I'm Jenna out there (on the stage)."

Afterward, the night still relatively young, I retreated to the hotel lobby—or what's left of it. I found no bar but a loungy type of area where someone had set up a DVD player atop an '80s-era TV. The documentary about Marta, now dated itself, played in a loop. Encased in glass were mementos from Marta's heyday—frilly hats, richly embroidered costumes, playbills and the like. I leaned in to get a look and felt a presence behind me. It was a woman, bent with what looked like extreme osteoporosis, shuffling down the hallway toward one of the few rooms still habitable.

You wouldn't suppose that was . . . ?

Well, yes, who else would it be at this time of night in such a lonesome, remote venue? Even infirm, even hobbled by age and memory, she moved with a kind of grace.

Making Contact

November 2015
Site: Fort Irwin National Training Center
County: San Bernardino, Mojave Desert
Population: Classified (part of U.S. Armed Forces Command)
Elevation: 2,454 feet

If only it had a more distinct reddish tinge, this parched landscape 45 miles northeast of Barstow would look a lot like the images we've received of the terrain on Mars—except, of course, that we now know Mars has more water than California.

Such a setting in the vast Mojave Desert just seems right for a government-run operation called the Goldstone Deep Space Communications Complex, home to NASA's 14 uber-powerful deep dish antennas constituting its Deep Space Network, fondly shortened to DSN by acronym-loving federal employees.

Here, amid miles of boulder-strewn nothingness accented by a few hillocks bearing the barest three-day stubble of sagebrush, these massive and sensitive antennas are in constant electronic communication with such peripatetic vehicles as the Mars Rover, the Phoenix Mars Lander, probes exploring Saturn and Jupiter and, still sending out signals after all these years, Voyager 1, the spacecraft launched in 1977 that has accrued some impressive frequent-flier miles (like 6.5 billion and counting). Who knows, these dishes might even be in contact with Matt Damon, the actor who was starring in *The Martian* at the time of my visit.

Along with DSN complexes in Spain and Australia, the "intelligence from alien realms" gleaned at Goldstone is funneled to the Jet Propulsion Laboratory (JPL) in Pasadena for analysis and dissemination.

It is, to be sure, mind-blowing to imagine that enormous hunks of metal "dishes," outfitted with highly sensitive amplified receivers, can pick up the faintest of transmissions from spacecraft equipment that, in the words of NASA press material, give off only "20 watts, about the same as a refrigerator light bulb." By the time it hooks up with a Goldstone antenna, the signal power "can be as weak as a billionth of a billionth of a watt." Yet, even with fading power, JPL scientists, like teenagers sharing snaps of their muscle cars, can routinely show us high-res images of the Mars Rover traversing the Red Planet.

So a trip to Barstow, the go-to Interstate 40 exit for those with small bladders who, you know, have to go, was necessary for something other than nature's calling. Actually, Barstow is just home base for this quasi-military maneuver. It's 45 minutes off Interstate 15. But the journey is a lot more complicated than that. We're talking much advance planning. There are two layers of security and bureaucratic hoop-jumping, since NASA leases land at the Fort Irwin National Training Center, but neither pose major logistical headaches—unless you hail from outside the United States. Foreigners have to apply weeks, sometimes months, in advance and are subjected to NSA-level background checks. We Americans, though, simply need to call or email Goldstone's peppy and professional public outreach coordinator, Leslie Cunkelman, a few days in advance. Providing we can produce a valid photo ID, proof of car insurance and car registration, we're good to go.

Before I get to the cool antennas and satellite dishes, allow me a digression to muse about the curious, polite but slightly unsettling encounter that civilians face with military personnel and federal-government security guards.

Maybe it's just me, but it seems there's some major power-tripping going on. When I pulled into the Fort Irwin Visitors Center, the first of three gantlets to run through, I encountered a line six deep of workers and delivery men handing over their papers, stating their business, posing for a mug shot, then waiting for their laminated Fort Irwin day passes. A man in front of me, whose long gray ponytail partially obscured the Harley-Davidson logo on his jacket, told the Army officer (either very buffed or wearing a flak jacket underneath his uniform) that "I'm here to serve papers. Been here before." A few clicks of the keyboard, and the process server was off to carry out his pleasant task.

I, however, ran into trouble. It wasn't because my car registration was in the name of a large media outlet—the officer displayed no antipress bias—it was just that my name had not appeared on that morning's Goldstone Deep Space Network roster of tour-goers. Not on the list? You don't exist. This necessitated several phone calls and walkie-talkie dispatches before it was cleared up. I sensed from the officer's body language (erect spine, pursed lips, narrowed eyes) that Goldstone ranks pretty low on Fort Irwin's list of priorities, being mere tenants and all.

Gantlet No. 2: the fort's main gate, a pebble's throw from the visitors center, where another officer examined my badge's mug shot, then stared at my face, then back at the badge before waving me through. I had the gall to ask for directions and his perturbed expression signaled his annoyance. "First left," he sighed. "Look for the sign."

The third gantlet was the Goldstone gate, where Cunkelman waited with an all-business security guard in a reflective vest referred to only as Mr. Christian. He asked for my badge and driver's license. In stepped a khaki-clad guard whose badge read "F. Hicks." The two conferred for a good five minutes about whether to issue me badge No. 4 or No. 6. (Six it was; I didn't want to ask what happened to pass No. 5.) Then Hicks handed me a clipboard with a waiver attached and said I was to initial each line as he read the rules aloud, rules that ranged from "Don't take pictures of military equipment" to "Do not feed or do anything with" the mountain lions, bobcats, burros and tortoises that roam the desert, to "The water, do not drink it."

At last, Cunkelman took over, leading our caravan of four cars to a drive-by only of the Apollo Station, which features a 26-meter (85-foot) antenna built in 1966 for moon missions but now hooks up with a variety of unmanned orbiting satellites. Then we did another drive-by, this time of the BWG (Beam Waveguide) cluster of antennas, built in the 1990s for a host of deep-space missions.

Finally, the main attraction: the Mars Station. We parked and craned our necks at the looming 70-meter (230-foot) dish attached to a base 21 stories tall. The dish was "offline" that morning for maintenance, but that didn't quell the excitement of my fellow tour-goers, Cheryl Gaj of Thousand Oaks and Mike Zahra of Toronto. (Zahra, a Canadian engineer, had to fill out paperwork in advance and, being a foreigner, was given a thorough going-over by a vigilant series of Fort Irwin guards, oh yes indeed.)

Whereas the scientifically inclined Zahra and Gaj wanted to delve into the intricacies of signal reception, I, the erstwhile English major, just made corny Matt Damon jokes about the movie *The Martian*. Cunkelman humored me. "There's a direct link here to Matt Damon, actually directly into my cellphone," she said. "Anyway, this Mars 70-meter antenna was built in 1966 and took 3½ years to construct."

All data and images beamed from deep space to the dish go to JPL in Pasadena. But behind us stood the SPC (Signal Processing Center), where, well, the data is processed going Pasadena-bound. The adjoining DSNOR (Deep Space Network Operations Room) is where engineers stare intently at VMs (video monitors) and DSs (data screens), occasionally pushing buttons and clicking mouses (CMs). "From each of their desks, they can control two antennas at one time," Cunkelman said. "Projected there on the back wall is a portion of JPL's seven-day schedule for tracking. It's color-coded. Green means it's tracking right now."

A soundproof glass partition separated us from the desk jockeys behind the consoles. The worker closest to us, a man in sneakers, was slurping coffee and scanning five screens from his desk. "He's in charge of moving the antenna to point," she said. "All the other screens show equipment so that he knows he's in lock with the spacecraft and the data streaming one way or two way is functioning. Looks like it's tracking Planet C, which is a mission to Venus."

Fascinating, but what's that showing on the smaller screen farthest to the right on his desk? It looks like—wait, it is!—the home page for the *Washington Post's* website.

"They still do have a regular desktop computer and access to Google," Cunkelman said. "They aren't completely cut off from the real world."

It only seems that way on the long drive back to civilization—or, at least, Barstow.

One Town, One Man, One Dream

February 2015
Town: Jacumba Hot Springs
County: San Diego
Population: 561
Elevation: 3,212 feet

The man who owns this town cultivates no regal bearing, displays no gaudy Trumpian affectations, exhibits no megalomaniacal tendencies.

David Landman just looks like any other middle-aged guy on a lazy Sunday afternoon, hunched over a bowl of chicken soup at a handsome, varnished wooden bar, a half-drunk pint of beer at his elbow and a golf tournament flickering on the TV over his right shoulder. He chats up the bartender, Lacy, laughs at some witty remark, unfurls a paper napkin to dab his close-cropped white beard that, along with his thinning dome of silver hair and khaki shorts and sandals, makes him resemble Papa Hemingway kicking back in Key West.

You would never suspect, by appearances, that this is the man who owns that handsome varnished bar, the man who employs Lacy and everyone else at the hot springs spa and resort he also owns on Old Highway 80, the main drag along this town wedged between Interstate 8 and the imposing fence at the Mexican border in far eastern San Diego County. Landman, in all, owns 29 parcels of land, including many boarded-up businesses, a few single-family bungalows, a partially drained (but ecologically rebounding) lake, pungent mineral wells and scores of tumbleweed-strewn fallow dirt lots. And, on the other side of the freeway, tucked against the border of Anza-Borrego Desert State Park, he owns the De Anza Springs Resort, a popular nudist site.

Laid-back as he is, downright unassuming, there is one thing that gives Landman away: He's wearing a black T-shirt with the phrase "Victory Is Mine" emblazoned on the front.

Victory over what, you might ask.

Landman, in his late 60s, is the first to admit he never set out to, essentially, buy a town. He swears it all was "by mistake." Things like this just seem to happen to him and his wife, Helen. He shakes his head with equal parts amusement and bemusement. He also is quick to add, philosophically, that no one really owns the land; you're just a caretaker. But try telling that to the few remaining descendants of the Kumeyaay, the native tribe that pretty much was massacred and driven out by the end of the 19th century.

But Landman, like most land barons, shied away from talking politics or genocide of Indians. He will get really animated, though, talking about how he wound up here. The way Landman tells it—he uses the phrase "long story short" often, but do not believe him—he sort of stumbled into a career in mortgage banking in Northern California after a bleak Willy Loman existence selling wholesale clothing, and when his bank firm got bought out by a company that got bought out by an even bigger company, he used a "golden parachute" in 1997 to buy, on a whim, a rundown RV park at the Jacumba exit off Interstate 8 and turn it into a "clothing-optional" resort that now ranks among the top 10 in the nation by those who judge such things.

That success, while satisfying, didn't exactly infuse Landman with the naked ambition to take over majority control of Jacumba, whose population, 561 in the 2010 census, is far exceeded by its elevation, 3,212 feet. Seems that, long story short, a cabal of residents who called themselves the Jacumba Revitalization Committee approached him four and a half years ago to buy the town's centerpiece property, the Jacumba Hot Springs Spa and Resort, which had fallen on hard times as its out-of-town owners had fallen in deep arrears. (The town is pronounced "ha-coomba," which sounds kind of like the snort of amusement Landman gave when first approached with the deal.)

Landman deferred. People persisted. He begged off again and again. The resort, once fashionable, had become a dump. He'd be crazy to take it on. They kept plugging away. They wore him down. He relented, finally, in 2012.

"I didn't want much part of it at all, really," he said. "Put it this way: The roof over the hot tub was in the hot tub. These people (in town) kept saying, 'We'll throw this in.' Turns out I found out the note holder (on the hot spring) was living in Temecula (in Riverside County). We met at a Marie Callender's. I made him an offer that day and he said, 'Well, my family meets every Sunday for dinner, and I'll run it by them and see what we can do. By the time I got back home two hours later there was a phone call from him, saying, 'We accept your offer.'"

For $1.5 million, he now owned the hot springs resort. But wait, there's more: By purchasing the promissory note, Landman also had acquired about 80 percent of downtown, which amounts basically to a four-block stretch of Old Highway 80 and a few side streets, as well as some land in the foothills with views overlooking that stark russet fence that runs along the U.S.-Mexican border.

"That's what I mean when I say 'by mistake,' because we didn't know 29 properties were secured with that note," he said.

First thing, Landman set about legally changing the town's name to Jacumba Hot Springs. Long story short, it was a branding thing. Then all he wanted to do was refurbish and reopen the spa and hot springs, which was a flourishing operation before a series of managers representing a Chicago-based ownership group apparently ran the resort into the ground. That, and maybe open a nice restaurant, cloth napkins and all, as part of the restored grounds.

What to do with all these empty storefronts?

"That was a good question," he said, laughing.

Landman is quick to point out that he technically does not own the entire town, not everything lock, stock and denuded landscape.

He doesn't own the tiny grocery store on the main drag, nor a couple of dilapidated wooden storefronts without tenants. Some residents, of course, own their own homes on the few streets jutting out from the main artery of Old Highway 80. The county owns the community park, the library and youth center; the federal government owns the post office. An artist collective called the Institute of Perception, headed by Kirk Roberts, owns a swath of land on the hillside.

Landman's purchase, though, raised expectations and eyebrows among locals. Headlines in the *San Diego Union-Tribune* ("He Holds The Keys To Jacumba's Future") and the *San Diego Reader* ("Jacumba Trusts the Naked Guy") only heightened the anticipation/anxiety.

(Brief aside: The Landmans live at De Anza, that clothing-optional resort 4 miles from downtown, but outside those confines, he remains fully clothed at all times and, scurrilous rumors to the contrary, has no plans to turn Jacumba Hot Springs into a clothing-optional town.)

"I think a few people thought at first, he might try it, turn the town into Nakedland," said Alta Rose, behind the counter at the Mountain Sage Market. "But Dave, he's a pretty good guy. He's started to fix it up a little bit. He did real nice with the spa and refurbished all of that. He's got a nice bar and restaurant in there. It's expensive. I like the fish and chips. I've got a daughter-in-law that works (at the hot springs), two granddaughters that work there, my grandson works there. So it's good for employment."

But . . .

"I've seen a lot of people try to 'help' the town," Rose said. "Basically what people do, from my experience, is they think they're going to refurbish everything, the whole town. Well, you can see. Everything's empty across the street. The rents are too high on those two buildings. Both of those are Dave's. It's really hard to keep a business here. My husband and I (at one time) owned Rose's Propane. I had Rose's Video. I used to own this store. Now, I just work here."

A Jacumba resident, T.J. Farr, interposed himself. Farr, a veteran, lived in Jacumba until 1974, when he moved elsewhere in California. He's back now and not liking what he sees.

"The hot springs, they used to be right across the street in the park, and it was free and open to the public," he said, referring to the source of the springs, where water now is pumped a block east to the hot springs resort's pools and Jacuzzi. "I don't see how they can take away the springs, close 'em. Isn't it a natural resource?"

Rose shook her head.

"Well, T.J., it goes with the town," she said. "The person that buys that town gets the springs."

"Damn shame."

What befell Jacumba is what turned many a California desert town into a ghost of itself. Interstate 8 plowed through in the 1960s and replaced what had been the two-lane Highway 80, which ran from San Diego over the mountains and right through Jacumba on its way to the state line and Yuma. Under the new configuration, Jacumba now was 2 miles from the flow of traffic, a small town's lifeblood; it might as well have been 20 or 200 miles away, because people stopped coming. The Hotel Jacumba, so lavish in the 1920s that it drew Hollywood stars, the Barrymores and such, to springs boasting a comfy 104-degree temperature, helped build up the town's population to triple digits. Post-freeway, the population dipped and the hotel fell into disrepair. Only that brick chimney remains, and it's mostly obscured by weeds and accumulated sand.

You would think that, given Jacumba's decades of being down on its luck, it would welcome anyone willing to open his wallet. But because he's lived near Jacumba since the late 1990s, Landman said he's not surprised by the reaction to his bulk purchase. One town wag nicknamed him "The Duke of Jacumba," and "the name stuck," he said.

"Some of (the residents) were against it," he continued. "To some people, bringing any new business in town, they were against. There are people who live up here that want no progress at all. So, yeah, there was some negativity. Fortunately, most people are for it. They want to see this improved."

To the charge that in slightly less than two years he has yet to find tenants for the spiffed-up storefronts on the main drag, Landman preaches patience. And he also points out that "there are investment opportunities available" for anyone wanting to partner with him in filling those storefronts.

"Well, they've all been renovated," he said. "You wouldn't believe what these places looked like."

Much of Landman's time and money these past few years has gone into the town's signature property—the hot springs. It wasn't just a sagging roof over the mineral springs hot tub that needed fixing. The rooms were trashed and the previous managers of the resort "cut the pump lines (to the springs) on their way out. The place hadn't seen a coat of paint maybe in decades."

"Long story short," he said. "The place was in bad shape."

The 24 rooms (rates range from $99 to $129 a night) have been overhauled and now sport hardwood flooring and a desert southwest motif. He's opened Tepary Southwest Grill, whose large dining room is adjacent to the Raven's Nest bar, which serves as a meeting place for locals most nights. An in-house massage therapist has been added, and both outdoor mineral pools are large enough for lap swimming, while the indoor hot tub featuring a skylight is large enough for a party, which is what took place one recent night when more than a dozen San Diegans descended on the resort to celebrate someone's 50th birthday.

"It's a nice little spot," said guest Jong Park, who owns a bistro in Ocean Beach. "Their restaurant is good and reasonable. This is a good place to come, hang out, party, wake up in the morning, have breakfast, drive back home. That's the thing: You feel like you're far away, but it's close (to San Diego)."

In the years since the reopening, the resort has attracted mostly weekenders from San Diego (about an hour's drive) and Yuma (90 minutes), but also passing groups of motorcyclists and car clubs, even a few bicyclists making their way from Florida to California, or vice versa.

"We've been on about 15 (cross-country cycling) blogs of people who've stopped and stayed here and loved it," Landman said. "Another selling point for us is that in the summer our temperature (averages) about 92. That's 15 degrees cooler than the desert and warmer than San Diego."

Good weather, in other words, to lounge by the mineral pools. But Landman acknowledges what is empirically evident as soon as you drive into town—there's not much else to do in Jacumba.

The resort provides a folder of "Things to Do" in each room. It mostly consists of three short hiking trips in town that visit significant places (the lake, mineral spring and decaying site of the Old Vaughn Hotel, circa 1920; Jacumba Peak; and the "Chinese Castle," built by a businessman in the 1920s as a second home) and another hike that starts from a trailhead at De Anza, the clothing-optional resort, and heads into Anza-Borrego Desert State Park.

Landman has plans, though, to turn the town into a mini–Taos, N.M. He foresees art galleries and boutiques moving into his empty storefronts. "We got one guy thinking of taking this (husk of a) gas station next door and turning it into a high-class auto restoration shop," he said. "You know, the type of cars that sell for $100,000 to $900,000. We're hoping he'll have a showroom outside under the canopy and maybe he'll teach welding and auto shop."

First, he needs more people to flock to the place. De Anza has a steady stream of visitors due to its high profile in "naturist" circles, but the hot springs resort still is an "undiscovered gem."

"This has been more work in two years than De Anza's been in 15," he said. "Yeah, you could say there's been some hassles."

Owning a town—or the vast majority of one—is not all it's cracked up to be. "Way more work than I wanted at (age) 67," he said. "The biggest hurdle, frankly, has been dealing with the county and permits. Like, we inherited a (toxic) burn site where it hasn't been used since the '40s, but, somehow, the county found out that it was there, and now they monitor it every three months (to make sure Landman follows environmental regulations). It just sits there and I have to maintain it. I apparently need to put more topsoil on it, more fencing up, no-trespassing signs. It hasn't been a lot of money; just a hassle.

"The hotel is running fine. The bar is running fine. The kitchen we've had problems with. We've had five different executive chefs, including one who cooked at Applebee's for 17 years, but he couldn't cook, well, breakfast. Long story short, didn't know how to make breakfast, but insisted on the morning shift for personal reasons. Another guy did OK on the cooking but was shaking down the waitresses, like, 'Give me your tips, or I'll cut the brake lines on your car.' I'm like, 'Oh my God.' The problem is, in a small community like this, the talent pool is pretty shallow. But the kitchen (staff) now is phenomenal. I'm just telling you the challenges."

This is not what people want to hear, Landman knows. They want to hear about how it's good to be king, how fulfilling it is to be the master of all you survey. And he does love it, truly, he does.

Long term?

Well, long story short . . .

"When we get this going," he said, "and people will come up to me and ask whether (one of his parcels) is for sale or for rent, I'll say, 'Yes.'"

Still Getting Kicks on Route 66

September 2012
Town: Oro Grande
County: San Bernardino
Population: 1,030
Elevation: 3,000 feet

They glisten and glint in the kiln-like Mojave summer sun, a forest of emerald, amber and ocean-blue starkly offsetting the unwavering beige desert canvas.

Driving along historic Route 66, also known as the National Trails Highway, it might first appear a mirage—a two-acre grove of tall, stately metal trees, some as high as 18 feet, with bottles for branches. Upon closer inspection, you see they are topped with items as idiosyncratic as a half a surfboard, a manual typewriter, Mrs. Butterworth's syrup containers and a rusted door from a burned-out Chevrolet.

If you don't feel an overwhelming desire to stop the car to have a look-see at this place called Bottle Tree Ranch, then you must've been born without an iota of curiosity.

Mouth agape, you tentatively pass through an open gate and wend your way through a wonderland of folk art. What you can't see, at least initially, through the maze of steel, glass and reclaimed detritus is the low-slung home that belongs to the creator.

Not to worry. Elmer Long, on the far side of 60, normally will see you before you see him and will wander over to say hi and patiently answer whatever questions might arise.

The artist himself could be considered a work of art, too, one of those friendly recluses who often alight in desert climes. He certainly looks the part: His Rasputin beard, snow white, cascades down his chest before separating into three stalactites. His skin, sun-seared and desert-parched, feels as thick and rough as hide when he firmly shakes your hand.

It doesn't take much prompting for Long to tell you his story, to tackle the inevitable "why" question and regale you with anecdotes. He has the routine down pat, because, he says, he's gotten thousands of visitors since the first tree sprouted on his parcel about a decade ago.

The short version: He grew up in Manhattan Beach, in Los Angeles County, son of a deaf aviation engineer who liked to take his son to the desert for camping trips and to collect bottles. After a stint in the Marine Corps, young Elmer decamped to Oro Grande to work in the nearby cement plant. Being his father's son, he collected bottles and discarded items in the desert and mountains for years, until his collection nearly rivaled his father's garageful of bottles.

"It just kind of came to me," Long said. "I took my dad's bottles and what I collected. So I put one (bottle tree) up in a corner here and, shoot, within a half hour, someone was taking pictures of it. I did it for two years. And I figured it's more fun to do this than (to) work, so I retired in 2002. I've never looked back."

He wasn't looking to open a roadside attraction, he said. He neither sells anything nor buys anything, and he insists he's no artist or attention-seeker. It's just his innate neighborliness that leads him to allow total strangers with cameras to tramp through his front yard.

"That's just an accident that I bought a place (on Route 66)," he said. "I think everything I've done is an accident. My whole life I've gone from this to that with no real plan."

That may be a slight overstatement. Long and his wife of 40 years, Linda, have carved out a pretty good life in the high desert. They were able to put three sons through college—the third and youngest is now at California State University, Long Beach—yet live simply.

In fact, for a few years, the Longs lived off the grid. Now, his only concession to convention is electricity from solar panels. They cook with a wood stove, wash clothes by hand and hang them to dry inside (they'd scorch outside).

"I make all our food," he said. "I'm the cook. I make spaghetti sauce by the ton, and it'd be hard for you to find something as good."

He's reluctant to show visitors the inside of his humble abode, featuring plywood floors he laid himself, but he wanted to show off the kitchen sink. It's a beaut: He fashioned it out of a discarded hospital gurney he sawed in half. The shelves above are molded from rusted movie reel canisters.

But his chef d'oeuvre is what's in the front yard. The Bottle Tree Ranch is in the tradition of bottle-tree folk art found throughout the country, mostly in the Mississippi Delta. Long, though, stops short calling himself even a folk artist. He's just a guy wielding a welder who happens to possess thousands of bottles and bric-a-brac, ranging from a military rifle from 1896 to roller skates from 1906 to antique adding machines, gas pumps, airplane propellers, even a military bomb (thankfully not live).

"That, I found in a store for $25," he said. "But you do find bombs out here in the desert sometimes. I don't mess with them."

Long will, however, pick up anything else that he strikes his fancy on his walkabouts. He'll lug it home in his pickup truck.

His overall aesthetic?

"Whatever grabs me," he said. "I started out with my dad's bottles. He and I used to collect them in the '50s. We went camping and went into dumps. They were pretty. My dad was an interesting man. You're not going to find too many people who'd leave Manhattan Beach and go out in the desert and dig a hole to find bottles. You just aren't. This is really a tribute to my dad. He never did anything with the bottles. But I think differently than other people."

He shielded his eyes from the harsh morning sun with a hand and surveyed his handiwork. He fell silent, seemingly lost in thought, and I felt the need to pick up the conversational slack.

"This is really extraordinary," I ventured.

He gave such a full-bellied laugh that his beard fluttered.

"It's something, all right," he said.

The Bard of Antique Cars

May 2015
Town: Bard
County: Imperial
Population: 3,814 (includes neighboring Winterhaven)
Elevation: 138 feet

Never underestimate the power of deep familial feeling, coupled with gnawing regret and a healthy fear of boredom, especially in the desert. It can lead to certain extreme behavior and creative flights of fancy, make you lose any sense of proportion and engage in an activity others might find inexplicable.

Such as, well, opening your own roadside attraction, on a road deep in the heart of Imperial County's ag fields that even Google Maps has trouble locating, dedicated to nothing but antique cars and assorted automotive accessories.

Johnny Cloud (his real name, swear; he'll whip out his driver's license as proof), whose eponymous museum sits on a significant wedge of land surrounded on all sides by row upon row of lettuce, says on the phone that you can't miss the place, once you finally figure out where York Road starts somewhere outside the (by comparison) metropolis of Winterhaven. A large, hand-painted sign greets you: "CLOUD MUSEUM: Over 120 Vintage Vehicles." So, too, does one of Cloud's border collies, Jack, who's lying in the mud just off the roadside.

You pass through a corrugated tin fence and, here it is, rows of old-timey vehicles, some rusted and rickety, others refurbished to a gleam. Here, too, comes Cloud, adjusting his straw cowboy hat and kicking mud off his boots.

His handshake is firm, and you can feel the calluses that denote years of toil. Truth is, though, Cloud, in his early 70s, doesn't farm in the desert anymore. His days of growing cotton, alfalfa and wheat are long past. He leased the acreage out to big national agriculture companies almost 25 years ago. That, it turns out, is one reason he turned to collecting antique automobiles. The others—preserving the memory of his father and trying to reclaim his lost youth—he'll gladly tell you about.

"I got a Model T Ford out back that belonged to my father," he said. "I collected two or three Model Ts when I was in school and stuff and on the Indian reservation in the desert. And I sold them when I started chasing the girls. I always regretted it. They'd sure be worth a lot more (now) than what I sold 'em for. One I sold for $75, a complete Model T."

A rueful head shake, but he continues.

"You ask why I built this? After I leased my farm out, I just about went crazy with nothing to do. So I started collecting junk, and this is what I ended up with after 25 years collecting."

Junk? Hardly. Untold dollars went into these early-model car purchases, so there's got to be some pride of ownership there. And Cloud, like the archetypal laconic farmer, nods and says, "Proud of all of them."

That's when Cloud leads you past muddy rows of rusted cars into the covered portion of the "museum," where rebuilt and lovingly detailed cars from the 1920s and '30s reside, safe from the elements.

He stops in front of an off-white truck with black fenders, grill and trim and a polished wooden bed behind the boxy enclosed cabin. A sign draped around the hood ornament reads:

Make: Ford
Model: "TT" Closed Cab Truck
Year: 1926–27
Price New: $515
History: This truck belonged to my father in Yuma, AZ.

Unbidden, Cloud launches into an anecdote.

"Eighty-one years ago, my parents lived in the Yuma valley, southwest of Yuma. My mother started labor one night. My dad jumped in the old truck, started it up, went into town, told the doctor. The doctor came up to the house and delivered my sister—she's 10 years older than me—and, luckily, it was a moonlit night because his headlights were all burnt out. That's a true story. My dad couldn't afford headlight bulbs."

He only laughs when you ask if the truck is rare and valuable.

"Oh, no," he says, "it's not. It was just my dad's."

Which, actually, makes it not only rare and valuable but one of a kind. But Cloud doesn't seem the kind of guy bent on introspection or into philosophizing, so you don't argue.

"Here is one of my rarest, a 1922 Chevrolet Model T truck," he said, moving down a row of gleaming chassis. "When I found the thing, I contacted the Chevy club, and they said they only knew of five still in existence. There may be more that they don't know about, but it's still rare."

You keep wanting to bring up monetary figures, but Cloud won't bite.

"Yeah, it's probably worth something," he said. "I just find (cars) anywhere and everywhere. You never know. I don't do the Internet. I go to four swap meets a year in California—San Diego, Long Beach, Riverside and Bakersfield. These are put on by antique car clubs. They have the old stuff. I have no idea how much I've spent. I keep no records. It's a hobby. I just buy something if I like it and put it in here."

Interesting that Cloud eschews the Internet, because his museum has a handsomely designed website touting his collection and giving all-important directions to the place.

"I don't know anything about computers or the Internet," Cloud said, "but a neighbor down here, his grandson came to visit down here (in 2007).

He came to the museum. He likes old cars, and he just put a Web page up there. He does Web pages for congressmen back in Washington, so I guess he knows what he's doing."

Has it drawn visitors to his attraction?

Cloud shrugged and scratched the wet coat of his other border collie, Jill, tagging alongside.

"Guess so," he said. "It's not really about drawing people."

Good thing, too, because finding the place amid the maze of brown desert sands and the green squares of ag fields is, as Cloud says, pert-near impossible. But he likes it that way—an attraction that exists mostly for the builder himself.

One Big-A** Hole in the Ground

October 2013
Town: Boron
County: Kern
Population: 2,253
Elevation: 2,025 feet

Odd thoughts come to you on the road, the mind lulled by the deadly combination of mundanity and inertia into strange reveries as the broken white lines roll under your feet.

Finding myself recently on a vast, forsaken stretch of Highway 58 in the Mojave Desert, with the only thing to look forward to being a stop at a convenience store to gas up, I posed a challenge to myself.

To wit: Could I write about a visit to the Borax Visitor Center, a corporate tribute to the caustic hand soap and household cleaning solvent that spawned a 1950s TV show, in this one-horse—but 20-mule-team—town without inducing spontaneous narcolepsy in readers and myself?

The task seemed enormous, big as the 700-foot-deep, mile-long hole in the ground that serves as Boron's raison d'être. So many times over the decades, while driving to Las Vegas or taking the long way to San Diego, I had zoomed past the beckoning Borax billboard and left that Boron off-ramp in the dust, not feeling a whit of remorse for missing tales of heroic mules hauling rocks from pits.

This time, though, I flicked the blinker and headed toward an erector set of grim, gray buildings and snaking towers amid an ocher landscape. Already, I was questioning my judgment.

Writing about dirt? Has it come to that? I mean, really?

For those who've stuck around, permit me to give you what we in the journalism racket call a teaser to whet your reading interest.

In the next, oh, 500 words, you'll read about:

- Your clueless narrator nearly getting nailed by a train.

- A kindly docent who may wind up getting fired in the wake of his honesty.

- Ronald Reagan's second-best acting performance.

- Souvenir calcimine rocks that look like something they cook and smoke on *Breaking Bad*.

- The existential ennui that comes from staring too long into an abyss.

Gosh, who knew exploring the site of the world's largest deposits of the fifth element on the periodic table could be so pulse-pounding?

The drive in off the freeway offers a peculiar pull. The industrial skyline, the only thing vertical within miles, seems close enough to touch. Yet, you keep moving and, mirage-like, so does it.

Upon finally reaching the site of Rio Tinto (the British-Australian multi-national that acquired Borax U.S. a few years back), you get a taste of the company's dry (make that arid) wit on a sign: "Maximum Speed: 37½."

Full disclosure: I may have been pushing 37⅞ in the turbo-charged company hybrid car. But I came to a complete stop at the railroad tracks just before the entrance. A train, about eight box cars in length, inched along the tracks at about the same speed as my osteoporotic mother-in-law ambles. Five minutes passed, almost 10, and the train still blocked the only path to the center.

Did I consider doing a U-turn and abandoning my assignment?

Yes, reader, I did.

But then the train, as if sensing my irritation, chuffed and clattered and started, excruciatingly slowly, to reverse itself. When it had almost cleared the intersection, I started the engine and hit the gas pedal. That's when the train jerked and started moving forward once more. I cleared its cow catcher with mere feet to spare.

Slightly shaken, I followed arrows to the visitors' center up a man-made berm (sign: "Speed Uphill: 23").

According to Borax's website, 126,845 people have visited the center since 2011. All I saw was an empty parking lot with a replica of a 20-mule-team wagon in front of a handsome, single-story building. That, and a portable toilet. No cars. Inside, I saw lots of pretty, shiny rocks sheathed in glass displays as if the place was housing the Hope Diamond. A brass plaque told me it was "ulexite."

"Here ya go!" a voice behind me barked.

I nearly tumbled into the precious ulexite. Before me stood a kindly docent, an éminence grise wearing a nametag: Gene Van Horn.

He was holding out a laminated card affixed with four chunks of real, honest-to-goodness minerals mined at the plant: borax, colemanite, kernite and the aforementioned ulexite ($NaCaB_5O_{98}H_2O$, for those keeping score at home). On the flip side, a handy explanation with this self-congratulatory tidbit: "Borax ships approximately one million tons of refined borates to customers in nearly 100 countries."

I made small talk with Van Horn. We were the only two people in the center, after all. He said he worked in the plant for 55 years but now is retired. I asked if much had changed in his time.

Uh, oh . . .

"A lot has changed," he said, sounding none too happy. "They changed owners and it's not the same. Different rules and regulations in the plant. You're not a person, you're a number."

As if remembering his PR job, Van Horn quickly recovered and pointed me toward exhibits showing all the household items that contain this special mineral: footballs, magnifying glasses, frying pans, hammocks and detergents ranging from Tide and Cheer to the classic Borax your grand-mother used.

"It's used in about 3,000 things," Van Horn said. "There's hardly not anything you can't pick up that doesn't one way or the other have some (boron) in it."

The docent was informative, but the 10-minute company film in a sepa-rate room featured our future pitchman-in-chief—Ronald Reagan. He hosted the 1950s TV show *Death Valley Days*, a model for product place-ment. On YouTube, check out the Gipper rubbing axle grease on his palm and then using Boraxo Waterless Hand Cleaner to miraculously wipe it clean.

When the film ended, the curtains covering the floor-to-ceiling windows parted and visitors were treated to a sweeping view of the open pit. This machine-made concavity lacks the grandeur of, say, the Grand Canyon, but you can't help but entertain deep, meaningful thoughts as you peer into its vast depths.

Big hole, man. Big fuckin' hole.

I then hopped in the car and made it to San Diego by nightfall.

2

Set Loose in LA

The sun is a joke. Oranges can't titillate their jaded palates. Nothing can ever be violent enough to make taut their slack minds and bodies. They have been cheated and betrayed. They have slaved and saved for nothing.
—Nathanael West, *The Day of the Locust*

Tip the world over on its side and everything loose will land in Los Angeles.
—Frank Lloyd Wright

In Search of LA Noir

April 2012
Town: Los Angeles
County: Los Angeles
Population: 3,884,000 (more moving in daily)
Elevation: 233 feet

It was a dank, rain-sodden Raymond Chandler kind of morning, as if some omnipotent auteur had rung up the studio and ordered a classic film-noir sky. Cumulonimbus clouds the color of a snub-nosed revolver hovered with ominous intent, and tires on slickened freeway lanes gave off a sinister, knife-sharpening hiss.

Only a sap would be out on a day like this, searching for the seedy, serrated soul of LA noir.

Yet tourists often come here, searching for the Los Angeles of the 1930s, '40s and '50s. They seek remnants of a period when the city was an incubator of tawdriness, a place where corruption, double-dealing and unchecked passion gave rise to a literary and cinematic genre that to this day captures the imagination.

Fitting, then, that the weather would cooperate and set the mood. But, really, the sun has never served as a nourishing, warming presence in LA noir; rather, it's a carcinogenic inferno bent on mocking desperate dreamers with incessant, incongruous cheeriness.

Already this morning, fueled by too many black and bitter cups o' Joe, you've swung by the Southern Pacific Railroad Depot in Glendale. Scene of the crime in the seminal noir thriller *Double Indemnity*, you picture a hunch-shouldered, stubble-jawed Fred MacMurray skulking around the tanned Mission Revival structure, not stopping to admire the twisted columns or handcrafted ironwork.

Now, you head downtown and to the Hotel Barclay (né Hotel Van Nuys), one of Chandler's haunts and the setting for the gruesome ice-pick-in-the-neck murder scene in his novel *The Little Sister*. All that remains is the art deco sign; the hotel has long been shuttered, its windows cracked and duct-taped.

Move along, bub. Nothing to see here.

Plenty to see at the nearby Millennium Biltmore, the famous, swanky downtown hotel that once hosted the Oscars and retains its ornate, retro opulence. This was, legend has it, the last place the Black Dahlia (aka Elizabeth Short) was seen in 1947 before her dismembered body was discovered in a weedy patch south of town.

That's a real-life murder, pal, not some made-up movie plot. (Although, this being Los Angeles, where fact and fiction can quickly meld, it eventually became a feature film.) In its day, the Black Dahlia case—still unsolved—created a media frenzy: Think O.J. Simpson trial to the nth degree.

In the expansive lobby, featuring a stained-glass ceiling and marble fountains with water trickling out of lions' mouths, you try to picture the Black Dahlia in her low-cut black dress, snapping gum and batting heavily mascaraed eyelashes as she slinks out the door toward her fate.

You approach a dame behind a desk. She has an alluring smile, one that can make even the most cynical wise guy ask impertinent questions. She says her name is Nicole Solum. Claims she's the hotel concierge. You have no reason to doubt her.

"We get people bringing it up all the time," she says. "Sometimes, we get tour groups. Sometimes, they'll ask if (the Black Dahlia's) ghost haunts the halls."

What of it? Is it true about ghosts? Spill it, sister.

"Well, this is an old hotel," she says, leaving the answer dangling. "We don't mind people asking. We even have a cocktail in the bar called the Black Dahlia."

No time to imbibe the novelty Black Dahlia martini made with Absolut Citron vodka, Kahlua and Chambord raspberry liqueur. A teeming metropolis awaits.

You hightail it to Hollywood Boulevard and Musso & Frank Grill, where in a back room celebrated writers of the era (everyone from Chandler to Nathanael West to F. Scott Fitzgerald and William Faulkner) used to convene to rinse away brain cells after selling out and penning noir scripts.

Upon arrival, you see that the landmark restaurant is smack dab in the middle of the area's cheesiest tourist trap, an area best avoided unless you want to beat yourself up with existential ennui.

Make a sharp right on Ivar Street and search for West's rented cottage, the place where he wrote *The Day of the Locust*. In the novel, he calls Ivar Street "Lysol Alley" and says the rooming house was "mainly inhabited by hustlers, their managers, trainers and advance agents." Now, it appears little more than a clean, middle-class neighborhood of apartment buildings and bungalows. Under the gentrified facade? Well, who knows?

Hollywood Boulevard can quickly wear on even the most resolute cultural gumshoe, so you travel west on Santa Monica Boulevard to the blood-red exterior of the Formosa Cafe, away from the tourist hordes. Back in the day, this watering hole was said to be a police-protected hangout for gangsters, molls, prizefighters and bookies.

Moviegoers may remember the Formosa as the setting in the neo-noir 1997 flick *L.A. Confidential*, where a detective played by Guy Pearce says to a bleached blonde in a booth that "a hooker cut to look like Lana Turner is still a hooker; she just looks like Lana Turner," while worldly partner Kevin Spacey smirks because he knows it really is Lana Turner sitting there.

Los Angeles is so movie-saturated that you forget the crimes were real. A trip northeast of town to the Los Angeles Police Historical Society Museum—housed in a decommissioned police precinct headquarters— slaps some sense into you. It also makes you realize that the city's noirish-ness both predates the film genre and mutated into a surrealist noir in the '60s and beyond.

A museum dedicated to the LAPD might at first come off as a mug's game for noir fans, given that the Rodney King and Rampart corruption scandals are not mentioned. Yet the museum provides plenty of grisly exhibits about cases that defined the city, from the Black Dahlia to the Manson Family and beyond.

Remember the 1973 Symbionese Liberation Army shootout in South LA? It is memorialized pictorially and on video. Evidence includes gas masks and pipe bombs retrieved from the SLA safe house and a red-and-black serpent flag like the one Patty Hearst posed in front of after her "Tanya" transformation. Remember the 1997 North Hollywood bank robbery shootout and daylong hostage situation played out on live TV? The museum shows mannequins dressed in the bloodstained body armor of the robbers and chillingly displays the bulletproof bank teller's window with gunshot indentations intact.

But it's the traditional period pieces that best recall the noir era. Jail cells remain from the 1940s. Batons and blackjacks merit their own display case, as do gangster-period machine guns. Lurid headlines, often flanked by fingerprints and mug shots, from the period's infamous kidnappings and murders line the walls. But, in an only-in-LA twist, fiction mingles with fact with tributes to Jack Webb (*Dragnet* fame) and the TV show *Adam-12*.

As you wander the drafty floors of the old police station, the museum seems to tell you that the good guys (the cops) always won in the end. It's a sunny and sanitized display, right down to the life-size cutout of former Police Chief Daryl Gates, toothy grin and all, at the front desk.

Your noir brain, however, recalls that line in Orson Welles' *Touch of Evil*, filmed in nearby Venice: "A policeman's job is easy in a police state."

Seeking answers, you buttonhole the flatfoot in charge, museum director Glynn B. Martin, a retired cop, whose enthusiastic handshake crunches your metacarpals.

"These are all materials given to us through court processes or the DA or the Police Department," he says in just-the-facts-ma'am tone. "We go through the formal disposition process. We're a stand-alone nonprofit but obviously work in close cooperation with the department. For the Black Dahlia (exhibit), robbery-homicide has an entire file cabinet with tens of thousands of pages of materials and photographs, so we were able to draw from that. But nothing gruesome. We're not a ghoul show."

Sanitize it if you must, but noir can be gruesome.

Quoth Chandler from *The Long Goodbye*: "Out there in the night of a thousand crimes, people were dying, being maimed, cut by flying glass, crushed against steering wheels or under heavy tires. People were beaten, robbed, strangled, raped and murdered."

Where to see the lurid underbelly? Tipsters point you to the Museum of Death on Hollywood Boulevard. There, beyond the serial killer and suicide cult memorabilia and the room dedicated to the embalming process, lies the California Death Room.

Not for the squeamish, it shows graphic photos of actress Sharon Tate, murdered by the Manson Family; even more hideous severed-torso police shots from the Black Dahlia investigation; and a wall dedicated to later serial killer cases—the Hillside Strangler and the Night Stalker.

You approach two young women, who don't look to be the type to frequent a joint like this, but here they are. They say they're tourists from Memphis, Tenn. They look honest, wholesome, not yet beaten down by the naked city. You take them at their word. You ask why they've come here.

"This kind of thing always intrigues me, you know," says Hannah McCaleb. "Like, we don't know what death is so we want to come and find out as much as we can."

Cohort Felicia Hankins, unfazed by the carnage, adds slyly: "We know all about Manson. And I've seen the Black Dahlia movie. We had some chicken for lunch and then came on over here."

The femme fatale who runs the Museum of Death, a dazzling redhead named Kathy Schultz, says she has gotten death threats from people who say "we should not be promoting serial killers, these despicable people." She adjusts her horn-rimmed glasses and casts a gimlet eye on you: "Look, I love life and all aspects of life. And part of life is death."

You leave and can't get that William Holden line from *Sunset Boulevard* out of your head: "Funny how gentle people get with you once you're dead."

Dusk approaching, the sky becomes, in West's words, "one of those blue and lavender nights when the luminous color seems to have been blown over the scene with an airbrush."

You have one last stop. You drive south on the freeway 20 miles to Rancho Palos Verdes and Green Hills Memorial Park. You're looking for Charles Bukowski's grave. It's been said that Bukowski's gritty, dissolute poetry and prose brought LA noir into modern times.

Certainly, he had the seediness part down. At least two dozen bars in LA boast that "Bukowski drank here" before his death in 1994. You're told that Bukowski fans, in tribute, often drink, smoke and fornicate upon his grave.

All you see at plot 875, with its headstone overlooking Palos Verdes mansions to the right and the port of San Pedro to the left, are two wilted flowers in a cup, rain-soaked and missing a few petals.

His epitaph reads: "Don't try."

A perfect noir image.

Downtown Goes Upscale: A Gentrification Tale

February 2016
City sector: Downtown (DTLA)
Square miles: 5.84
Population in 2000: 27,849
Population in 2015: 52,400

Not even noon, on a weekday, no less, and the line for entrance to the Broad Museum was long and lemming-like. It took up a good two blocks, formidable city blocks, in a town not known for pedestrian traffic. Black-clad, whippet-thin museum workers tried mightily to corral this docile yet teeming mass of art-loving humanity, directing the herd northward. It wrapped around Grand Avenue, snaked clear down Second Street, then doglegged left onto Hope Street. Finally, mercifully, the queue petered out at the last entrance to an underground parking garage.

Wait time to gain admission? Two hours, maybe three. Who knows? Who cares?

The Broad, on a winter's day in 2015, was new and shiny, the latest jewel in downtown Los Angeles' undeniable revitalization, so people gladly waited with an intensity once seen only in Depression bread lines. Across Second, the sun glinted off the metallic wings of the Frank Gehry–designed Walt Disney Concert Hall, which looked as if it might levitate and soar off, but few seemed to notice. Heads were lowered, not in supplication but at their handheld screens, a few retro outliers opting to read from text imprinted on emulsified wood pulp. They brought provisions, too, bulgogi beef from a nearby Korean food truck, boba tea from a joint on Hope, kosher hot dogs sprouting sauerkraut from a street vendor whose jaunty wool driver's cap seemed pilfered from studio wardrobe.

Every few minutes, incremental progress could be detected. The line shuffled forward, sometimes gaining a giant leap of a whole yard, prompting people to look up and, good Lord, actually make eye contact with fellow would-be museumgoers.

"I knew it would be a long line," said Echo Yang, from the Orange County 'burb of Brea. "But not this big. I've been planning this since September, since it opened. They said there's always a line."

No line, by the way, at the Museum of Contemporary Art, diagonally across Grand, where Warhol and Rothko, Rauschenberg and Pollock awaited. But MOCA was old news, so last century. Got to genuflect at the ever-changing altar of the new, this latest gift (yes, free admission!) to the city by Eli Broad, real estate developer and philanthropist, that features Warhol and Koons, Rauschenburg and Basquiat—essentially the same lineup of modern-art icons as at MOCA. Got to literally rub shoulders with the Broad's perforated white carapace, flippantly dubbed by architecture critics a "supersized cheese grater" (*Guardian* [U.K.]) and a "distorted waffle" (*Independent* [U.K.]) with the "color and texture of gefilte fish" (*New York Times*). Got to, you know, make the scene.

"Well, it is new and all," said Tiana Griego, a Hollywood resident who, with devout patience, had gutted it out to the upper third of the line with friend Jesus Soria. "Everybody's gonna check it out."

Visiting the Broad wouldn't be worth it, the sentiment runs, if you could just walk right in. Where's the exclusivity in that? Where's the buzz, the social cachet? These days, nothing bolsters a person's trend-seeking, social-influencing bona fides like hanging in downtown Los Angeles. This would've been a ludicrous, not to mention dangerous, proposition even into the early 2000s. But downtown's population has swelled from 26,000 in the 2000 census to 52,000 as of 2014. Civic boosters branded this example of an urban renaissance, and its ubiquitous acronym was attached to streetlight poles and public transit stops and even spawned a mural of a beatific woman, whose ethnicity seems purposely ambiguous, looking down on the corner of Sixth and Spring, a nimbus of golden light swirling over her raven locks adding religious overtones. Its title: Our Lady of DTLA. Its purpose, according to an artist statement on the website for the nonprofit

Mural Conservancy of Los Angeles: "She is a celebration of life & love here in downtown poised to host this new incarnation of DTLA into the future."

DTLA? Old-timers might remember when that could well have stood as an admonition to day-trippers or office-working commuters as the sun sets: Don't Tarry Long Angelenos.

Now, though, Los Angeles boasts a burgeoning cultural hub (Broad, Disney, MOCA) in its Bunker Hill neighborhood. It offers expensive and exclusive bars and restaurants, some of which occupy erstwhile bank vaults, power-company offices and long-shuttered department stores that look quasi-dilapidated yet somehow still regal in a Norma Desmond way. Live-work lofts, whose ground floors are leased to businesses such as designer pet boutiques and hookah lounges, line once-bleak Spring Street. Charming boutique hotels, such as the Standard and the Figueroa, have made strides in attempting to blot out blight, as has the massive Staples Center sports and entertainment complex that anchors DTLA's far-western flank.

Skid Row endures, of course, its sidewalk encampments and high-profile poverty serving as a stark juxtaposition to all the sidewalk seating at bistros mere blocks away. Crime has hardly been rinsed clean, like so many coupe glasses at clubs with red-velvet ropes. In September, that violent crime in the downtown corridor increased 57 percent, and property offenses almost 25 percent, over the same period the previous year, the *Los Angeles Times* reported. A new type of crime has blossomed, the paper stated: "Creeper" burglaries, in which thieves will snatch smartphones and purses from tables while heads are turned. Mayor Eric Garcetti called the rising homeless population a public emergency and has taken steps to find shelter for the growing numbers.

Such incidents perhaps are inevitable, given the tension of downtown's rapid transformation, gentrification being both a boon and a burden.

The boon is obvious: more money pumped into the civic bloodstream, resuscitating its municipal heart. No longer can critics (especially those haughty New Yorkers) whine that Los Angeles has no center. Garcetti, speaking at the Broad opening, called the museum the "crown atop downtown," his implication being that DTLA now has ascended to a kingdom worthy of such laurels.

The burden may be less obvious to visitors: the economic migration of longtime residents, many Latino, from downtown, priced out of their neighborhood. South Broadway, the bustling retail boulevard once dominated by Latino businesses, eateries, jewelry stores and bodegas, is in mid-transition. Family-run taquerias try to stay open amid the proliferation of trendy bistros, whose wafting aroma of kale and coconut stir-fry compete with that of deep-fried chicharrones. Mom-and-pop businesses are pushed out by chains, as the likes of Walgreens are forcing businesses to find other digs. The clatter of construction cranes, razing and rebuilding the western half of Main Street, is the sound of success to civic boosters, but a symphony of sorrow to those bent on maintaining history.

"Let me ask you this: What's the majority (ethnicity) in California? Hispanics," said Richard Blitz, owner of Farmacia y Botanica, a pharmacy that deals in Mexican prayer candles and folk medicine, which will lose its lease at the end of January. "When you gentrify you're displacing the majority of your population. They make it too damn expensive for people. The developers come in and build. They started in Silver Lake, then Echo Park (both neighborhoods north of downtown), moving east. Boyle Heights is next. And, of course, here in downtown. There's no place for (longtime residents) to go."

Atwater Village, north of Silver Lake and southeast of Griffith Park, is another nearby neighborhood experiencing gentrification, said resident Monica Chavez. She lingers with her children and friends at the new 24,000-square-foot plaza outside the Broad, shaded by century-old Barouni olive trees replanted by the same landscape architect who designed New York's High Line public park. She sits on the repurposed tree-trunk benches, ringed by dymondia, and said she harbors mixed feelings toward DTLA (she didn't use the acronym, which might be telling).

"Oh, it certainly is a different world," Chavez said. "Years ago, you didn't want to be here. We spend a lot of time here now. We also spend too much money here. But there is the problem of people not having anywhere to go because of rent and cost of living."

Such ambivalence is common among Angelenos. Carol Thompson, in her 70s and a native, grew up playing on the erstwhile "railway" that ferried people up from Hill Street to Bunker Hill. She can point to most any building downtown and say what used to be there. Change, to her, is inevitable. She does not begrudge "progress" but does not want to see the city lose sight of its heritage.

"You know, people always think downtown was not a good area in the past, but that's not true," she said. "It was very upscale in the '40s and before that, too. It had a real economy here. The department stores were upscale—

Bullocks, Robinson's and the Broadway—and the restaurants down here had a lot of class, a lot of continental fine dining for the time. About the mid-'50s is when I noticed it changing."

Now she's noticed it changing back.

"What they need is more of a mix, in terms of prices for lofts and apartments," she said.

Her lunch companion at Grand Market, the venerable (since 1917) open-air arcade of dining and produce markets, Shirley Chasin, of Studio City, added a positive note: "At least the development people are embracing the (existing) architecture and history and are no longer just willing to demolish the old LA."

Chasin brought up the preservation of the Bradbury Building, said to be the oldest commercial building in downtown (1893). With its dizzying staircases featuring ornate iron railings and marble steps, as well as a sweeping skylight and open-cage elevators, the building had fallen into disrepair before a 1990s makeover. Before restoration, director Ridley Scott used the building for a key scene in the film *Blade Runner*, cinematically reveling in the Bradbury's shabby-chic vibe.

To those whose idea of the "Old LA" extends only as far back as the 1980s, the idea of preservation might strike a chord of curious incongruity. Visitors overwhelmingly like the changes. They like feeling safer and like the nightlife.

Traveler Tamer Shaaban, from Washington, D.C., was dining at the Grand Central Market's sidewalk tables on Broadway, in front of the trendy restaurant Egg Slut. As he was talking, a homeless man lugging a bulging Hefty bag rummaged through the trash receptacles for plastic bottles and recyclables. Neither cast the other a glance, though Shaaban later acknowledged that gentrification can't be all bad if he's able to enjoy a sunny afternoon al fresco.

"It's the cost of luxury," he said of DTLA's ambitions. "In my opinion, it feels like (Los Angeles) is still on its way, not quite done yet. There's definitely places where it's been built up great. But, then, you'll run into pockets of the old LA."

Old and new LA meld at hipster haunts such as the Edison (its pitch: "Industrial cathedral crafted from the architectural artifacts of LA's first private power plant") and the Croker Club (pitch: "Drink inside the vault . . . of the old Crocker Citizens National Bank"). Hoteliers are snatching up historic buildings, as well. Two years ago, the Ace Hotel (and performance space) converted a 1920s office building on Ninth and Broadway.

But it's the new-new of DTLA that has newcomers, mostly the loft-dwellers, downright giddy. Brigham Yen, a marketing and real estate businessman, has started a blog called *DTLA Rising* which unabashedly cheerleads for the area's growth. He recently breathlessly reported a rumor that an Apple Store might open in an abandoned theater on Broadway. When downtown's first Whole Foods Market opened on Eighth and Grand, Yen enthused, "Some might say the opening of Whole Foods means Downtown LA has truly arrived—for good."

Hype rings hollow without results, though. Success stories can be found any evening at any number of nightclubs. These are trendy dance clubs offering artisanal cocktails, not Bukowskian dives serving Schlitz. The Pattern Bar, on Ninth Street in the Fashion District, is a prime example. Back in DTLABG (Before Gentrification), the Fashion District cleared out by nightfall. Now, with nearby lofts and reason for those working in the fashion industry to hang around after clocking out, the place is hopping.

"It's the house music and the DJ curation," said Eduardo Meza, Pattern bartender and cousin of co-owner Alejandro Meza. "We get the young people, 21 to mid-30s. But we also get people who work here. That's really what we're most known for, our drinks, named after fashion designers." (To wit: the Chanel: "Tequila reposado, orange liqueur, fresh cilantro, organic agave, serrano pepper and fresh lime.")

Pattern Bar has lasted nearly five years, which, given the churn of the restaurant/bar business and DTLA's short memory, qualifies as real staying power. Soon, it might even graduate to venerable.

Back in line at the Broad, where that new-museum smell had yet to wear off, the line's movement was glacial but inexorable.

Lisa Naslund and her two teenage sons, from Torrance, joined the queue back on Hope Street, near the parking garage. It was 2 p.m. now, and they were halfway up Second Street. They were confident they could gain entrance before the museum closed at 5 p.m. Even if they didn't get a lot of time to take selfies in front of Jeff Koon's porcelain *Michael Jackson and Bubbles*, even if by some chance the line clogged like the 405 Freeway at rush hour and they didn't get in, their day trip to DTLA would not be wasted.

"I was just thinking that I'd love to come here more," Naslund said. "Maybe go to the Grand Market or find some great noodles. It'll be a good experience for the guys because Torrance, you know, is a bedroom community. We need to come to the city more, I think."

A Spiritual Antidote for Urban Ennui?

December 2015

City sector: DTLA

Percentage of Hispanic population in 2000: 36.7

Percentage in 2015: 25

So there I was, walking down Broadway in this most impersonal of cities and wondering why I felt so cold and hollow even though it was 72 degrees in mid-November, when I glanced up after crossing Third Street. I saw, literally, a sign. It was in red, with an all-caps script: *Se Hacen Limpias. Haga Su Cita.*

My long-forgotten college Spanish dredged up a crude translation, something along the lines of "Become clean. Make your appointment."

A spiritual cleansing, I assumed. I'm fully capable of tending to my personal hygiene, thank you very much, and this corner store, whose sign read "Farmacia y Botanica Million Dollar," didn't appear to be the kind of place that offers trendy high-colonic cleanses. (Go to the Westside, Century City or Santa Monica for that.) No, this seemed to be a drugstore where the secular and the saintly, the spiritual and the medicinal, commingle.

The window displays, which an innocent might first mistake as fronting a folk art museum exhibit, confirmed it.

There was an 8-inch figurine of San Lazarus, eyes mournful, expression hangdog, leaning on crutches while suppurating wounds decorate his bare chest. There was San Simon, spiffily suited and sitting on a throne like a total boss, stogie between his lips, a bulging bag of coins in one hand, a gold cane in the other. There was the bust of a raffish, mustachioed dandy with bedroom eyes, identified cryptically as "Jesus Malverde." And there she was, *Santa Muerte* herself, the venerated personification of holy death, begowned in frilly lace, holding a scythe, her high cheekbones so pronounced because it's just her grinning skull.

Curiosity—Who are these icons? What's their significance? Can they help me?—compelled me to enter.

At first glance, you don't even recognize it as a pharmacy, so overwhelming are the statues and figurines that seem a sectarian mix of Roman Catholicism and Yoruban-inspired. The eye next goes to the colorful candles and rows of holy water, promising everything from a cure for your hemorrhoids to success in the weekly lottery. Then you notice the richly adorned alcoves, serving as temples to the saints, and side rooms offering card readings and the aforementioned spiritual cleansings. But look closer and, yeah, you do see Band-Aids, ChapStick and Tylenol.

No surprise that a store such as this existed downtown, given that this stretch of Broadway long had been a Latino shopping stronghold. What was surprising: that Farmacia y Botanica Million Dollar survived a decade's worth of gentrification that has seen many Latino businesses, and their clientele, priced out. So this would be a feel-good story, something to lift spirits, most notably my own. You know, that whole plucky-underdog angle, tradition triumphing over trendiness.

But not five minutes after Richard ("Call me Dick") Blitz, the 77-year-old *farmacia* owner, greeted me with a metacarpal-crunching handshake did he disabuse me of such sappy notions.

"There was a loophole in our lease," he said, bluntly. "We'll be out by the end of January."

And he was right. A few months after my visit, the pharmacy closed. Word is, a trendy boutique is on the way, where you may not be able to cleanse your spirit but certainly can fill your closet.

Blitz, who owned the shop for decades, was in full acceptance mode when I visited. He has seen the Million Dollar Theater building go through many incarnations and was matter-of-fact about the closure. No hand-wringing, no crowdfunding campaigns to forestall closure. He complained about the evils of the "G-word" (gentrification), sure, but even those protestations seemed halfhearted. Nope, Blitz knew he didn't have a prayer.

True, *farmacia* regulars can find other Santeria botanicas in more Latino-populated sectors of Greater Los Angeles. But, as the travel website Atlas Obscura noted in an early write-up, "This one is an eccentric among eccentrics."

Mostly, that was due to the sheer volume of religious fetishes. They lined every wall, filled all display cases. The altars (yes, more than one) dedicated to *Santa Muerte* were strewn with monetary offerings, coins and dollar bills. People left notes, wishes for illnesses to be healed or straying spouses to return. There were candles marked *Destrancadera* to unblock one's path to happiness; others under the heading *Leche de la Mujer Amada* (milk of the beloved mother), whose astral essences promote intimacy and attraction; a bathwater called *Separación: Rompe Amores* (love breaks); and water called *Tapa Boca* (mouth cap) to stop others' gossip. You also could buy bath herbs called *Miel de Amor* (love honey). Directions: "Mix well and stay in tub about 7 minutes while bathing and reflect on desires."

"We used to light hundreds of candles in here and people would come and pray," Blitz said. "The city came in and shut down the candle burning. Guess they were worried about their high-rises going up (in flames)."

Ask Blitz about the origins of the statues, or even about the ingredients sprinkled on the candles to cast spells, and he quickly called over one of his employees to explain.

I pointed to the ceramic visage of San Simon, the one surrounded by money bags and bling, and Blitz called, "Gladys, San Simon? *¿Qué? ¿Suerte?*"

"Yes," Gladys answered in English. "It's for good luck. For money, actually."

Next, I pointed to the statue of the mysterious Jesus Malverde.

"I know that one," he said, smiling. "Jesus Malverde is for marijuana, right, Gladys?"

The reason Blitz was not well-versed in Santeria religious lore?

"I'm Jewish," he said.

When queried to explain his cross-cultural entrepreneurship, Blitz said, "About 10, 15 years ago, I had to get more business, so we came up with the candles and (spiritual) water things. (The store) just evolved slowly."

Blitz said he respects all religions and the rituals and totems used therein. He was just providing a service to his Latino customers. He added that "We never sold anything bad, no evil spells. Praying for your daughter? Fine. Love? Money? Fine. But nothing bad. We could do it. We don't. We can't control what people do with the candles."

So, sort of a don't-ask-don't-tell policy?

"Yeah, you might say that," Blitz said. "But I used to warn people and say, 'If you wish bad on somebody else, it'll bite you in the ass.'"

A Full Plate of History

January 2016
City sector: DTLA
Cost of meal at Clifton's in 1935: "Pay What You Can"
Cost of meal in 2015: $14

The Jell-O molds, they are a-quiverin'. All lined up along the cafeteria rows, they seem alive, almost sentient, swaying like drunkards on petite white dessert plates whenever diners reach out and snatch up squares of sweetness. These chunks of gelatinous sugar and collagen come in colors not often found in food that Michael Pollan would recommend, electric blue and traffic-cone orange. Globules of fruit hang suspended in the jiggly mass, though a positive identification of the exact berry embedded therein proves murky. Little matter: It's Jell-O, so it's going on the tray, no questions asked.

Isn't that just so, so Clifton's?

As with the over-the-top faux woodsy interior, replete with taxidermied animals posed in mid-snarl amid a lush redwood forest motif, on Broadway and Seventh Street in the heart of downtown Los Angeles wouldn't be the same without its signature wiggly confection that once sold for 35 cents but still seems a bargain today at $2.

This old-school cafeteria, which served hearty, stick-to-your-ribs fare such as roast beef and whirled peas and chicken-fried steak and mashed potatoes to hungry, often homeless, Angelenos since Depression times, has endured a depression of its own. Closing in 2010 after 75 years, when the last of the Clifford Clinton family could no longer make a go of it, Clifton's was bought for $3.6 million by retro-loving developer Andrew Meieran, who seemingly owns half of downtown.

Five years and $10 million in renovations later, it's back and drawing crowds—maybe not the sheer numbers, estimated at 15,000 a day, that flocked there in its heyday, but Clifton's is definitely a must-stop for Southern California natives bent on a nostalgia trip and tourists wanting an "authentic" LA experience in a town where history often is subsumed by a craving for all things new.

It's the same, but it's also different. It's been praised by wistful nostalgists but also panned by strident purists. It still serves the comfort-food staples—chefs are said to consult recipe cards unearthed from 1935—but has added an uber-healthful salad bar, vegan and gluten-free options and the seemingly obligatory craft-beer bar. The original kitschy outdoors theme for the interior endures, but Meieran and his design minions have supersized it, most notably adding a three-story, 40-foot steel and concrete redwood tree that looks so lifelike it puts cell-tower "trees" to shame.

Compared to more-upscale downtown establishments, many of which Meieran built and owns, Clifton's remains something of a bargain. A hearty turkey dinner with all the fixin's will set you back about $14. That may not seem affordable to the homeless and those hovering near the poverty line—who, historians note, dined on a pay-what-you-can basis back in the old Clifton's, circa World War II—but Meieran has made an effort to retain some of the original's civic-mindedness. To that end, 10 percent of the workers are from the homeless program Midnight Mission or are at-risk youth.

But, to be sure, Clifton's no longer is an extension of the down-and-out bread line. Original owner Clifford Clinton, whose parents were Salvation Army missionaries, dubbed his cafeteria the "Golden Rule Restaurant"—i.e, you got a square meal even if you couldn't pay. But even during the height of the Depression, Clifton's was much more than a gussied-up soup kitchen. Back in the day, it drew an eclectic mix of notable Angelenos. How eclectic? Try L. Ron Hubbard, Jack Kerouac, Ray Bradbury and Nathanael West among its regulars. In later years, filmmaker David Lynch occasionally slid into a booth.

These days, you're more likely to find the technorati, rather than Hollywood glitterati, holing up here. At least, that's the way it's been hyped since its reopening in fall 2015, based on the scores of Instagram feeds featuring campy interior shots of Clifton's. *Los Angeles Times* architcture critic Christopher Hawthorne recently opined that "this spiffed-up temple of idiosyncrasy" is geared toward a "target demographic (that) probably first learned about its rebirth on a glowing screen of some kind" and that these young influencers "may reminisce about (their first) visit on a third (visit)." History, Hawthorne worried, might be shunted aside because "new kitsch has been laid alongside well-scrubbed old kitsch."

A recent visit somewhat refuted such traditionalist fretting. During the weekday lunch hour, the line stretching outside the door was 20 deep, with nary a man-bun, Converse-wearing hipster in sight. The only people with blue hair were elderly women with unfortunate dye jobs. People held canes, not selfie-sticks. For sure, there were non-AARP customers, but they had come with their parents who, back in the day, came with their parents, and so on.

The line parted near the door, where a party emerged from the dimly lit dining area to the brightness of Broadway. Brothers Ernie and Edward Garcia, along with their mother, Virginia, all of Claremont, were expressing a voluble Yelp-like review people could overhear.

"We were born and raised on Clifton's, and I gotta say . . . it's not the same," Ernie said.

Virginia: "The food is dry."

Edward: "The aesthetics is nice, but that's as far as it goes."

Ernie: "Knowing there's so much history and all the (stuffed) bears and stuff like being in a forest, that's a nostalgia thing for us. But the food is not real Clifton's. Clifton's was such comfort food. It was just bad."

"Dry," Virginia repeated.

The Garcia family's assessment apparently did not dissuade those in line. Nobody left. Maybe they had read that Clifton's pastry chef is none other than Michael Luna, who has worked for Gordon Ramsay and Wolfgang Puck and at Le Foret in New Orleans. Maybe they just wanted to eat whatever was available in a campy setting. Or maybe they just had a craving for Jell-O.

People milled about, necks craning to take in the five-story facade with the burnished marquee saying "Living History" and "Cabinet of Curiosities" rather than the original "Meals for Millions Foundation" and "Food Service Training School." Just then, another diner emerged, Catalina Maravilla, 64, of Burbank.

"I haven't been here for 34 years," she said. "I used to come all the time back then. I've been waiting for it to reopen. The restaurant itself, the decorations? I am extremely pleased. A few details are different, like the stairs are different and a lot of those (stuffed) animals are new. But I think it's lovely."

The food?

"Listen," she said, index finger pointing upward. "I'm picky, extremely picky. I used to come all the time for the traditional ham. And they don't have it now! They ask me inside, 'Is everything OK?' I said, 'No, you have no ham. Where is the traditional ham? I was coming for the ham.' That's the only dish I care about. There were other Clifton's, you know, in Century

City, Cerritos and Covina. All closed. I went to all of them. And the reason I went was for the ham. Now, no ham. Very sad. I talked to the manager. I opened my big mouth. I want ham."

Even without ham, the offerings along the bustling cafeteria lines and stations could be daunting, resulting in a paralysis of choices. Row upon row of macaroni and potato salads in small porcelain dishes are lined up next to legions of fruit cups and steaming cauldrons of soup. That evocative throwback feel is broken when you reach the salad bar, thoroughly 21st century. Its sign may be in a '50s font, but it touts ingredients as being "locally sourced, always organic," providing the diner with the exact location where the field greens (Blue Heron Farms, in Watsonville) and heirloom tomatoes (Tutti Frutti Farms, in Lompoc) are grown.

The Hot Line and Carving Station feature barbecue ribs, roast beef, fried chicken and baked mac-and-cheese, all cooked in the 10,000-square-foot kitchen on the fifth floor and transported, via dumbwaiter, to the first-floor steamer tables.

That's basically how the food was prepared in the old days. You don't get a lot of "presentation" and "plating" at Clifton's; they'll pile on the stuffing and slop on creamed corn without a thought to aesthetics—as it should be.

"This is like grade school all over again," Gordon Sneddon of Whittier said.

But grade-school cafeterias don't feature a taxidermied mountain lion that stares at you when you're noshing on a tri-tip, or keep the place so dark you're almost in need of a miner's lamp, or waft big-band music from the speakers.

Because it's cafeteria-style, Clifton's is perfect for downtown workers wanting to grab a quick bite for lunch. But people tend to linger, take a postprandial stroll, check out the many nooks and alcoves, wildlife dioramas, the fossilized dinosaur eggs, the 4.7-billion-year-old bronzed meteorite embedded in a bar made from the century-old altar of a Boston church, the waterfall, and, of course, that 40-foot faux redwood that serves as a centerpiece in the atrium.

Lounging on a couch positioned at the base of the tree, where a fireplace warmed customers even on a 72-degree day, Jonathan Taylor seemed well-sated after his meal.

"The best roast beef I've had in a long time," said the classical guitarist from Los Angeles. "I had what I call the Standard: roast beef, mashed potatoes, cranberry sauce. That bartender over there knows his drinks. He took 10 minutes to put that absinthe rinse in my drink. He's not a hack. He knows his proportions and how to chill. That's a good sign."

Taylor looked around, utterly content to watch the diners come and go and gawk at the stuffed animals. Like so many others, he had come to Clifton's in decades past. But, unlike some others, he doesn't pine for the old days. He likes Clifton's just fine in its current incarnation.

"Can you imagine, during the Depression, the lines out the door here on Broadway?" Taylor asked. "People think it's bad today. They have no idea of 35 percent unemployment. Clifton's was the only food some people got. Compared to that, today we've got it pretty good."

True, that. You can leave here full and not spend a lot of money. Plus, there's the Jell-O. There's always room for Jell-O.

A Touch of Venice

November 2014
City sector: Venice Beach
Population: 40,885
Elevation: 13 feet

We were not asked to stand back and picture the scene. No, thanks to the wonders of technology and more than a little gumshoe detective work, we were able to stand in the shade under one of Windward Avenue's few remaining colonnades and watch a scene from Venice Beach's past play out on Jonathan Kaplan's iPad.

When Kaplan tapped the screen held in front of his torso, suddenly the vivid, Technicolor Sunday freaky spectacle of this self-styled beach community faded, replaced by a murky, inky noirish nightscape—the celebrated three-minute tracking shot that opens Orson Welles' classic *Touch of Evil*, shot in 1958 in exactly the spot where we were standing. This was the climactic scene, as it were, of Kaplan's three-hour Vintage Venice Reel to Real Tour that illuminates the area's storied and sullied history as filtered through movies shot on location over the decades.

"So it begins behind Larry's," Kaplan said, pointing to the popular bar across the Windward traffic circle, near Ocean Front Walk.

Venice Beach has a long history of being a location for film noir and other bizarre Hollywood movie and music happenings. Jonathan Kaplan leads a tour which starts and ends at the giant mural inspired by the Orson Welles movie *Touch of Evil*, filmed in Venice.

We looked down to the screen and saw a man running on the street toward a 1956 Chrysler New Yorker convertible. The man placed a ticking bomb in the trunk.

We looked up to that spot and saw some trustafarians loitering with intent, exuding cool and ganga fumes in the midmorning breeze.

We looked back to the screen and saw a couple walking down the sidewalk of the fictional Mexican border town of Los Robles—he in a suit, she in a calf-length skirt—framed by lighted pillars. They get in the car and pull out on the street.

Pause . . .

"See those arches they had back then," Kaplan said. "Columns of them, all up and down Windward."

Look up, and notice that only two sets of columns remain on the north side of Windward and none on the south side, where a tattoo parlor and bar now stand.

Look down, and see cart vendors and peasants with goats scurrying across the street—Kaplan: "Don't think they had goats in Venice in 1958"—

to avoid the slow-moving Chrysler, which makes a left turn to another street, then a right.

Pause . . .

"There on the left, those columns, is the old St. Mark Hotel," Kaplan said. "Not there anymore. Oh, and don't get too attached to that car. Well, you'll see."

Look up, and see that a low-rise souvenir shop is at the St. Mark location; it's obscured by street performers break-dancing for a buck.

Look down, and the car passes another couple walking down the middle of the street, where the camera shows a radiant Janet Leigh and Charlton Heston, made to look Mexican with makeup and a mustache, cavorting without a care in the world as they head west, seemingly in step with Henry Mancini's Latin-tinged theme song. Both the car and the couple stop at the U.S. Customs and Immigration checkpoint.

Pause . . .

"That's the former site of the Neptune Theatre, which, for the movie, had a big false canopy in front of it," Kaplan said. "That is now Big Daddy's (pizza)."

Look up, and crane your neck across the alley to Ocean Front Walk, near Market Street, where bikini-clad women and shirtless men nosh pizza and sip smoothies as a parade of roller-bladers, bike cruisers and gawking tourists pass.

Look down, and watch as Leigh and Heston walk around the car, which drives off as Kaplan jokingly mimics the line spoken by the woman in the car ("I've got this ticking noise in my head . . ."). Leigh and Heston kiss as the pan shot ends with an explosion. Then, a quick cut to Heston, with the neon lights of the Paradise bar shining behind them.

End of scene . . .

"You can see there's a continuity error, as they are now suddenly farther up (Ocean Front Walk), and you can see the columns of the (current) Sidewalk Café just behind them and the fake canopy in front of the Neptune Theatre where they just were, now far behind them," Kaplan said.

Film clip over, Kaplan finished up an exhaustive morning of strolling the streets and alleys of Venice—not the last remaining canals across town; that's another tour entirely—by showing us the ornate carving of faces on the columns and the Renaissance and Byzantine design flourishes and explaining how the colonnade is one of the last remaining artifacts from entrepreneur Abbot Kinney's turn-of-the-century vision of Venice Beach mirroring its Italian counterpart.

Most of Kinney's works—the lagoon and canals downtown, the two "pleasure" piers, the "Race Through the Clouds" roller coaster, biggest west of the Mississippi River, the World's Fair–like midway with rides such as the Dragon Slide and attractions such as the Streets of Cairo and Temple of Mirth—have long since been razed, the water filled with dirt, covered with asphalt and concrete, visions of a wondrous Coney Island of the Pacific all but forgotten.

But not completely.

Because of Venice's convenient location near Hollywood, and its unusual architecture and landscape, filmmakers over the years have used it as settings for hundreds of movies. And Kaplan, a longtime Venice Beach resident and TV writer by profession, has sifted through the vast celluloid dustbin of history and unearthed clips that show visitors what the place looked like in days of yore. He started his side touring business, Vintage Venice, as a hobby, and it has turned into almost a consuming passion.

Clips he shows visitors date from Mary Pickford's *Never Again!* (1910) through the Chaplin/Keaton/Laurel and Hardy era, musicals such as *Hollywood Cavalcade* (1939), noir classics such as *Touch of Evil*, and too many 1960s and '70s films to mention (*Mother, Jugs & Speed* or *Roller Boogie*, anyone?), as well as footage featuring Jim Morrison and the Doors cavorting on the streets, the site where the Eagles played their first gig and a house once occupied by Manson family members.

Entertaining as it is to watch the old clips, the important thing is to focus on the setting. Venice Beach itself, remember, is taking its star turn.

"What's neat about seeing all these movies is you can kind of see LA's history through Venice movies," Kaplan said. "In the old days, all the movies shot here showed this place as Coney Island of the Pacific. Later on, it was like these down-and-out movies like, well, *Down and Out in Beverly Hills* and *Cisco Pike*, which is about a washed-up country star now dealing drugs. Now, you can see Venice used in movies for these hip things. It's all like having home movies of LA, but it's all done by professionals.

"And the thing is, I'd say most of the people I take on tours are locals, though I believe Venice is No. 2 behind Disneyland in tourism, with about 17 million a year. But people live in LA 40 years and don't know (Venice's) history. They might just think of Venice from the '80s and '90s as the 'Slum by the Sea' before the money came in. They don't realize this once was a magical place of dance halls, attractions and movie stars. There's not a lot left, but I've found enough (footage) to see things if you know where to look."

Like any savvy Hollywood writer, Kaplan shows more than tells on the tour, which loops around the north and western parts of the community before heading back along the oceanfront. He makes liberal use of his iPad as well as old-timey photos he keeps in a black leather binder.

But a little exposition was needed to put the Venice clips in context. He told the story of Kinney, developer, conservationist, renaissance man, how he came to Southern California to cure his asthma, fell in love with the coastal burg south of Santa Monica and wanted to replicate it in the Venetian style—canals, lagoons and all—and how he basically bought and transported the St. Louis World's Fair midway to the town, constructed a pier and the oceanfront walk to make use of the water, but also built two elaborate bathhouses for those preferring to swim indoors.

Kaplan flipped through vintage photos, some colorized but most faded black-and-white, that showed the impressive size and scope of the amusement park and piers. Three Australian tourists, Jane Pierce and Jan and Brendan Wayland, said they could hardly believe the intersection at which they were standing (Main Street and Grand Avenue) once was under water.

"That must've taken (Kinney) forever to build," Pierce said.

"It actually took Kinney less than a year," Kaplan said.

Enough talk, though. We stood on Main Street as Kaplan cued up the first clip showing the now-filled-in canals in 1910, as Pickford glided along in a boat in *Never Again!*

"That's America's Sweetheart at the beginning of her career," Kaplan said. "This might be the only scene left, which I found in a compilation."

He paused the iPad, pointed to the screen.

"See that house with the gable a couple of blocks down? It's there (in the clip)," Kaplan said.

Next clip: A scene from *The Sheik of Hollywood* (1923) showing stars Fred Caldwell and Gale Henry riding the giant roller coaster with the ocean in the background.

"We're at that very spot," Kaplan said. "It stretched from here all the way to the beach."

He then led us to the corner of Main Street and Westminster Avenue, a nondescript intersection bordered by an elementary school and dog park.

"You don't need me to tell you that this is the most historic intersection you'll see today," he said. "What? I take it you're not impressed. This was important for one day only and that day was January 10, 1914. An event was happening here in Venice and a Hollywood producer wanted to cover it but couldn't get his favorite actor. So he settled on this kid."

With that, he tapped in iPad and on the screen came frenetic footage of Charlie Chaplin in hat with mustache and cane, on a street that looked vaguely like Main Street of today.

"You are now standing in the very spot where the Little Tramp was born," Kaplan said. "His first time in that character. Look down this way, there was a roller coaster back in the lagoon. Basically, Chaplin's like Borat 100 years ahead of his time, screwing around with the crowd. No one has any idea who this insane person is or that he'll be the most famous person in the world by the end of the year."

Kaplan replayed the short clip twice, then put the iPad away. "But again, you didn't need me to tell you that because you can see the wonderful statue the city's erected to Charlie Chaplin on this important spot," he said, sarcastically.

(There is no marker.)

Clips, both visual and audio, came about every five minutes during our Sunday stroll.

He cued up the Doors song "The End" when he reached the "blue bus" stop that Morrison immortalized in verse. When we stopped on Main Street in front of the faded facade of the original Gold's Gym, he flipped to clips of Arnold Schwarzenegger as a muscle-bound lad in *Pumping Iron*.

He showed the pagodas on Ocean Front Walk where Nick Nolte and Richard Dreyfuss chatted in *Down and Out in Beverly Hills*, the beach-side retail store where Steve Martin and Sarah Jessica Parker got a "high colonic" in *L.A. Story*, the oceanfront bathhouse scene from Buster Keaton's 1928 film *The Cameraman*, a clip from the musical *Hollywood Cavalcade* that gives a glimpse of the original Venice Pier, and another clip from *The Sheik of Hollywood* showing that electric trams used to shuttle Ocean Front Walk visitors from hotels to the amusement park.

Nothing if not thorough, Kaplan spent more than an hour on the beach and Ocean Front Walk, playing clips and pointing out places of note, such as the apartment where Morrison spent the summer "on a diet of canned beans and acid, writing poetry we all now know," he said, smiling.

But Kaplan turned serious when he took us to the winding concrete bike path lined with palm trees.

"I'm going to show you know the thing that took me the longest to find," he said. "It's kind of my crowning achievement. This one took me a lot of sessions coming out here. I'm a little proud of this one. . . . People, we're going back to 1977. Do the curves on the bike path look familiar? If they do, it might be because of this . . ."

He whipped out the iPad, tapped the screen. John Ritter is riding a bike along the path, with the TV show's title, *Three's Company*, flashing in front of him and then . . . wait for it . . . Ritter falls off his bike onto the sand. End of clip.

The Australians nod but don't look overly impressed. I asked, "Did you get *Three's Company* in Australia?" They nodded. Tough crowd.

"Right where we're standing is where he fell off his bike," Kaplan said. "It was hard to figure out because there was like a dozen curves. But then I figured out it was by the green pagodas. But then there are three sets of green pagodas. I narrowed it down, but then I was like, 'Hmm, I looked at the film and there were these tiny little palm trees. Where are those now?' I finally figured it out by the tree pattern where he actually fell off."

Pierce: "Well done!"

Kaplan smiled, perhaps thinking that *Three's Company* is not as famous a '70s TV show overseas as it is here. Perhaps a little gun-shy, he then asked the Australians if the movie *White Men Can't Jump* (1992) made its way to the outback. The trio nodded enthusiastically.

"OK, well," Kaplan said, stopping at a parking lot near the oceanfront and Rose Avenue. "Let me show you one of the basketball scenes."

After 30 seconds of Wesley Snipes and Woody Harrelson going at it on an outdoor court, Kaplan pushed pause.

"Look, there's the hotel (on the walk) right there (in the frame)," he said. "They shot the basketball scenes right in the parking lot. The thing is, the real basketball courts farther down are a city park and they couldn't keep it closed long enough for filming, so they just set up courts here in parking lot. . . . So, everyone goes down to the basketball courts and says this is where they shot *White Men Can't Jump*. But they are wrong. Now you know better."

After three hours of seeing the sights and squinting at the screen, I felt I knew Venice like a local. Kaplan, in fact, said we now knew Venice's old canal district better than 90 percent of Venice residents. He's part of a neighborhood group trying to preserve the district.

"The good news is, about 60 percent of the old Craftsman houses are still here," he said. "The bad news is, literally, only one house is protected (as a historic site). A lot of money is coming into Venice now. It's not the Slum by the Sea anymore. These houses might get torn down for mansions. We might be about to lose a neighborhood."

We ended up back on Windward Avenue, under a giant black-and-white mural called *Touch of Venice* on the side of Danny's, a bar and restaurant that in Orson Welles' time was a chop suey restaurant. In the mural the colonnade is lit, the "Venice" sign glows brightly, as Heston and Leigh stroll Windward Avenue with the doomed Chrysler New Yorker trailing them. Inscribed on the bottom left is a message that captures that feel of the Reel to Real Tour: "Like a dream I remember from an easier time . . ."

Get on the Garish Bus

August 2013

City sector: Hollywood

First star on Walk of Fame: Actress Joanne Woodward, 1960

Year of the Victoria's Secret Lingerie Model's star: 2007

Once you step foot aboard the garish red 24-seat TMZ tour bus, parked just off garish Hollywood Boulevard where glazed-eyed tourists in ill-matching outfits dodge garish characters dressed as Michael Jackson, Marilyn Monroe and Elmo, you sacrifice all claims on dignity and can no longer hold the moral high ground.

You have officially become one of those people—the celebrity-obsessed, the gossipy gawkers who care infinitely more about Kim and Kanye than, say, the Syrian conflict. Like, maybe if Bashar al-Assad got in a booze-fueled car wreck with Bieber on Sunset and Doheny, then, like, *maybe* I'd pay attention.

For the next two hours, you will cruise the teeming streets of Hollywood and Beverly Hills, where every aspect of celebrity bad behavior will be, well, celebrated and mocked in equal measure.

Good taste? Fairness? Compassion?

Sorry, bub, you surrendered all that at the Starline Tours check-in counter when you plunked down $55 to be entertained and titillated by lurid tales of this modern-day Babylon.

Really? What did you expect, a sober, even-minded Ken Burns documentary?

This is TMZ, the pop-culture-besotted website and TV show that mines the depths of Tinseltown scandal and disseminates it to the slavering, slack-jawed masses. It doesn't take itself or its subjects all too seriously, though it prides itself on the scoop. Scoop, in this case, being anything from an A-lister overdosing in a bathroom stall to a sex tape featuring a wayward child star.

In case you still harbored any sense of decency, TMZ tour guide (and one of the show's producers) Nasrene Nikpora quickly sets you straight about the "celebrity safari" upon which you are about to embark.

"Some people get on the tour bus and think they're way too cool for TMZ," said Nikpora, through a wireless mike in the front of the bus. "I'm like, dude, the secret's out. You're on a red bus. People are gonna see you around town. Chill and have a good time, or I will embarrass you if you look like a sourpuss."

You look around, and no one else looks chastened. They had no reason. They have gone out of their way to take the tour—one couple traveled from Romania, another from Australia—and they equate TMZ as part and parcel of the Hollywood experience.

And the bus itself is almost a rolling TV show. It's equipped with four video monitors and a booming sound system so that when a bus stops at an infamous location of celebrity malfeasance—say, Winona Ryder's Saks Fifth Avenue shoplifting caper—Nikpora can roll the tape after giving the introduction. The live guide and the canned voice serve as a snarky, often hilarious tag team.

Mostly, tourists say, the setup provides a you-are-there realism.

"We watch the TV show and wanted to see what they do," said tourist Michelle Moreira, from Miami, who brought her teenage son Lewis. "It gives you the inside, what's really real about these people."

TMZ's astounding success—eight years after its debut, it's arguably grown into America's go-to gossip source—is a prime example of how the barriers blur between reporting on celebrities and becoming a celebrity.

Call it the Seacrest Line, in which a measure of fame comes from basking in the refracted light of the truly famous.

But, unlike lightweight competitors such as *Access Hollywood* and *Extra*, TMZ is more obnoxious than obsequious, at once lambasting and venerating its subjects, yet all the while acknowledging that its very existence depends on a steady stream of mockable exploits.

Just as TMZ—its name, by the way, stands for "Thirty-Mile Zone," a movie-industry term too boring to detail here—hoisted celebrity-reporting to new heights, its foray into bus tours attempts to do the same thing to Hollywood tourism.

As the *Los Angeles Times* opined before TMZ's maiden voyage in 2011, "younger visitors are more interested in the happenings of reality stars such as Kim Kardashian than the homes of actors Lucille Ball or Lionel Barrymore."

It doesn't take long to discover that on a TMZ tour an incident such as Britney Spears' head-shaving exploits of 2007 is considered the stuff of sepia-toned newsreels. The Fatty Arbuckle scandal? Well, that belongs with those Ice Age fossils at the La Brea Tar Pits, old-timer.

You get a sense of TMZ's short shelf life of fame at the very first stop—the Roosevelt Hotel, at 7000 Hollywood Blvd., just a crack rock's throw from the famed Grauman's Chinese Theatre.

"Miley Cyrus was just caught with Justin Bieber there the other day," Nikpora chirped into the mike. "They might be dating, might not. I don't know whether you care. But there's really big stars who stay at the Roosevelt."

Nikpora paused, a Jack Nicholson–like smirk spreading across her face.

"Like Honey Boo Boo child," she added. "That one make you wanna holla?"

Then, Nikpora rolled the tape, and an announcer with a voice so abrasive it could corrode metal continued.

"The Roosevelt Hotel, home to Teddy's nightclub, one of Lindsay Lohan's favorite hangouts, probably because her ex-girlfriend Samantha Ronson DJs here," the voice intoned.

A few tour-goers snapped smartphone photos of the Roosevelt's facade, its stately 1920s Spanish Colonial architecture.

"And, if you're over 50," the voice continued, "this is where JFK would allegedly sneak in through the laundry room to hook up with Marilyn Monroe back in ancient times."

You don't have time to muse on presidential affairs. The bus doesn't linger anywhere. Like a shark, it's always moving forward. Lots of celebrity hot spots to hit, not a lot of time, especially with LA's notorious traffic.

Next up, a block down on Hollywood Boulevard. Nikpora pointed to an El Pollo Loco and rolled tape:

"Before there was Angelina, before there was Jen, there was only one love in Brad Pitt's life—El Pollo Loco, specifically the one coming up on your right. Yes, it was at this exact fast-food restaurant that Brad Pitt got his big break—standing outside dressed as a chicken. Soon, Brad went from handing out flyers at the joint to hiring them as caterers on his films. And that is clucking awesome."

The raunchy pun elicited chuckles from the group, which was game for anything. No prudes aboard. But the next two stops didn't exactly send pulses racing—the Seventh Veil, a strip club where Mötley Crüe filmed its video for "Girls, Girls, Girls," and Gardner Street Elementary School, where Michael Jackson attended the sixth grade.

But when Clarence the bus driver pulled over at the corner of Sunset and Courtney, Nikpora asked, "You people from Romania and Australia, do you know what we find on street corners in America? Hookers!"

Roll tape: "(This) is where Hugh Grant made the worst decision of his life, and no, we're not talking about (the movie bomb) *Did You Hear About the Morgans?* It was here that Hugh picked up prostitute Divine Brown for a $60 good time in his car. But when cops noticed his brake light flashing on and off, the whole thing blew up in his face. And hers."

Nikpora cringed, even blushed a bit when glancing at the few teenagers on the bus. Still, her snark won out: "Aren't you glad you brought the kids today on the TMZ tour?"

The stops came fast and furious after that. Highlights included the Laugh Factory (8001 Sunset Blvd.), where *Seinfeld* star Michael Richards' racist rant derailed his career; the Body Shop strip club (8250 Sunset Blvd.), where actress Megan Fox reportedly had a "fling with a lesbian stripper named Nikita"; and the Chateau Marmont, best known to old-timers as the hotel where John Belushi OD'd in 1982.

But, as the tour instructed, the Chateau is known for so much more. Nikpora noted that "Lindsay Lohan, America's sweetheart, lived here for 46 days and racked up $43,000 in expenses. Crazy! That girl spent $500 one day just on alcohol." Then the TMZ video played a 911 call from actor Josh Hartnett outside the Chateau, asking for medical assistance because he had diarrhea.

Nikpora: "TMI, Josh!"

It could be argued that the whole tour is "too much information." But the tour group was ready for anything, from the Viper Room, where River Phoenix died, to the Four Seasons Hotel, venue for Paris Hilton's sex tape, the courthouse where "Lindsay Lohan wrote F.U. to the judge on her fingernails."

The only thing missing from this orgy of celebrity slagging was in-the-flesh celebrities. Nikpora told the group to be on the lookout and that if a real live celebrity was spotted, she'd film the specimen from the bus. "You'll all be on TMZ!"

There was only one close call 90 minutes in. Nikpora paused in her spiel near a valet parking area and swiveled her head.

"Oh my gosh," she said, "I thought that was what's-his-face for a second, Anderson Cooper?"

A voice from the back shouted out another name.

"Who'd you say? Richard Gere. Oh, that works, too."

All that could be determined is that it was a slender man with gray hair.

The prime spot for trawling for celebs is one of the tour's final stops—the Ivy, an upscale bistro with a white-picket fence patio on Robertson Boulevard. Clarence idled the bus's engine across the street from the eatery and, in an instant, someone on the bus yelled: "That's the 49ers quarterback!"

"Colin Kaepernick?" Nikpora asked.

She grabbed her video camera, hustled out of the bus with two tour volunteers and tried to approach Kaepernick and a small entourage. But the quarterback, known for his scrambling ability, turned on his heels and walked down the street out of camera shot.

She returned, empty-handed of footage, but smiling crookedly just the same.

All part of the freak show, folks.

Hollywood Is a Dead Town

April 2015

Exploiting the dead is distasteful. I think we all can agree on that. Let the departed, dearly and otherwise, rest in peace. For when we die—sorry to plunge you into existential despair, but it will happen—our dignity and right to be treated with a modicum of human decency should not expire with us.

And yet . . .

In spite of my better self, I was drawn to a twisted, shameless and undeniably fascinating Hollywood tour called Dearly Departed: The Tragical History Tour, which for $50 will expose the seamy underbelly (no doubt liposucked, to leave a better-looking corpse) of the glitzy TV and film industry and those often-flawed personages who populate it.

Gawd, I'm such a bad person. Something, probably buried deep in my childhood subconscious, makes me find allure in the lurid. Forgive me, please.

Or, better yet, go on the tour yourself and see if I'm wrong. Discover whether the three-hour excursion into the dark side of Tinseltown truly is as tasteless as a Twinkie, and with about as much nutritional value as edifying brain food, as well.

I didn't walk, so much as slink, into the Sunset Boulevard offices of Dearly Departed one recent Saturday for its afternoon thanatic outing. (There are, please note, more specific packages, such as the Helter Skelter Tour of sites and the Carpen-Tour, tracing the bright career and sad demise of the seminal '70s songstress, but those are for hardened veterans; the general Tragical tour is sort of the gateway drug.)

Like a naughty schoolboy ducking into a peep show, I tightened the draw strings on my hoodie. When I opened the door, I was greeted with wall-to-wall Death of the Stars mementos, from Lana Turner's favorite gold-plated cigarette lighter (she died of throat cancer) to Marilyn Monroe's last (unpaid) telephone bill to Rock Hudson's bedpost and Rolodex to a chunk of the tile floor from the bungalow where Rudolph Valentino died.

I also was greeted by the toothy grin and alarmingly strong handshake of Scott Michaels, Dearly Departed's owner, who quickly provided me with absolution for my prurient interests—or, you might say, merely delivered cogent, if sophistic, dissembling disguised as incisive social commentary (you decide).

"Ten years ago, when we started this company, everyone was giving us the stink eye whenever we passed anyone's death house," Michaels said. "Now there's not a single company that doesn't pass Michael Jackson's death house. Things have changed. I mean, look at the tabloids, you know.

"This is 100 years' worth of deaths. A lot of names of the dead on our tour aren't thrown around anymore. But their deaths are so interesting that perhaps somebody, after taking the tour, might be inspired to rent one of their movies. It may not be the way (the stars) wanted to be remembered, but then again, attention is attention in this town. They are public figures. Just because you're dead doesn't mean it stops."

Michaels does have a point. When is the last time you've thought about William Frawley (the droll Fred Mertz on *I Love Lucy*) or Brian Keith (beloved *Family Affair* patriarch) or Marie Prevost (silent-screen diva turned pop-song subject)? They all are featured on the tour, though details of these stars' demise didn't exactly send the hearts of the 11 women (no men, sans yours truly) on the bus fluttering like when guide Brian Donnelly got to the climax-like Whitney Houston-Marilyn Monroe-Michael Jackson tragic triad.

"We love this (tour), and this is our fourth time," said Kourtney Robb, part of a gaggle of gawkers up from San Clemente. "It's a guilty pleasure."

Kind of like chocolate except with more bite.

Once you delude yourself into thinking, "Privacy be damned; these are celebrities and nothing's off-limits by our click-bait, sleazy social-media standards," you can sit back in the van's plush seats and spend three hours being driven around the streets of Hollywood, Westwood, Beverly Hills, Century City and West LA with the manic running commentary of Donnelly, whose database-size knowledge of the sites and circumstances behind stars' deaths makes him a walking, talking celebrity pseudo-coroner—or maybe just an amateur obit writer. (Big props to Donnelly, by the way, for not once succumbing to euphemism: Stars died; they did not "pass away" or "cross over" or "find eternal rest." OK, he did use "kick the bucket" once, but in a thoroughly ironic context.)

Donnelly weaves a narrative around each death, peppered with pun-laden quips and occasionally unbidden Roger Ebertian critiques of subjects' acting chops. Only occasionally does he resort to props, such as distressing

911 emergency recordings he cues up on the dashboard CD player. He manages, with impressive hand-eye motor skills, to navigate through gawd-awful LA traffic while pointing to the architectural anomalies of a certain apartment house where a B-movie actor expired and engaging his guests in witty chitchat. His delivery resembled nothing less than the sped-up voice rattling off side effects in TV drug commercials.

As the oversize van—white and black with the company logo embla-zoned on the sides, though I really think they should consider switching to a hearse—barreled west down Beverly Boulevard, Donnelly rendered the crowd slack-jawed by his rapid-fire *Rain Man*–like litany of the celebs who were "pronounced dead" (note the subtle distinction) at Cedars-Sinai Medical Center:

"GeorgeBurnsGracieAllenMinnieRippertonFrankSinatraSammyDavis JuniorHarryCohnSammyKahn (breath) GildaRadnerJohnnyCarsonLucille BallRiverPhoenixRebeccaShaeffer (breath) EazyEBiggieSmallsElizabeth TaylorSherwoodSchwartzChuckConnersErnieKovacs (breath) Michael ClarkeDuncanErnestBorgnineDonKnotts (breath). . . . But not Michael Jackson—that was at UCLA (Medical Center)."

Not everybody in the van—tour-goers ranged from mid-20s to mid-50s; the tour, for obvious reasons, restricts minors—knew all these stars. Little matter.

Donnelly considers it his job to immortalize those forgotten of the silver screen.

Take his "tribute" to Prevost, the sultry silent movie star who (for a while) made a successful transition to talkies and made 121 films before, alas, dying alone at her nondescript apartment in the Aftonian, 6230 Afton Place, Los Angeles. Donnelly pulled the van over, put it in park and turned to face his audience.

"There's this book called *Hollywood Babylon*, and because of that book, Marie Prevost is known as 'The Woman Eaten by Her Dog,'" Donnelly said. "Complete bullshit. Repeat: They wrote that her dachshund ate her. (The author) got three parts of the story correct. She was a woman. She owned a dog. She died. Yes, it was a while before they found her body. But a dog wouldn't do that. The dachshund did bite her, not to consume her but to wake her up—like any dog would do when they see you sleeping. But the story has (persisted) for years."

Here, Donnelly cued up the CD player and this chorus from the great Nick Lowe filled the van: "She was a winner / That became the doggie's dinner . . ."

Before veering back into traffic, he made a final comment about the unfortunate pop-culture peccadillo of turning rumor into fact: "For instance, Mama Cass did not choke on a ham sandwich. She died of a heart attack. Now, it is true that she died in the same room Keith Moon died of a drug overdose four years later. Coincidence. That's all it is."

Like the old chestnut that "comedy is tragedy plus time," details of the long-ago deaths seem easier to absorb than those of stars in our cohort.

When Donnelly rolled by the Beverly Hilton Hotel, where Houston died of a drug overdose in the bathtub of Room 434, he played the 911 tape from February 2012. Most listened staring at the floor. Silence afterward. To his credit, Donnelly played it straight in detailing the events and even made a self-deprecating remark.

"Her family bought every stick of furniture out of the hotel room," he said, "and word is they had it destroyed. I don't know if they actually did, but I heard they didn't want the bathtub winding up someplace weird—like in our office. I mean, Scott has Karen Carpenter's sink, for God's sake."

Apparently, there is no precise end to a celeb mourning period, no expiration date when it's OK to have a little respectful fun with a death. Not long after Donnelly's rather sober telling of the Houston saga, he drove by the Highland Garden Hotel, at 7047 Franklin, in Los Angeles. In Room 105 in 1970, Joplin died of an overdose. A huge Joplin fan, Donnelly wove a story about how he has spent the night in 105—"a 47th birthday present to myself"—and "laid out masking tape where Janis' body was." He said the room is a tourist attraction, and the hotel is just fine with that. "People hide notes to Janis in the room," he added.

The stories just kept coming. We passed Bungalow 3 of the Chateau Marmont, where John Belushi died in 1982; saw the front entrance of the Viper Room in West Hollywood, where River Phoenix died in 1993 (and heard another disturbing 911 call, made by little brother Joaquin); stopped briefly at the Afton Arms apartments on El Centro Avenue in Los Angeles where Red Hot Chili Peppers guitarist Hillel Slovak OD'd; and spent considerable time at apartment No. 4 at 120 Sweetzer Ave. in Hollywood, where young actress Rebecca Schaeffer was murdered by a stalker in 1989, a crime that led to several anti-stalking laws.

The Los Angeles Dead Tour visits the final resting places of many
Hollywood Stars. Here, Kourtney Robb of San Clemente, a tour-goer, kisses
the headstone of Marilyn Monroe's final resting place.

So much loss. So much wasted life.

Nobody promised this "tragical mystery tour" was going to be a laugh riot.

To lighten the mood—and I know this sounds odd, but it helped—Donnelly drove us to where many big names are buried. He handed us maps with names and arrows—Burt Lancaster, Natalie Wood, Brian Keith, Jack Lemmon, Rodney Dangerfield (inscribed on headstone: "There goes the neighborhood"), Truman Capote, Don Knotts, Walter Matthau, Merv Griffin ("I will not be right back after this message"), Farrah Fawcett, Roy Orbison, Billy Wilder ("I'm a writer, but then, nobody's perfect"), Dean Martin and, of course, Marilyn Monroe.

"Have some fun here," he said, jumping out and running around the side to open the doors.

Nearly all the women on the tour—every single one of the San Clemente contingent—made a beeline to Marilyn's grave.

There was a crowd, and people waited patiently for their turns. Donnelly warned there might be lipstick smooches on the headstone, and there were. Robb reached in her purse and unsheathed her hot-pink lipstick and added a new coat. Then she bent slightly over—kind of like Marilyn's iconic pose on the subway grate, actually—and planted a kiss next to her name.

"Eww," she said, daubing her lips, "hope I don't catch something."

Celebrity Pets Laid to Rest

July 2013
City: Calabasas
County: Los Angeles
Population: 24,153
Elevation: 978 feet

When it comes to our pets, even the most cynical, nihilistic or evil among us get all teared up and sappily sentimental when their beloved companion shuffles off this mortal coil. Hey, Hitler doted on his dog, Blondie, and Saddam Hussein was said to be a major cat fancier.

So, truly, pet lovers span all generations and ideologies.

But there's a certain type of human companion who is a breed apart, who so venerates his dearly departed fluffy, scruffy or scaly amigo that he will drop major coin to make sure it is laid to rest with all the pomp and ceremony of a state funeral.

These are the people whose pets occupy the nearly 40,000 plots—and expanding, of course, since death is a recession-proof growth industry—at the 90-year-old Los Angeles Pet Memorial Park and Crematorium, 10 acres of verdant hillside in the San Fernando Valley.

It is said to be the nation's second-largest pet cemetery—a park in New York City gets top billing—and, this being LA, it is saturated with celebrities. That's celebrities of the four-legged variety. At least one of the "Petey" terriers from the old *Our Gang* movies calls this place home, as does Tawny, the lion who acted in *Tarzan* films, and Hopalong Cassidy's horse, Topper.

"A lot of celebrities bring their pets here," said Marie Beavers, second in command to park manager Emad Whitney. "Some we can talk about; some we can't. Privacy, you know."

Humphrey Bogart's dog, Boots, is here, not far from Rudolph Valentino's Great Dane, Kabar. Charlie Chaplin's cat, Scout, has a plot, as do various species of pets belonging to such noted celebs as Peter Falk, William Shatner, Diana Ross and Lauren Bacall.

"We also have the horse from the original *Lone Ranger* movies somewhere, and of course, you've got to see Tawny the lion," Beavers said. "He's got a huge headstone with a photo of him with a (house) cat on his back. Apparently, they were raised together, and now they're buried together. We've got everything here: fish, turtles, squirrels, lizards, chimps, ferrets. A lot of hamsters. We've even got a boa (constrictor). We don't discriminate."

There are, alas, no maps of celebrity plots, but Beavers offered to get someone from the ground's crew to lead me to the notable resting places. But not before she showed off the dazzling array of caskets for animals of all sizes, from an itty-bitty mouse to a hefty hippo.

"We have carbon fiber caskets, and we have a gentleman here who makes custom pine caskets all the way to expensive hardwood, like you would find for a human," said Beavers, who handed me a price list ranging from $699 to $1,115. "We can put most anything in there except horses. Horses don't go in caskets."

The natural question is: Why do it? But Beavers takes the query almost as an affront.

"Listen," she said, "I've been in the death-care industry a lot of years, with humans. I was an embalmer and a funeral director. I've been working here about a year, and I see a lot of similarities.

"We have to bury our humans, OK? We don't have to bury our pets. But people who come through this door, their pets are very important to them. They become children. They replace children. They replace spouses. They become that important. That's why we have a viewing room, where visitations take place, and why we hold services."

Some are simple memorial services with a tasteful burial; others more lavish.

"We started having butterfly releases—a mass release or individually wrapped (butterflies) so each person releases it—at services," Beavers said. "Dove releases, too. I can get you a rabbi, a priest, anyone you want. I'll get you a limo. Whatever you want. Why can't we do it for our pets if we do it for our people?

"A lot of people come in and ask, 'What's normal?' I say, 'Forget that. What do you want? I can get it for you as long as it's not too illegal or too immoral.'"

Each month, pet lovers from throughout Southern California are invited to the memorial park for a candlelight vigil at dusk to remember the departed. The procession begins at the St. Francis of Assisi statue and ends at the hillside mausoleum. People tell their stories. It often gets emotional.

"We had a woman whose cat died, mauled by two rottweilers," Beavers said. "Her grown son blamed the woman. The woman's friend said, 'It's an animal. Pets are property. Get over it.' But this woman couldn't stop crying (at the vigil). She told her story through her tears, and I almost started crying because it was like a Lifetime movie. Every one of the 50 people at the vigil came up and hugged her."

The heartless might dismiss this as wretched excess, as people with too much money wallowing in First World problems.

But here's a challenge: I defy you to spend a half an hour strolling the grounds here, reading the headstones and not be moved by the genuine feeling expressed.

Some are simple: "1958–1974. Our Fifi. She gave so much and asked for so little."

Some are elaborate: "Elby. August 1990–June 2005. My sweet Elby, an extension of me in another form. Keep my place next to you in heaven warm. I cherish you with all my heart and I will see you soon. Your loving mom, Vicky."

And some, like this headstone inscription for a cat named Borden (1985–July 10, 1999) just begs for further explanation, maybe even novel-length treatment: "Borden. Died of uremic poisoning at 3:30 a.m. due to kidney failure 7 hours before he was to be euthanized and it's all my fault. Richard."

My favorite headstone, though, is one of the oldest and simplest: "Sport: 1928–1937."

TV Show Taping: Laughter on Command

March 2014
City: Burbank
County: Los Angeles
Pop.: 103,340
Nickname: "Media Capital of the World"

On any given day, the biggest cluster of stars in Los Angeles is not centered in Beverly Hills or Brentwood, nor seen sunning on the beach in Malibu, nor attending a Lakers game at the Staples Center. And they sure as hell stay away from Hollywood Boulevard.

No, these glamour-pusses, these Beautiful People, most often congregate in . . . Burbank.

Yeah, Burbank, the punch line for Johnny Carson and so many others. Burbank, the smog-enshrouded, traffic-choked hell on earth.

Why Burbank? Because, like Willie Sutton said about robbing banks, that's where the money is. Most of the television produced in Southern California comes out of Burbank studios—ABC, NBC, Warner Bros., Walt Disney Co., Marvel, Nickelodeon, etc. Naturally, then, fans are drawn, moth-to-flame-like, to Burbank to waste an entire day and most of a night to wait like former USSR fishwives in bread lines to get into TV show tapings. Against advice from, well, pretty much everyone I know, I took the plunge and drove, willingly, under no coercion whatsoever, to Burbank.

Let me start off by clueing you in on several things to know before your brush with celebrity:

- Getting free tickets, at least to shows shot at Warner Bros. Television Studios, is as easy as a mouse click, but it will be the last easy thing in the process.

- It's a major time-suck, hours of queueing and waiting, waiting and queueing, even before the six-hour taping of a 22-minute sitcom, and you will never get back those precious grains of sand through the hourglass.

- A sturdy bladder is essential, for once you've gained entrance to the hallowed inner sanctum that is the stage set, potty breaks are all but verboten.

- You are forced to break up with your smartphone for the duration, cause of much separation-anxiety and weeping at the parting.

- You must be peppy-on-command—THIS PUMPED UP!—and laugh uproariously at a punch line, even if it's the 12th time you've heard it.

All right, so if I haven't dissuaded you yet, you must really want to see TV magic being made, or else Marge is being a major pain in the rear. Anyway, what follows is one man's experience at a midweek taping of the CBS Monday night hit *2 Broke Girls* in the beige, hulking Quonset hut known as Stage 21.

Actually, it begins before you even reach the studio lot. The ease with which you can reserve tickets and print them at home lulls you into thinking you can just stroll right onto the set, no problem. Sure, it says to arrive "at least one hour" before the 5 p.m. taping, but they always say that, right? And there was something in the fine print about how the ticket doesn't always guarantee a seat, yadda, yadda.

Still, knowing the Los Angeles freeway system, I gave myself plenty of time to spare. But when I pulled into the parking garage at Gate 8 at 3:30 p.m., most of the first floor was filled with people, close to 300 in all, in shorts and flip-flops sitting on portable rows in front of a *2 Broke* sign.

My crack research had told me most stage sets seat an audience of about 150, 200 tops. Despite the odds, people seemed in good spirits and not at all concerned that two hours of waiting might end up being fruitless. There was no organized front of the line; people sat haphazard, holding their printed-out "ticket" in one hand, their picture ID in the other. So far, this was about as glamorous as waiting at the DMV. I sat in the front of the fifth of six rows, almost as far away as you could get from the gate where the audience would be led.

Several scurrying Warner Brothers "pages," clad in black pants and white shirts and carrying clipboards and walkie-talkies, wielded enormous power, and they certainly seemed to be tripping on it. Same for the blue-uniformed rent-a-security, stamping your hand ("right hand on right thigh, sir, palm down"). After about 20 minutes, the pages pointed to a row of about 15 people, seemingly at random, and summoned it forward. This, of course, was after the "VIPs," none I recognized, were ushered in.

Passed over, I unsheathed my iPhone to kill time.

"Oh, you don't want to do that," a woman across the aisle said to me. "Can't bring in phones. Better take it back to your car."

Bernice Reddy, who lives in the San Fernando Valley and was taking her friend from Minnesota, Jeanette Murphy, to the taping, knows whereof she speaks. Reddy and Murphy graced the audience of the *Dr. Phil* show last year and *The Tonight Show with Jay Leno* the year before that. I took a chance and hustled back to the car to stash the phone and lucked out. I didn't miss a cattle call.

A few minutes later, a particularly bossy page stopped at the row in front of me. "No one here needs to pee." (It sounded like a statement, not a question.) "OK, come with me."

Two more rows were selected, and I wasn't liking my chances. Every time the bossy page clopped by in her heels, we audience-wannabes gazed up hopefully, like refugees waiting for the last helicopter out of a war-torn country.

Finally, the damnedest thing happened. The page stopped at the head of our row, pointed a Lee Press-On nail at me and said, "I'll take you five." We hustled into line. Turns out, we were the last ones selected and, fortunately, we were ushered out before the bad news was broken to the rest of those losers.

Another page had us line up, single-file, like kindergartners on a field trip, and marched us out of the lot, past Forest Lawn Drive, through not one but two TSA-like security checkpoints and onto the lot. As we passed trailers and sets for *Hart of Dixie* and *Two and a Half Men*, people gawked and tittered. At last, we reached Stage 21 and found the only open seats left were in the last row, with limited sight of the set below (because of the overhanging lights).

We were told they were filming Episode 319, titled "2 Broke Girls and the Kilt Trip," to run on St. Patrick's Day night. It was then my Irish luck kicked in. A page asked, "Is there anyone here by themselves?" I was the only one (yeah, I know, such a loser), and I was ushered to the front row seat, reserved for a no-show VIP.

I barely had time to gloat, because a large bald man named Roger at the foot of the seats bellowed into a microphone, "PUT YOUR HANDS TOGETHER. WE WANT YOU FIRED UP."

Roger is what the TV biz calls the "warmup," a comedian employed to prime the audience to laugh. Roger would be our guide and sidekick for the next 4½ hours, telling jokes, between takes and scene changes, that ranged from how bad the traffic is in LA to how cold it is in Chicago. Roger promised us candy and T-shirts. He promised us cupcakes, sandwiches and water. He even promised cold hard cash if we'd make a lot of noise.

"You are the most important part of the show," he told us.

(Quick aside about the plot: There are these two girls in Brooklyn, see. And they're broke, right. They work at a diner and try to get a cupcake side business going when not firing off sexual double entendres and innocuous ethnic slurs at other cast members. The show gets boffo ratings.)

Then Roger introduced the cast, and the audience did Beatles-on-Sullivan-decibel screams for the two stars, Kat Dennings (as sassy Max Black) and Beth Behrs (as erstwhile rich girl Caroline Channing). Poor Garrett Morris (who plays Earl, the cashier at the diner where the show is set). Once, he was revered on *Saturday Night Live*; now, he gets just polite applause.

"You guys were great," Roger enthused. "Of all the audiences we've had, you are without a doubt the most recent."

Then, the taping began, and the audience was instructed to either stay deathly quiet or laugh wildly. No in between.

It was easy to do, at first. But by Take 7 of the first scene, in which the girls sell cupcakes to a redheaded Irish mom with a flock of redheaded kids, we knew what was coming but still had to laugh "spontaneously." Max's scene-ending bon mot, "Or in your case, 'Erin Go Training Bragh'?" just wasn't as funny after the seventh time. That scene, all of maybe three minutes, took 45 minutes to tape. Not only did they take it from the top several times, but they did many "pickups," which Roger told us meant do-overs of individual lines.

That was one of the many nuggets of TV lingo Jolly Roger shared long into the night. All told, the cast taped five scenes and the audience was shown two "playbacks" (scenes shot previously, such as in a cab on a street, and played on the monitors to get audience reaction).

Had it not been for those playbacks—essentially cutting out two scenes—we might have been holed up until 'round midnight, forced to laugh on command. But every time the audience's energy started to flag, Roger served as a human amphetamine drip, cajoling us to emote. He made good on those promises of goodies, too. We got bottled water at 7:07 p.m., cupcakes at 7:23, T-shirts given away at 7:51, sandwiches at 8:09, candy at 8:25 and more candy at 9:27 as the final scene wrapped. People left looking wearied, as if they'd just sat through Wagner's *Ring* cycle.

I wondered why it took so many takes to shoot a handful of scenes, when it all could be spliced together in postproduction (another term Roger threw at us). I mean, this was *2 Broke Girls*, not the Royal Shakespeare Company's *Two Gentlemen of Verona*. That's because show creator Michael Patrick King, bedecked in blue blazer and tennis shoes, apparently is a perfectionist. His production team, at least 20 strong, followed him, flock-like. Not once, the whole night, did King laugh. He barely broke a smile. Mostly, he stood with arms crossed and brow furrowed, staring into the quad-screen showing the camera angles and halting takes to give stage direction.

I left sure of at least one thing: There's nothing funny about the making of a comedy.

The Valley Gets Some Respect

April 2016
City sector: Chatsworth
Unofficial designation: San Fernando Valley
Population: 37,102
Elevation: 978 feet

It's a long day livin' in Reseda
There's a freeway runnin' through the yard . . .
—Tom Petty

Tommy Gelinas likes that song, "Free Fallin'." Truly, he does. Killer guitar riffs. Nice hook. Sure, it sort of slags on his beloved San Fernando Valley, but then, doesn't everybody? Gelinas accepts it. Doesn't like it. Calls it a worn-out stereotype, certainly not the Valley he knows. But he abides, mostly.

Not to say Gelinas condones what he calls Valley bashing—"the LA haters hating on the 818ers," 818 being the Valley's area code—but he understands the impulse by snooty types from "over the hill," those in the Los Angeles Basin who wouldn't think of careening down the Sepulveda Pass into the hazy scrum of the Valley, unless they wanted a better deal on, say, bathroom tile than they could get in Santa Monica or Brentwood.

Think of the Valley as New Jersey to LA's New York, a reliable punching bag and punch line.

Gelinas adjusts his horn-rimmed glasses and nods vigorously when a visitor to his Valley Relics Museum, situated next to Tile Clearance Inc. in a Chatsworth light-industrial complex, reels off a litany of Valley slights from over the decades: Johnny Carson and *Laugh-In* putting down "beautiful downtown Burbank"; the up-speak vacuity of Moon Unit Zappa's "Valley Girl" ("It's like, fer sure, gag me with a spoon"); TV weathermen references to smog so thick it's like "inhaling iron fillings"; the grim movies of native son Paul Thomas Anderson, including *Boogie Nights*, detailing what in recent decades has become a major Valley industry, porn.

Taking a long pull from a can of Rockstar Energy Drink to gird himself for what, knowing Gelinas, promises to be a lengthy response, the voluble curator of 60 years of Valley memorabilia instead is brisk, clipped and to the point.

"The Valley has endured enough bashing," he says. "It's been stripped, and it's been pillaged. I'm like, you're not gonna do it here anymore, not on my time. Look, we've always been underrated, got a bad rap from the LA haters. But they never had an understanding of what the Valley was. But part of it is our fault. When people talk doo-doo about the Valley, it can be hard to defend it when there's nothing left in terms of history. This was, I mean, is the world's most famous valley."

Gelinas makes this bold proclamation while sitting in a booth salvaged from the erstwhile Sherman Room, a once-swanky steak-and-lobster-and-high-ball Van Nuys restaurant, lovingly restored in the museum to all its Mid-Century Modern splendor, right down to the green Naugahyde upholstery.

A sweeping look at the artifacts attests to Gelinas' deep affection for the Valley. You spy everything from the neon sign that once graced the original Henry's Tacos (an early '60s "Gringo Mexican" forerunner to Taco Bell) on Tujunga Avenue in Studio City to uniforms from the 1976 movie *The Bad News Bears*, shot at Chatsworth's Mason Park, to bric-a-brac from the old Palomino country-and-western bar in North Hollywood.

Impressive and nostalgia-laden as it is, it doesn't seem to bolster Gelinas' bold contention that the San Fernando Valley reigns over all the other valleys in the world. There is no official designation, after all, and it's all a matter of criteria. One would not normally rank the San Fernando Valley

Tommy Gelinas, unofficial historian of the San Fernando Valley, started his museum because he felt the Valley gets no respect.

up there with Yosemite Valley and the Lauterbrunnen in Switzerland. But Gelinas swears it's no hyperbole—"You take the San Fernando Valley and compare it to anywhere in the world," he says, "Switzerland, New York, Chicago, San Diego. Wherever. I mean it. Anywhere in the world."

Another slug of Rockstar, and Gelinas starts ticking off reasons until he runs out of fingers, making a pretty darn good case for his Valley to be the top, at least among urban/suburban places. Be prepared for a soliloquy worthy of Shakespeare—or, at least, a rapid-fire TV pitchman:

"Why do I call it the World's Famous Famous Valley? Well, first, like you said, it was mentioned in that Tom Petty song. Open up (high school) yearbooks from the Valley. Oh, John Elway, Granada Hills High. Robert Redford went to Van Nuys High. Marilyn Monroe went to Van Nuys, too. James Cagney's ranch was at O'Melveny (Granada Hills). Huge ranch for Cagney. Lucy and Desi were married in Canoga Park. Their ranch was in the Chatsworth area. The Valley: home to the stars. Even right up until Ronnie James Dio died, he was living in Encino. Johnny Cash lived in

Encino and Liberace, too. Clark Gable, Gene Autry, Roy (Rogers) and Dale (Evans). I can go on and on. Mr. Hertz, the rental car guy, he had a ranch. Zeppo Marx and Barbara Stanwyck had the Marwyck Ranch right up here.

"Why? It was rural and safe. A lot of dirt roads and ranch homes. We were one of first to legalize horse racing. Devonshire Downs, man. People would get out of glitz of Hollywood and mid-Wilshire and escape over the hill. That racetrack, it was beautiful. Devonshire Downs also had the Newport '69 concert festival, where Janis (Joplin) and Jimi (Hendrix) played prior to Woodstock. I'm just giving you the pop-culture info. I could go back to the 1800s, if you want.

"And trees. Man, we had trees. Land. Still dirt roads into the '60s. Good prices for homes. Raise a family. Have horses. We had jobs. Produced 62 million Firebirds and Camaros. We produced Marantz stereos, JBL speakers, Fisher components, Infinity stereos. Rocket engines and some of the best war planes that defended the USA. We also invented the sport of BMX. Did you know that? Made the best BMX bikes in the world.

"Of course you know about cruising Van Nuys Boulevard. Thousands of spectators and hundreds and hundreds of the most amazing hot rods, Harleys, choppers, dune buggies every Wednesday night. The air was filled with that '60s glitter. You had air-brushed Ford and Chevy vans with wood paneling and shag carpeting. Van Nuys Boulevard on a Wednesday was like going to the Vegas strip. Young girls everywhere. Good-looking guys everywhere. Hells Angels, too. People used to hang out from 7 o'clock to 2 in the morning . . ."

Note how Gelinas slipped into the past tense during his reverie. Much of the manufacturing is gone, others seeing their glory days in the rear-view mirror. But it all still lives on in Gelinas' mind. And he seeks to keep memories alive for other longtime Valleyites.

"My tagline is, cherish what we had and preserve what's left," he says. "You need to be proud of where you come from."

Gelinas, 52, is so proud that he has accumulated more than 15,000 pieces of Valley lore over the past 18 years. A native son—"I was conceived in Sherman Oaks and popped out in Burbank"—Gelinas says he never felt the urge to leave the Valley. His father was an actor (and later inventor) who met his future wife at Republic Studios in Encino, where she was a switchboard operator. They found a home in the Valley, like so many young couples in the early 1960s, and had nine children. When Tommy came of age, he didn't think about leaving the Valley. And why should he? He could more easily start his T-shirt business ("We produced 150,000 T-shirts a week, all licensed to, like, SpongeBob Square Pants or Britney Spears and Iron Maiden") here as over the hill, where leases were outrageous.

He has kids of his own now, and likes the family values evident in the Valley. Too, he's a sucker for nostalgia and hopelessly smitten with the Valley of his youth. In fact, even in middle age, Gelinas still looks boyish. Wearing a black baseball cap on backward, and slightly askew, and a gray hoodie that covers his arm sleeve of tattoos, he looks like he's ready to hit the trails on a dirt bike.

"I've been called the 'Unlikely Curator,'" he says. "I don't want to call myself cutting edge, but. . . . Look, I have a home and $3,000 suits in my closet. People look at the tattoos and my hat and make assumptions. But don't judge a book by its cover. Just like the Valley, you know."

It always comes back to the Valley. If you called Gelinas obsessed with it, you wouldn't be too far off. He relishes showing off his "finds," which range from vintage signs like the scoreboard from the old North Valley Little League to a 1975 Cadillac convertible, with longhorns and silver dollars on the chassis, belonging to Western-wear entrepreneur Nudie Cohn. There's a story behind each item. One Gelinas likes to recount is his acquisition of the sign outside the erstwhile White Horse Inn that, in Gelinas' words, "used to light up Northridge where there was nothing else going on." The restaurant closed in 1997, and Gelinas spoke to the owner about salvaging the sign. The owner remained noncommittal.

"People celebrated bar mitzvahs, graduations, proms, anniversaries there," he says. "The building stayed abandoned. I circled it almost every day for more than a decade. I watched the sign wither away. Someone threw a stone and put a little hole in it. Then, one day, I'm driving by with my wife, who was pregnant, and they're tearing down the building. I slammed on the brakes. My wife says, 'What are you doing?' I had to stop it. I told the workers it was a sacred Indian burial ground. Then I called up the owner and said, 'I'll stop this construction if you don't give me that sign.' He said, 'OK, Tommy, OK.'"

In the early days of collecting, Gelinas relied on his own wiles to salvage Valley stuff. These days, people contact him via Facebook or the Valley Relics' website. Gelinas has acquired so much memorabilia that he has had to store the excess in another building in North Hollywood. He opens the

Chatsworth museum for five hours every Saturday, and he strolls the aisles reminiscing with fellow Valleyites.

On a recent Saturday, two men reveling in past lore, Jaime Gallegos and Bill Garza, of Canoga Park, said they felt transported.

"The Palomino!" Garza, 70, said. "I remember the Palomino. That sign. People probably figured all this stuff went to the dump. It's surprising to see it again."

Younger Valleyites, who weren't even born when the signs were torn down, appreciate the pop-culture history lesson.

"My dad, he told me everything about the Valley," says Patricia Siegel, 26, of Mission Hills. "We'd be driving around and he'd say, 'I remember there used to be a restaurant there,' and I'd say, 'OK.' He'd recognize a lot of the stuff here. It's nice to see the Valley represented. I think people get the wrong impression. For one thing, not all of us use that 'fer sure' crap voice. We don't talk like that."

For sure, uh, surely, they do not.

Behind Scientology's Doors

June 2015

City sector: Hollywood

Reputed members of Scientology worldwide: 15 million

Number of people working front desk at L. Ron Hubbard Life Exhibition: 3

This big blue marble on which we dwell has more than its share of disputatious religions—pick a creed, any creed—but only one holds the distinction of offering as a place of worship, or at least education, a historic building that lights up at night in the heart of one of the nation's most touristy areas, Hollywood Boulevard.

Yes, Scientology.

Seems incongruous at first blush, but not if you step back and take a look at the 1924 Hollywood Guaranty Bank Building or, better yet, step inside and ogle the ornate Beaux Arts lobby.

You'll find the venue makes perfect sense. After all, this is a belief system that boasts many movie industry notables (Tom Cruise, John Travolta), was founded by a screenwriter and pulp-fiction author (L. Ron Hubbard) and reportedly has enough assets to fund its own bank. And as for the location, well, Scientology's proselytizing—they are known to hand out the booklet *The Way to Happiness* on the sidewalk—is considered just another part of the whole mind-bending Hollywood Boulevard experience.

I can't tell you how many times over the years I passed by the Scientology digs without giving it a second thought—and certainly without considering popping in. Then again, visiting religious shrines is something that tourists (and travel writers) do. When in London, you go to Westminster Abbey; in Rome you see the Vatican; in Salt Lake City, Temple Square. So, when in Los Angeles, why not make a pilgrimage to the religion that, for good or ill, is closely associated with the city?

Besides, the sign out front said they give free(!) tours of the L. Ron Hubbard Life Exhibition, which fills the lobby and mezzanine levels of this gorgeous building boasting restored marble flooring and a tile drop ceiling with ornate wainscoting. Would it be merely a clever ruse to lure you in and indoctrinate you into Scientology's precepts, as detailed in its urtext, *Dianetics: The Modern Science of Mental Health,* and school you to conquer what they call the "reactive mind?"

Only way to find out is to take the tour. Two other sets of "tourists" mingled in the lobby before the bronze bust of Hubbard, front and center, and a wood-paneled display of 15 photographic portraits of the man, with all-caps lettering dubbing it "The L. Ron Hubbard Series." None wanted to give me their names, for some reason, but they consisted of three 30-somethings from Cincinnati and two grandmotherly types from Maryland.

Before I could ask their motivation for entering the gates of Scientology, we were herded by a fresh-faced docent who resembled Kelly Clarkson, circa Season 1 of *American Idol.* She didn't give her name and no one felt compelled to ask. She led us beyond a set of double doors to the sanctum sanctorum of all things L. Ron.

It was a finely appointed, museum-quality exhibit: long, well-lit hallways with stage sets depicting scenes from Hubbard's early life, his swashbuckling early days as a "world traveler" seeking wisdom in the East, his career writing genre fiction (sci-fi, westerns, adventure) and his time as a Hollywood screenwriter. This last display consisted of a movie marquee with the title in lights, "L. Ron Hubbard's The Secret of Treasure Island," which our fresh-faced docent (henceforth referred to as FFD) said "broke all records for all movies at that time, a box-office success."

In the heart of Hollywood, in what used to be the historic Hollywood Guaranty Bank Building, is the world headquarters for Scientology.

Reality check: According to the Internet Movie Database, *The Secret of Treasure Island* was the 210th top-grossing movie of 1938.

OK, so maybe FFD was exaggerating a tad. But the display showing a becapped newsstand vendor standing before row upon row of magazines all featuring the science fiction prose offerings of L. Ron cannot be disputed. The man was so prolific that you wondered whether he suffered from hypergraphia.

"He wrote *Battlefield Earth* in 1982," FFD said, "to celebrate his 50 years of being an author. To this day, it's one of the most popular science fiction novels."

Reality check: According to the website bestsciencefictionbooks.com, *Battlefield Earth* doesn't crack the top 25 most popular novels, a list that includes people named Asimov, Herbert, Bradbury, LeGuin.

But, really, why be such a factual stickler? Just accept that the tour's first 15 minutes amounts to a Hubbard hagiography.

It's what comes after those first 15 minutes that starts to unsettle.

We were led to the wing devoted to *Dianetics*, the 1950 tome that FFD said was "the first book ever written on the mind."

Reality check: A real whopper, that claim. See: William James and Sigmund Freud's oeuvres, for instance.

FFD herded us down a hallway, brightly lit and stacked floor to ceiling with copies of *Dianetics* behind glass cases, and into a theater where "I'll show you a short video . . ."

Uh-oh, here it comes.

I'll spare you a line-by-line dissection, but its point was that *Dianetics* can cure you of "negative thoughts, self-doubts, unreasonable fears" by pointing out that "all your painful experiences are stored in a previously unknown part of the mind, called the reactive mind." The narrator's warm baritone clashed with overwrought acting of couples arguing over money, a parent slapping a child, a man either in deep existential anguish or extremely constipated.

After the 10-minute video, FFD walked us upstairs and asked us personal questions, such as our professions. Our group had a paralegal, an interior designer, a bank teller and a limo driver. I didn't lie. I told her "writer," after which I detected the slighted arch of her eyebrow. Then she asked us, "What have you heard about Scientology?" Silence. Seconds passed. I felt bad for FFD, so I blurted out, "Tom Cruise." Somehow, she both smiled and frowned at the same time.

"Pretty much everything you hear in the media is baloney," she said with a dismissive hand wave, but no real bitterness. "Scientology actually comes from the word 'scio,' which means 'knowing,' and 'ology,' the 'study of.' So it's the study of knowledge or knowing how to know. It is a religion, but it's an applied religious philosophy. . . . Let me show you this. It's called an emotional tone scale, the first scale to accurately predict human behavior. Come closer. It's OK."

FFD proceeded to tick off the 24 attributes of the ETS, waving brochures and what seemed akin to a personality test some gun-ho corporate human resources director might administer. Next up, a contraption called the E-Meter, short for electro-psychometer. It resembled a 1950s gizmo that the paralegal mistook for a lie-detector device. It consisted of a console with a big knob and a glass window holding a needle that whipped around like a windshield wiper. Attached to the console were two cords with metal handholds at the end.

"What it does is show when a person has a thought," she said. "You hold these and there's a tiny bit of electricity that goes through you and back into here. It's used in counseling. The thoughts will affect the needle on the dial. Wanna try?"

One of the women from Maryland was game. She grasped the hand-holds while FFD twisted the knob. The needle swung deep to the right, then back to resting position. "You had a thought just then, right?" FFD chirped. "Pretty cool, huh?"

I took a turn. As I grasped the metal holds, I felt no current of electricity. The needle wasn't moving, either. FFD twisted the knob, and the needle jumped to a vertical position. I asked her, "What are you doing with the dial?" She said, "Oh, basically calibrating."

Next came another video, about seven minutes long, concerning marriage and Scientology's role in fostering a better relationship.

Reality check: How many times has Tom Cruise been married and divorced? (Three.)

In any event, we learned two terms in the video ("overt," an act you do but wouldn't want done to you; and "withhold," keeping such acts to yourself). Warm baritone narrator: "By withholding the overt, you fall out of communication . . . at the very root of divorce."

Finally, after passing through an archway saying "The Way to Happiness," we were back in the lobby and then on the street, a place I was profoundly happy to be.

A Second Place to Shrink From

May 2014

Turns out, you haven't escaped the clutches of Scientology when you exit the shrine to L. Ron. FFD (Fresh-Faced Docent) handed you a laminated card, good for one free admission to another museum just down the block:

"PSYCHIATRY An Industry of Death Museum."

Oh, I just had to stop by, even though the title was poorly punctuated, sans colon.

I briskly made the walk, past the Subway, distracted by promiscuous American Apparel billboards hulking overhead and checking out the new e-cig business, Puff In Vaporium, across the street from the Blessed Sacrament School. Suddenly, there it was: a large poster showing a bed with ominous leather foot and arm restraints and the word "psychiatry" in blood red letters.

A museum dedicated to maligning, possibly slandering, an entire healing profession? Count me in.

I craned my neck to get a look at the building, white-and-blue stucco with an official seal and an important-sounding name: "Citizens Commission of Human Rights International." Its facade gave off the feel of high seriousness, as if you were about to enter the U.N. building. I looked in one of the windows and saw a giant photograph of a baby bottle filled with pink pills, the caption reading, "Every year, 2,000 prescriptions for anti-depressant drugs are written for children under 1 year old."

I could've just walked on by. Maybe I should have. Even if I hadn't been handed the card by FFD, it was obvious this was a "museum" with an agenda, a not-so-hidden one. Let me say I have no issues with psychiatrists, psychologists, anyone in the mental-health field. I know many people who swear by them, and only a few who swear at them.

Almost immediately, I was pounced on by a volunteer, a middle-aged librarian type whose perkiness was surpassed only by her zealotry. She didn't give me her name, but she sure gave me an earful about the CCHR, how it was cofounded in the 1960s by Dr. Thomas Szasz, an emeritus professor of psychiatry at Syracuse University, and the Church of Scientology and how . . .

She never mentioned the S-word. I wanted to interrupt and mention the Tom Cruise-vs.-Matt Lauer "psychiatry is pseudo-science" showdown on *The Today Show* in 2005, and how other stars/Scientology adherents like Anne Archer and Priscilla Presley have spoken about the issue.

But I kept quiet. Just before she finished, she finally came clean: "(Scientology) just helped Dr. Szasz cofound (the organization) because no other people would fund it back then. What we do is survey and track everything that goes on in mental health. We're trying to reform it."

I asked her about the museum, and she said it opened in 2005 to give an overview of the history of psychiatry, its supposed dubious practices and the role it plays in modern society. (I later contacted the American Psychiatric Association for comment about the museum; it declined.)

"You've come on a busy day," she said. "We have medical students here touring and doing workshops. How much time do you have? It'll take about seven hours to really study what the museum's about. If you don't have that long, I'd suggest you go right to the DSM (*Diagnostic and Statistical Manual of Mental Disorders*) Room and the School Classroom (exhibits). We have millions of kids on drugs. They're turning them into zombies."

Seven hours? Really? Spending that long in any museum would drive me crazy—perhaps not the wisest choice of words in a place like this.

I told her I had an hour, adding that my ADHD prevented me from spending any more time. To her credit, she got my lame joke and laughed, told me I couldn't take photos inside but didn't flinch when I whipped out my notebook. She handed me a museum tag to plaster on the front of my shirt, then pointed to a purposely rusted wrought-iron arch and doorway graced with a quote from the third canto of Dante's *Inferno*: "Through me the way into the suffering city / Through me the way to the eternal pain / Through me the way that runs among the lost."

Well, that certainly gives you pause before opening the door. And when I entered, I found myself in a padded room, and then an entryway where I was assaulted by the first of an onslaught of statistics and pronouncements, such as, "Every 75 seconds, somebody gets committed in this country against their will."

I took the volunteer's advice and breezed by exhibits about how psychiatry can be blamed for the eugenics movement, for the Holocaust, power walked past slogans such as "Torture and Death Sold as Miracle Cure," past renderings of people in straitjackets, in stocks, in cages, but I stopped at the Mind Control room, where footage of electroshock therapy was played. I had to stop because a gaggle of students from Everest Pharmacy Tech adorned in blue scrubs were staring slack-jawed at the hideous sight and blocked the path. I stopped again a few rooms down at a macabre walk-of-fame-type of display of stars—from Kurt Cobain to Sylvia Plath to Spalding Gray to Elliott Smith—who committed suicide. But far from suggesting these troubled souls needed help from mental-health practitioners, the museum seems to blame psychiatry for the deaths.

Moving on, I finally did make it to the DSM Room and School Classroom exhibits.

I watched a video with cleverly spliced sound bites, including this from Dr. Darrel Regier, vice chair of the American Psychiatric Association's DSM-5 task force: "We don't know the ideology of really any mental disorders at the present time." That was followed by heavy, two-beat base notes, Duh-DUM, like on *Law & Order*. Then the narrator, sounding like the voice-over people who do movie trailers, intoned as if hawking a horror movie and speaking of a clinical manual: "It's grown to 10 times its original size, and it labels everybody."

The schoolroom display featured desks and chalkboards and ran a video in a loop, insinuating that psychiatrists, in league with pharmaceutical companies, want to drug our youth and showing stats listing the growth of ADHD diagnoses in children, while running clips from *Fox News* about notorious school shooters, before lamenting that the United States "has fallen from ninth to 26th in worldwide academic standards."

My hour was up. I felt I'd "learned" enough. I went to lunch. The clerk at Subway gave me a smile that was almost sneer-like. Only then did I realize I was still wearing the sticker on my chest.

3
The Cities Within "The City"

San Francisco itself is art, above all literary art. Every block is a short story, every hill a novel. Every home a poem, every dweller within immortal. That is the whole truth.
—William Saroyan

Isn't it nice that people who prefer Los Angeles to San Francisco live there?
—Herb Caen

Curating a City's History

November 2015
City sector: Financial District
Population: 9,447
Square miles: 0.46

Heels, stiletto and blocky wingtip both, clack authoritatively along the cracked sidewalk of Post Street. Everyone seems in a hurry, this being the Financial District and all. Time is money, as they say, and money is these people's *raison*. Not a minute to waste, must make haste, which may be why a bank and a coffee shop are incongruously conjoined. *Care for a home loan with your no-foam latte, sir?*

Forgive these strivers, these hell-bent 21st-century Gold Rushers, if they fail to notice the demurely handsome Classical Revival building at 57 Post, its nine stories dwarfed by book-ended banking high-rises, its sedate setting overwhelmed by the chaotic clatter of foot traffic traveling between the Montgomery BART station and Union Square. Only a series of bare bulbs illuminate the ornately serifed, all-caps sign, easily missed, etched into glass below the granite-arched entrance:

MECHANICS' INSTITUTE
LIBRARY

Thing is, 57 Post probably predates any building or business along this teeming stretch of The City. Yes, even older than the hulking Wells Fargo monolith three doors down and across two lanes of traffic. The institute stood at 31 Post St. starting in the mid-1800s and, following the Etch A Sketch erasure of the 1906 earthquake, was rebuilt within three years in the same spot, albeit now christened 57 Post. And, over the years, through booms and busts, dot-com frenzies and high-tech meltdowns, the Mechanics' Institute has remained a solid and stolid presence in a city that purports to cherish its history but too often dismisses it as blithely as a techie's finger swipe on a smartphone.

Not that many denizens these days can fathom what might go on beyond the thick double-glass doors. They are just as liable to see the signage and wonder, Who are these grease monkeys? Why is their trade school in such a monied milieu? Are the library's shelves stocked only with begrimed manuals?

In reality, the Mechanics' Institute ranks as one of San Francisco's most dedicated cultural centers, certainly its most venerable. Its influence and reach may have ebbed and flowed over the decades, due to demographic shifts and the social whims of the populace, but it endures like a well-constructed, finely honed piece of machinery. A U-joint, say.

Created in 1855 by and for mechanics in the broadest sense of the word—artisans, fabricators, technological creators—its original mission was nothing less than to bring culture, creative learning and, yes, even a measure of civility to a wild, post–Gold Rush San Francisco. (Back in the day, yearly dues for this "members only" club was $6 and stayed at that price until 1975; now, it's $95 a year, still well within economic reach of most Bay Areans.)

These days, the organization's goal may be even more ambitious: to engage an overstimulated, easily distracted, tech-overloaded citizenry in thoughts and ideas beyond the ephemeral pixels scrolling across their screens, to show these high-tech "mechanics" that their most valuable tool may be their intellects.

At present, the institute seems to be making a modest impression. Its membership rests at 4,500, healthy compared to dips in the past decade, and in the past six months, 38 percent of new members are in the coveted under-40 demographic.

Now, as then, the institute houses a handsome library spanning two stories with nearly 200,000 volumes, catering to brows high and low, its works spanning *The Brothers Karamazov* and the oeuvre of the sisters Kardashian. Its fourth-floor chess room, home to the oldest continuous chess club in the United States, has welcomed such famous personages as Bobby Fischer, Boris Spassky and Anatoly Karpov, but is more widely known for its Tuesday night soirees in which a 7-year-old from Bangalore might square off against a 70-year-old Russian émigré. Its meeting rooms and lecture halls, once haunted by the likes of Mark Twain and Gertrude Stein, Jack London and William Saroyan, now host Pulitzer Prize winners and best-selling authors, both homegrown and far-flung, reading from and discussing their works.

Best of all, it seems, the Mechanics' Institute is a respite for the psyche, a place to plant one's feet and just think. Or read. Or sleep. All three activities were taking place one recent weekday afternoon in the pin-dropping quiet of the Beaux Arts–columned library, all high windows and low-slung leather armchairs.

Ralph Lewin, who in 2014 left his position as president of the California Endowment for the Humanities, a nonprofit partner of the National Endowment for the Humanities, to become the institute's executive director, swiped his card for a visitor to gain entrance. He spoke softly, so as not to disturb a patron furiously typing a database search or a man across the way slouching in a chair, chin on chest and finger marking the spot of a closed book. Four stories below, the ambient noise of the city could just faintly be heard, though not loud enough to distract the deliberative quiet engulfing the room.

"See that?" Lewin whispered, as he passed by an oak table with titles on display. A biography of kickboxer Mark "Fightshark" Miller rubbed spines with a biography of collage art master Jean Varda. Lewin gave a quick nod, as if to underscore the institute's egalitarian ethos.

"We're kind of a cultural oasis downtown, and people value that," he said, back in his fifth-floor office whose vintage pebble-glassed door evoked images of Sam Spade. "But also, as San Francisco is changing now, pretty dramatically, a lot of people in the cultural and literary world are being pushed out. One of the things we can offer is this space. We're reaching out to work in partnership with cultural institutions. That's important to us."

The institute may have been founded by mechanics and artisans who literally built San Francisco from nothing, but it quickly gained the attention, and financial backing, of various city movers and shakers. The same is true today. Though Lewin says the institute is just as diverse, culturally and economically, as in previous generations, the organization has built a solid endowment and is chaired by Matthew H. Scanlan, a CEO of an investment management firm. The biggest revenue stream, which keeps the institute afloat, comes from renting out office space in the nine-story structure, which the institute owns.

That's no small potatoes, considering the skyrocketing cost of San Francisco real estate. But Lewin said, in addition to attorneys and businessmen who populate the office space, the institute is home to a burgeoning cadre of literary and educational concerns that normally wouldn't be able to afford such a high-rent address. In recent months, Litquake, the nonprofit literary festival, moved its offices to the sixth floor, sharing space with the literary journal, *Zyzzyva*. The Writers Studio, something of a support group/workshop for budding novelists and poets, is another new renter, holing up on the seventh floor.

Finding a permanent meeting space for classes was important, said Writers Studio director Mark Peterson, adding that other literary concerns sharing the building is a pleasant bonus.

"I have to admit, I was not very aware of the Mechanics' Institute before this summer, but I think that it is a very relevant mission for our times, the desire for in-person communities is great, and the electronic assault on the places that many had gone to for this type of literary communion during the past 30 years has been rapid," Peterson said. "Most forms of electronic communities are shallow, and so any physical places that can provide greater depth to the interactions will always have a place in our social interactions."

Lewin speaks passionately about promoting a "safe, stable place for people in the cultural field," and literary agent Ted Weinstein, whose offices are on the fifth floor, says the place is fast becoming a hub.

No stranger to the building, Weinstein had been a member for two years and said he researched and wrote his first book in its library.

"I knew it was going to be really hard to write at the public library . . . and somebody said to me, 'Do you know about the Mechanics' Institute?'" Weinstein said. "She almost, literally, dragged me down there. I joined and started writing the book within 36 hours. Since then, I've tried to do the same with many others. I've gotten three new members for the library just since I've been here. That's because everybody who drops by for a meeting says, 'Wow, this is an amazing place.' On the way out, I take them for a tour of the library, and they're completely smitten and immediately march to the Mechanics' Institute office to sign up."

What attracts people such as Weinstein is the institute's democratic sensibility. This is no good-ol'-boys, exclusive Bohemian Club, nor is it a venue for Nob Hill hobnobbing or strictly the domain of effete elitists.

True, some events would be considered highbrow by anyone's measure—a screening of Federico Fellini's *Spirits of the Dead* in its CinemaLit series; a discussion of works by Laszlo Krasznahorka in its World Literature round-table—but there's also a "Brown Bag Mystery Reading Group" and, hewing to its "mechanics" initial mission, classes for people to brush up on skills such as creating PowerPoints.

Everything is applicable, Lewin said, in a fast-changing world in which fewer people need to learn how to work a lathe and more need to master a laptop. Yet, Lewin cannot help but look backward as he moves forward.

The institute's history, after all, is nailed to the hallway walls. Framed pictures by late 19th-century photographer Carleton Watkins feature the erstwhile Mechanics Fairs, sponsored by the institute, that wowed crowds as big as 600,000 with exhibits of then-cutting-edge technology (Eadweard Muybridge's kinetographic studies of people and horses in motion) and artisan goods (Levi Strauss' copper-riveted pants). But what strikes Lewin most is the populist, communal aspect to the institute, especially in its early days.

"I'm intrigued with the idea that in 1855 these carpenters and masonry workers came together and thought about the future of San Francisco," he said. "Their idea was kind of radical: to found the first library on the West Coast. . . . It was like your own private club, but open to everybody. It's astounding to me to think that it was so open—man or woman, black or white. Think about that in terms of the trajectory of American history. It really was at the forefront."

Likewise, the chess room, more than 40 tables with rooks and knights at attention, was originally meant to be a way for San Franciscans to blow off steam without devolving into the world of saloons, brothels and dance halls, according to historian Richard Reinhardt's history of the institute, *Four Books, 300 Dollars and a Dream.* The chess room, he wrote, "gave a man a place to get off the street, meet some friends and possibly even improve his mind."

Three computers are tucked in a corner of the chess room so that players can use them for research or to compete online against opponents worldwide. That's nothing new to the institute, though. Back in 1895, the institute's chess club challenged a club in Vancouver, Canada, to a long-distance match done via a telegraph connection made possible by Canadian Pacific Railway. (The teams each won one match.)

Several times over the institute's history, the chess room has been threatened with closure by the institute's board. Each time, efforts were rebuffed. Lewin says, at least during his watch, the chess room is here to stay. He led a visitor over to a "standings board," with nameplates of players affixed and their latest scores scrawled in chalk. It looks as if it hadn't been touched for years, maybe decades.

"See this guy, (Neil Falconer; sixth name from the top) on the board?" Lewin said. "He used to be on our board. Passed away. But he's still remembered here."

More than remembered, actually. Falconer embodies the spirit of the institute. He first stepped through the doors in 1938 as an Oakland high school student fond of chess. He became an institute member after serving in World War II and, having established himself as a prominent Bay Area attorney, was elected to the institute's board, becoming the longest-serving trustee in the organization's history. During that time, Falconer led a contentious internal fight to amend the institute's bylaws to ensure that it forever would have a place to play chess.

"This action was prompted by an attempt by the better-dressed members of the Institute to chase out what they perceived to be riffraff—namely the regular users of the Chess Room," according to a tribute to Falconer, who died in 2014, in the institute's newsletter. "Had it not been for (Falconer and fellow trustee Charles Bagby's) efforts to rouse the 300 or so Chess Room members to action, much of the fourth floor would now be rented out as office space."

However one defines "riffraff"—be they wearers of $3,000 Brioni suits or moth-eaten Goodwill print shirts—all are welcome at 57 Post St., provided they can cough up the $95 yearly dues. They'll gladly open the doors to non–San Franciscans—35 percent of current membership, in fact, come from outside The City.

Even stuffy, provincial San Franciscans, who delight in their disdain for tourists or people from outside The City, welcome visitors to the open doors of the institute, if not exactly opening their "Golden Gates" in the rest of the town.

Whoa, Dude, One Hella Flashback

August 2013
City sector: Haight-Ashbury
Population: 10,601
Square miles: 0.30

Before our groovy guide, Gaia, handed each of us a tab of "acid" that looked and tasted suspiciously like an innocent breath mint, before she told us about the Dead and Janis and the spot where members of the Airplane swore they saw a white rabbit, before the bus's shades went down and swirling, ever-morphing psychedelic images enveloped our senses— before all of that—the first thing she did was put a flower in our hair.

You know, just like the song goes.

If you're going to San Francisco
Be sure to wear some flowers in your hair

Mine, I stuck behind my right ear. Just to get into the spirit of the thing. Because if you're going to shell out $50 to take a two-hour tour on the Magic Bus, where you are hurled back to 1967, you've got to immerse yourself in full hippiedom. Otherwise, what's the point? Go take any number of the open-roof tours if you desire the "official" version of The City.

The Magic Bus, conversely, gives you what founder Chris Hardman says in the recorded introduction is "not a timeline of what happened to reality. It's about the dream, the dream of the '60s, about the things that should've happened, could've happened, as well as the happenings that actually happened."

That doesn't just mean that it will stop along the way at every Haight-Ashbury spot where Jerry lit a doobie, or Hippie Hill in Golden Gate Park. No, this bus is pimped out to the psychedelic max, brotha. Hardman is a celebrated multimedia artist whose work has appeared at the Smithsonian in Washington, D.C., MIT's Media Lab in Cambridge, Mass., and the American Center in Paris, and his vision for his hometown was to create a rolling, faux-lysergical interactive museum in which the bus windows could project images of the past at the precise locations where they took place decades ago.

Unveiled in 2010, the bus is wired with micro-video projectors pointing at each window, a killer surround-sound audio system to blare '60s rock classics and play sound clips from the likes of Allen Ginsberg, Timothy Leary and Ronald Reagan, and a bubble machine that constantly wafts the soapy creations out the tail pipe onto unsuspecting pedestrians.

All that, and Gaia, too.

Gaia claims not to be a '60s throwback; she swears she's *from* the '60s— transported here by love and good vibes.

(OK, her real name is Sophia LaPaglia, 27, an actress who grew up on a commune in Vermont's Green Hills and eventually made her way to San Francisco because "this is where I belong.")

But, for our purposes, she is Gaia, "the mother goddess here to take care of all of you." A flaming redhead with a cute, gap-toothed grin and a horribly mismatching tie-dye top and paisley peasant skirt, Gaia emoted with the raspy voice of a young Janis Joplin and exuded a Robin Williams– like manic energy.

In addition to providing comic relief, Gaia has to commandeer the video with a remote control, making sure the scenes on the screen correspond to where the bus is headed, be it Chinatown, North Beach, the Financial District or hallowed Haight-Ashbury.

Passing through Chinatown, Gaia guides us in deep-breathing meditation while the image of a hirsute Ginsberg intones, "We are all beautiful golden sunflowers inside." After the breathing work, the screens go up and we see the Chinatown of today. People are taking photos of the bus, while people on the bus are taking photos of those photographers.

Gaia apparently is into delayed gratification, because she kept hinting that we'd have a mind-blowing experience once we hit the Haight. But that was still a good half-hour away. We had to content ourselves with a spin around the Financial District, which actually was a hoot. With windows open, the Kinks' "A Well Respected Man" blared ("And he plays the stocks and shares / And he goes to the regatta") as we passed the Transamerica Pyramid.

"Look at it (the pyramid)," she said. "We've got all the little people working at the bottom and then just a few people at the top making all the money. It's the perfect shape of corporate America."

Then the screen descended and an ironic collage of conservative corporate images filled the screen, like outtakes from an old industrial film. It showed a clean-cut young man in a suit with the basso-profundo voice-over, "Working is part of growing up. You will all grow up someday. What do you want to be when you grow up?"

Then, a quick cut to Orwellian footage of factory drones, Pink Floyd's "The Wall" as accompaniment, followed by a montage of corporate slogans, such as "What's good for GM is good for America" and a commercial for Barbie's dream house.

The segment ended with Hardman, the narrator, saying, "The Magic Bus reminds us that the kids of the '60s didn't see these businesses as attractive but instead as prisons. When you got on a hippie bus, you weren't just a commuter. Buses were communes. You traveled by tribes, communed with nature, unlike city buses."

At this point, inching closer to enlightenment in the Haight, the bus pulled over to show the tribe . . . a Honda dealership?

"See the second floor?" she said. "That was the Fillmore West. The music scene: Jimi, Santana, Janis, the Dead. You paid $10, saw at least four bands, at least one a headliner, and you enjoyed unlimited free beverages provided by the audience."

Speaking of free nourishment, after we climbed Hayes Street and headed into the Haight, Gaia emerged with an Easter basket filled with colorful, individually wrapped fingernail-size "LSD tabs."

"Clear your mind, everyone, with this 'special candy,'" Gaia said. "Now, if this is your first time or it's been a while, just maybe start with just one; see how you're feeling before taking another. Of course, this is the Magic Bus, and you can do whatever you want."

Everyone aboard, even kids, slipped the candy under his or her tongue. Tasted like wintergreen. But if Gaia wanted us to pretend we were dropping acid, heck, why not play along? She lowered the screens and we saw vintage "testimonials" from LSD takers, first hyping the mind-expanding coolness of a trip then turning darker, with one hippie-chick saying, "After a while, things started to get crazy and my consciousness started to fracture apart . . ."

Our tribe seemed unfazed by the "candy." But Gaia apparently had to make sure, and she pointed to a colorful mural depicting Janis, Jerry and Jimi jamming.

"We have our first acid test: So this was a white wall this morning. But now, I see Jimi, Jerry. If you still see the white wall, let me know and I'll bring you more candy."

After a pit stop in Golden Gate Park—hey, even tripping hippies need to use the facilities—the tribe celebrated the free-love era by, well, watching footage of hippie hookups. The tribe laughed out loud when one girl told the camera, in all seriousness, "We had wonderful love affairs that lasted an hour."

Later, the mood turned darker, as Procol Harum's "A Whiter Shade of Pale" droned on. Gaia exclaimed, "Hold on to your good vibes. We're going into a bummer tunnel." The voice-over then told of peace and love turning to violence and the "scene" dissolving. Images of the assassinations of Martin Luther King Jr., Robert Kennedy and Supervisor Harvey Milk and Mayor George Moscone were shown as the bus passed City Hall, with John Lennon singing "Imagine."

Despite the buzzkill—more candy, Gaia, stat—the tour ended with a rousing reprise of Joplin's "Piece of My Heart."

Gaia bowed and thanked us, then awaited her next tribe.

Glasshole for a Day

June 2014
City sector: Nob Hill
Population 52,388
Square miles: 0.31

When you step into a bar in the Lower Haight called Molotov's, you've got to expect a certain attitude, a certain in-your-face atmosphere, replete with crusty characters who pull a moue as bitter as the cans of the Hamm's beer they crack open.

But when you're on the verge of stepping into Molotov's wearing Google Glass, Silicon Valley's first foray into wearable, interactive facial technology, you'd better expect sneers, leers, derision and maybe even harm to your person or pricey eyewear.

Even knowing the harsh milieu, my 24-hour immersion donning Glass would not have been complete without a visit to the site that has emerged as a symbolic ground zero of the simmering tension between technorati with their sleek, fancy devices and big, fat wallets moving into The City, and the less wired and monied citizenry feeling oppressed by the transformation of San Francisco from an unaffordable city to an egregiously unaffordable city.

It was at this very neighborhood bar—dimly lit, sporting blood-red walls accessorized by punk-rock stickers, with the crack of pool balls competing with the Giants on TV—that in February 2014 a loud, obnoxious and profane Glass-wearing woman saw her device swiped off the bridge of her nose and, while she gave chase, saw her purse and smartphone get whisked away as well. Shaken, she retrieved her Glass and posted the video the device recorded on YouTube. Naturally, it went viral and escalated The City's cultural war that ranges from rage about Google buses clogging streets to rants about rising rents.

Consider me merely an embedded correspondent in this ongoing skirmish. A newspaperman's salary hardly allows purchase of the $1,500 smart eyewear. Fortunately, the Stanford Court, a Nob Hill boutique hotel, has made it possible for anyone with a decent credit-card limit to strut like a techie peacock—snapping photos and shooting video through simple voice commands, sending them instantly to texting buddies, charting your pedestrian path with a map emerging, hologram-style, slightly above your right eye's field of vision. You can do Google searches and make phone calls as you power walk, a white glow emanating from the right frame. In short, you can make a spectacle of yourself in these specs (with or without tinted lenses) that weigh no more than a pair of Ray-Bans and come in many hues.

So why not take the hotel up on its one-night "Google Glass Explorer Package" offer, forking over $220 (plus tax) for the privilege of being envied by one subset of the San Francisco populace, reviled by another subset and just considered foolish by those with any fashion sense?

You cannot say I didn't know what I was getting into. Two days before my check-in date, an "assumption of risk, waiver of liability & indemnity agreement" popped into my inbox. I needed to sign and date this document, which said I "freely acknowledge" that "using the Device exposes me to many risks and hazards including but not limited to, collision with pedestrians, vehicles and/or fixed moving objects, becoming the target/

victim of criminal acts or assault, battery and robbery and risk of death, physical or mental personal injury, including but not limited to severe spinal or head injury." The legal form further stated that I was responsible for any loss or damage to the "Device" and that the "Releasee" (the hotel) would be "harmless of all claims."

Clearly, I was on my own here. But it's not as if the Stanford Court staff wasn't helpful. Oh, no, when I checked in, Austin Phillips, the director of sales and marketing, was there with a firm handshake and a glossy black tote bag bearing the coveted Glass, which though on limited sale to the public this spring has yet to achieve anywhere near mainstream use even in this tech Mecca.

Inside the bag was a brochure showing how to sync Glass with your smartphone and/or laptop—a somewhat laborious process for us Luddites, too boring to detail here—and, on the flip side, a tip sheet titled "Don't Be a Glasshole." Among the hotel's recommendations to avoid such an ignominious label:

- "Don't Be Creepy": Staring into the prism attached to the frame "for long periods of time" will look "weird to the people around you."

- "Avoid High-Impact Sports": Kite boarding on the bay is verboten, so is "skateboarding down California Street."

- "Be Polite": "In places where cellphone cameras aren't allowed, the same rules will apply to Glass."

Phillips seemed to have fewer concerns about a negative Glass experience than his own brochure expressed.

"People were equally as concerned when they first put cameras on phones," he said. "Like, whoa, you're going to film me? People freaked, but now they are OK with it. It's just a matter of time until people get used to it. There are a lot of places in the city saying Google Glass is not welcome, but our stance was to embrace the technology. The first thing we did was offer a free drink to any local person who came in wearing the Glass at our (lobby) bar. We gave away dozens of drinks that night. It was quite a sight. So, don't worry. You should be good to go."

With that send-off, I was free to explore The City literally through a different prism. I hoped not to be mocked or mugged while walking down teeming city streets tapping my right index finger to my right temple as if I suffered from a tic and shouting such militaristic commands as "OK, Glass. Record a video" and "OK, Glass. Share with circle."

But it would take self-esteem much higher than mine not to feel acutely self-conscious wearing Glass in public, especially when a user must sound like a schoolmarm carping "OK, class!" whenever giving the mandatory prefatory injunction "OK, Glass" to the device. (Oh, and a quick aside: Those in the know say to always refer to the device in the singular, Glass, since, don't you know, these are hardly mere glasses.) After adapting to the initial unsteadiness of trying to walk while peering up and to the right at the "screen," I felt confident enough to venture forth.

Not to Molotov's. Lord, no. You don't immediately face the angry hordes with untested weaponry; you test it out on easier subjects and go from there. Debuting my Glass at Molotov's would be like storming the beaches at Normandy without first dipping a toe in the water.

Union Square seemed a safe enough first foray. On the precipitous down-hill of Powell Street, some people coming at me did almost comic double takes and engaged in shameless rubbernecking. Others were too busy yakking away on their comparatively low-tech, handheld smartphones to pay any attention to my tricked-out eyewear. No one accosted me. Heck, no one even stopped me to ask about this technological marvel. Not even in line at Starbucks, where caffeine jitters usually make folks chatty.

Making a sortie into the Mission District, a hipster haven with pockets of Google resisters amid the trendy young urbanites, seemed a suitable challenge leading into a full Molotov's assault. The BART ride over was uneventful, and I was starting to think that people were just too caught up in their own tech bubble to look up and pay attention to anyone else.

That theory was summarily shot down as I walked past the 16th and Mission BART station toward Taqueria Cancun, where my college-age son reluctantly agreed to meet me for dinner. A mariachi trio glared at me as I passed, the accordion player curling his upper lip in obvious disdain while, nearby, a homeless man seemed to shake his coin cup with extra aggressiveness. OK, so maybe I was a little hypersensitive, paranoid even, but there was no disputing the intent of the dismissive headshake a 30-something hipster in a fedora, horn-rimmed glasses and 6-inch black beard gave as I neared the taqueria.

Once inside, waiting for my wary dinner companion to arrive, I caught out of the corner of my eye a young couple staring at me.

"I'm sorry for staring," she said. "But I've never seen one before."

I took that as an invitation to chat up Jennifer Jansonn and partner Noah Fichter, visiting from Portland, Ore. They agreed to a video interview, and they both giggled when I gave the "OK, Glass" directive.

"Is this investigative journalism?" Jansonn asked.

Just then, the video switched off at the 10-second mark—only later would I learn that 10 seconds is the default setting for video and you have to tap your temple to extend the run indefinitely—and started again. I asked them if they would ever buy Glass.

"No, no," Fichter said, without pause. "It's not that it looks silly or anything . . ."

"It looks a little silly," Jansonn interrupted.

"But," Fichter added, avoiding eye contact with me, "I don't think so."

My son arrived shortly thereafter. First words: "Gawd, Dad, take those off."

"No Glass, no burrito, son."

He relented. We ate. He made a hasty retreat soon thereafter, something about having to work early the next morning.

I decided I needed one more preliminary bout before Molotov's, so I ambled over to Dog Eared Books, the Mission's version of the uber-hip City Lights Bookstore in North Beach. As I browsed, I was startled when I tilted my head up to check the top shelf for Don DeLillo's novels. My Glass suddenly activated, a ping ringing in my Bluetooth-wired ear and the words "OK, Glass" flashing before my eye. (Only later would I learn that I had discovered the "head tilt" function for turning on the device without words or a tap.)

A clerk in a green trucker's hat eyed me as he shelved books. When I approached the counter to pay for DeLillo's *Great Jones Street*, hoping the literary purchase would offset any Glassholian presumptions the clerk harbored toward me, he asked me a question:

"What's it like? I have no knowledge of what it is you're experiencing behind those things."

I fumbled for a response. "It's, well . . ."

"Self-conscious?" he ventured. "Alienating?"

"Both," I said. "Do I look like a Glasshole?"

He smiled, and told me to enter my pin number for the purchase.

I could avoid Molotov's no longer. As I approached its fiery red facade, where several smokers lingered out front, my eye (and Glass) caught this sign in the window: "No recording of audio or video on the premises. You may be asked to leave if you violate this policy."

A bearded man with a cast on his right leg looked me up and down and said, in Tom Waitsian tones, "I wouldn't go in with that thing."

I compromised and turned off Glass' glowing prism. As I approached the bar, the pony-tailed, bearded bartender said, simply, "No," and turned around. He did not face front again for at least 30 seconds. By that time, I had taken Glass off and hid it in my jacket. He eventually took my beer order. I paid and told him I was a reporter working on a Google Glass exposé. This time, he said, "No comment," and turned his back once more.

I was able, however, to chat up a patron, Lower Haight resident Sam Clark, outside the bar. He said he was at Molotov's at the now-infamous Glass snatch caper. He said the woman was being rude—in essence, a "Glasshole."

"It was fundamentally a situation of not respecting other people's wishes," Clark said. "She showed up at 1:20 in the morning at a bar. It could've been any bar. It turned out to be this bar. She was making people uncomfortable. They asked her to stop and she would not."

Clark said he's not anti-tech. In fact, he said he works "in corporate communications for a tech company," though declined to say which one. (Not Google, though.)

"I understand there are periods of transition when people are uncomfortable with certain technologies," Clark added. "When people started texting in restaurants, that aggravated people.

"This is a private place. It's up to a private place to make a decision on what it wants to do. They made the decision: We'll bounce you."

Consider me bounced, then. I took my Glass and retreated to the Stanford Court. But first, I stopped at the Trader Joe's on California Street. In line with my bananas, I looked behind me and saw a slight man in a ponytail sporting—can it be?—a red, white and blue Glass.

I lurked outside until he bought his groceries, then chatted up the man, San Francisco illustrator (Marvel and DC Comics, among others) Justin Chung. Turns out, he was selected by Google in 2013 as an original Glass "Explorer." He exuded enthusiasm, said Glass has changed his life, made it so much easier.

"The only thing that separates us from animals is opposable thumbs and a superior intellect," he said. "But we lose the opposable-thumb advantage when we have to handle a phone and press all those buttons and look down. I have my hands free and I'm aware of my environment. I see people on the street looking down all the time and it's just too bad. They miss so much. With Glass, you don't miss anything."

At long last, I had found a member of my tribe—at least until my 24 hours with the Glass were up and I would return to life among the downward-looking rabble, alas.

Tenderloin Museum Honors the Squalor

August 2015
City sector: Tenderloin
Population: 25,067
Square miles: 0.35

Take a walk down Eddy Street. Resist the urge to walk fast with head down. Take in the acute, sometimes acrid, sensory details of these city blocks, the beating, arrhythmic heart of the Tenderloin. Be vigilant and streetwise, but don't succumb to fear, for there is much to see and experience in San Francisco's most notorious and misunderstood neighborhood.

A stoop-shouldered merchant sweeps the entryway of the Superette 128 market, careful not to disturb a homeless man and his dog, curled up sleeping nearby. Men linger outside the Herald Hotel, jawing and guffawing and swigging from 40-ouncers. Kids frolic on the swings and jungle gym at verdant Boeddeker Park, the roar of their playful squeals only partially drowned out by honking taxis and construction jackhammers. The marquee at the Tea Room Theatre ("All Male Entertainment") is lit but not yet open, same for the Power Exchange (hint: not a public utility building) a few doors down on Jones. Cops circle a man sprawled at a crosswalk, as a woman in a Marilyn Monroe T-shirt pushing a baby stroller tries not to look.

What's needed to fully comprehend this teeming street scene, this mingling of the ordinary and the sketchy, is context—historical and sociological perspective explaining such a rich urban milieu.

Context, conveniently, can be found at the corner of Eddy and Leavenworth, where the newly opened Tenderloin Museum has got it all covered.

A labor of both love and, well, labor by lawyer and Tenderloin activist Randy Shaw, the museum is three years in the making and $3.5 million in the building, with donations coming from local business owners, grants and philanthropists. At times during the process, Shaw admits he thought that with all the challenges the Tenderloin faces—poverty, homelessness, crime—what good will a museum do? "Maybe we should just open up another restaurant," he said, laughing. "But we kept at it. It was an ambitious goal, but we made it."

It is a goal mostly met, true.

The museum is a handsome, glass-walled space tucked into the ground floor of the Cadillac Hotel, the first of many SROs (single-room occupancy residences) that define the neighborhood. With archival photos, footage, recordings and yellowed newspaper clippings—augmented by artifacts ranging from a vintage pinball machine to peep-show viewfinders, from famous fan dancer Sally Rand to ticket stubs from the Black Hawk jazz club—it presents a history of the Tenderloin as a section of the city far richer than just a tawdry hub of gambling, drug use, porn and prostitution. Families have long lived here, churches long thrived, its sense of community evident in its embrace of all ethnicities, its tolerance shown by its acceptance of the gay and transgender populace long before the Castro became LGBT ground zero.

Where the goal might fall short is Shaw's hope that the museum will be a tourist draw, luring visitors away from obvious haunts such as Fisherman's Wharf, Golden Gate Park and Union Square and over to the 'Loin.

Shaw, author of the oral history *The Tenderloin*, knows what you might be thinking—is this dude deluded? But he believes the neighborhood can bring in tourist dollars. At times, he sounds like a super-positive realtor talking about a ratty fixer-upper having so much potential. His zealotry is so palpable, so contagious, that you want to believe him, regardless of evidence to the contrary.

The museum idea was spawned when Shaw led a successful neighborhood effort in 2007 to create a National Historic District for the Tenderloin. Now that the buildings, including the dozens of SRO hotels, were protected from the gentrification sweeping the rest of San Francisco, thoughts turned to commerce.

"We asked, 'How can we revive this community?'" said Shaw, who has dedicated his career in nonprofit advocacy to helping the Tenderloin and its residents, though he does not live there.

"What are our strengths? We looked at this low-income community with a long downturn, and we decided our strength is our history," Shaw said. "When we were working on the (historic district bid), we ran across all this great history. In the last chapter of my book on the Tenderloin, I mentioned that we just can't seem to get tourists to come here and spend money. A museum is a way to bring people in from the outside and build on our history."

Shaw hopes people will stop bad-mouthing the Tenderloin and actually see for themselves.

"We hired a professional company to do a survey to determine whether there was a demand or interest in a Tenderloin Museum, and we found out that people who'd never been to the Tenderloin were the people most afraid and were least likely to come," he said. "That says to us that the negative perception will change if we can just get people into the neighborhood."

In a perfect world, the museum should be a draw, mostly because it's as funky as the neighborhood itself. It's not afraid to highlight the less-savory aspects of the Tenderloin—the drugs, gambling and prostitution—while also celebrating the outreach to the homeless by churches such as Glide Memorial and St. Anthony's and community groups that advocated for transgender rights decades before Caitlyn Jenner emerged.

How could you not be captivated by a museum that features exhibits with titles such as these: Porn Is Born, Screaming Queens, Buying B-Girls, Placing Bets and Caged Teens? Along the way, you'll also learn about how activists worked for tenants' rights, how the Tenderloin served as a center for labor union organizing and how the neighborhood is the most culturally and ethnically diverse in San Francisco.

But, c'mon, wouldn't you rather hear about the tawdry?

To that end, there's a wonderfully kitschy archival video, circa early 1960s, about the Tenderloin that today comes off as almost a *Dragnet* parody. Flashing images of neon signs blaring "PUSSY CAT Theatre" and "LIQUOR," the basso-profundo narrator intones: "Every great city of the world seems to have an area given over to the fleshy needs of men. In San Francisco, this area is called the Tenderloin . . ."

Fleshy needs aside, the Tenderloin once was an entertainment hub. The Black Hawk jazz club drew the likes of Miles Davis and Thelonious Monk—you can listen to live audio recordings—and rock groups such as the Grateful Dead; Crosby, Stills, Nash & Young; Prince; and Herbie Hancock laid down album tracks at Wally Heider Recording Studio. In the post–World War II era and into the 1950s, bars (not just dives) and restaurants also drew visitors, before the Mitchell Brothers in the 1970s brought a different sort of crowd with their porn theaters.

Shaw has no illusions that the Tenderloin will be as trendy as the Marina or the Mission, nor does he want gussied-up, condo-laden streets ("We've passed strict land-use measures, so much of our housing is off the speculative market," he said), but he does pine for an economic upturn. "There's a great bar scene up near O'Farrell and Geary (streets) with Swig," Shaw said, "but the museum's in the central Tenderloin. That's harder to attract new businesses and people. But we're trying."

Walking back down Eddy Street, headed toward the Powell Street BART station, you see the neighborhood in a much more accepting light.

The homeless man and his dog are still asleep, the cops no longer surround the sprawled man and the kids at Boeddeker Park still burn off energy. An older man with a limp exits an SRO hotel, the Fashionette, and waits with you at a stoplight. He asks you for the time. You tell him. He smiles. "Man, 11 o'clock? I got me some good sleep this time." You cross the street together, then he limps off down Jones Street. Just another morning in the Tenderloin.

A Homeless Tour of the 'Loin

March 2014

We left behind the distinctive aromatic blend of maple bars and marijuana wafting through Donut World on Seventh and Market streets, sidestepped a supine homeless man moaning softly and dodged a swarm of loiterers later identified as fencers of stolen property.

Let the sightseeing begin.

Del Seymour, bedecked in black fedora and blue trench coat and clutching his signature leather briefcase, paused for a moment before launching into his two-hour tour of the Tenderloin, San Francisco's dingiest district, home to the homeless, to prostitution and the drug trade, but also to families

117

and schools, churches and good people just trying to get by. But before he could even utter a sentence, sirens blared as three patrol cars screeched to a halt across Seventh Street, on the lip of U.N. Plaza. Several firetrucks soon followed, as a handcuffed young man slumped in the gutter, his backpack getting a good going-over by the authorities.

Seymour laughed. Couldn't help himself.

"Damn, we've got something going on right here," he said. "People think I stage these things. I don't."

For the past five years, Seymour, a 65-year-old former homeless drug addict who once called a 6-foot empty refrigerator box home, has provided an insider's view of the one area of San Francisco where tourists rarely venture. He shows how local nonprofits are providing services, food, shelter and medical attention to the low- and no-income residents. He points out historic architecture and sites where significant civic events took place. He takes tourists into an SRO (single-room-occupancy) hotel, as well as a church where people sleep in pews weekdays. And, yes, he discreetly shows popular drug-dealing hangouts, a place where a second-floor "sweat shop" for garment workers supposedly is located, and introduces some of the neighborhood's colorful characters.

"I don't give you the ugly side," Seymour said. "I give you the real side. I don't want to glorify the ugly part, but you've got to tell the truth, man."

A two-hour descent by tourists into the Tenderloin's seedy underbelly might be viewed by some as craven slumming or poverty tourism, decried as insensitive to the less fortunate, as if people have come to view some twisted zoo exhibit of the down-and-out in their natural habitat.

But Seymour doesn't see it that way. He said educating folks about life in the Tenderloin might make people more compassionate, even demystify the district so it can begin to draw tourist dollars and thrive. Plus, in a city that showcases its many tourist attractions, why not the 'Loin?

"Years ago," Seymour said, "people probably thought Alcatraz wouldn't be a good tourist spot. Now, it's the most popular thing there is. Alcatraz is just a dirty, pissy jail. Well, I'll show you a dirty, pissy part of the city, but we got real blood flowing. Real people here."

He should know, having been a Tenderloin denizen for more than 30 years, 10 of which were on the street. After kicking alcohol and cocaine two decades ago, Seymour became a cabbie and fancied himself an amateur tour guide because "that's how you get tips." But when he got sidelined a few years back because of "too many points on my license," Seymour immersed himself in history at the library and learned everything he could about the Tenderloin's colorful past.

Such as, for instance, how the area got its name.

"Down on Taylor and Turk (streets), those used to be all butcher shops," he said. "The only meat they cut there was the tenderloin, because they had all the big hotels that wanted choice cuts. This was horse-and-buggy times, so you had to be close to your customers. So they called this the Tenderloin."

Seymour admits that his story behind the coinage might be disputed.

"Other people will tell you it's because that's where the police got the best part of their bribes," he said. "They'd divide the city like a cow and this was the choicest. And other people will tell you it was named after the prostitutes. But, man, I did the heavy research. I went way back in the history books."

Another thing in dispute: the exact boundaries of the district. "Mine is this: Market Street to Polk Street to O'Farrell to Mason," he said.

"Of course," he added, cackling, "if you live on O'Farrell, you're going to call that Lower Nob Hill. If you live on Nob Hill, you call O'Farrell the Tenderloin. If you need grants, you call your area the Tenderloin. If you want to serve the high and mighty dollar, you don't use the word Tenderloin. You say Lower Nob Hill or the Theater District."

Seymour, himself, has finally moved out of the Tenderloin. Between his veteran's benefits, his taxi wages (he drives a hack in Suisun City these days) and the donations he gets from giving tours, he and his wife, Luchell, now can afford to live modestly on Lower Nob Hill.

"But I still feel this is my home," he said. "I like showing it off to people."

He doesn't walk; he saunters. Seymour's never in a hurry. He wants people to take in the Tenderloin in its totality: the sights (juddering homeless and cellphone-yakking businessmen), smells (astringent urine in places, enticing ethnic food in others) and sounds (horns and sirens, ranting and laughter).

When he strolled the streets on this morning, people nodded at him. Seymour likes to call himself an "OG"—original gangster, one who's been in the thick of things for years and has earned street respect.

"People don't mind me bringing folks down," he said. "They know I'm doing what's good for the neighborhood. I'm teaching people."

He assures tourists—he does about three tours a week, more in the summer, he says—not to worry about safety. Yes, there are drug deals, auto thefts and the occasional homicide, but the reports of the Tenderloin's lawlessness are greatly exaggerated, he said.

San Francisco Police Department figures for 2013 show that the Tenderloin has by far the highest rate of narcotics arrests of 10 districts and has the third-highest rate of robberies and aggravated assaults, behind the Mission District and the Southern District (from the Ferry Building, south of Market to 16th Street). Bear in mind, though, that the Tenderloin is only 0.3 of a square mile, the Mission 2.7 square miles and the Southern 2.9 square miles.

Seymour scoffs at statistics. He believes people can visit the Tenderloin without fear.

"Some don't like coming here at night, but it isn't any more dangerous," he said. "It's only dangerous if you're in the drug trade. They aren't going to bother you. The number one thing you gotta know: There's a (drug-dealing) captain that runs every block. If someone tries to take your (photographer's) camera, he'll worry that someone'll call the police and shut this block down for a couple of hours. Well, he don't want this block shut down. Hurts business. He don't want any trouble with the police."

Seymour, in fact, has a theory about why the Tenderloin has a more laid-back aura than "menacing places" such as Compton, Watts or parts of Oakland.

"Maybe it's just because they are all medicated," he said. "I really think it might be because the drugs take the edge off."

It remains, however, not a place in which to let your guard down. According to the daily crime-mapping page of www.sf-police.org, 31 crimes occurred in the Tenderloin on the day I visited for the tour. One of the nine assaults in that 24-hour period was what caused the flurry of police and fire activity on Seventh and Market as we embarked. It was a stabbing, the site reported.

Yet, Seymour maintains the district is not a "hassle" to visitors because denizens have reached a detente with newcomers. The district is far from gentrified, but in recent years, tech businesses such as Twitter have moved in and tweaked the dynamic.

One newcomer Seymour likes to show off is the Cutting Ball Theater, an experimental troupe that has established a beachhead on Taylor Street. Last year, Cutting Ball produced a staged oral-history documentary called

Tenderloin, which played to packed audiences. So every time Seymour gives a tour, he knocks on the door and hopes managing director Suzanne Appel is around.

"We see ourselves as a bridge between people who've lived here for decades and people who are new from all parts of the city," Appel said. "We've reached out (and) offered pay-what-you-can tickets for those who live and work here."

Seymour asked Appel—probably for the edification of the tourists—if she feels safe working in the neighborhood.

"I've met a lot of people who live in the low-income housing unit next door, even the people standing on the corner, and we've built a (relationship)," she said. "Every once in a while, when I come to work, there will be somebody sleeping in front of our door. People on the street will help me out then."

Less than a block from Cutting Ball is the corner of Taylor and Turk streets.

Seymour stopped a few dozen feet before it. He lowered his voice.

"This is our big drug corner, ground zero," he said. "Crack and meth. People come from all over—Oakland, Marin, Sacramento, Solano—to buy and sell."

He paused and gently admonished a tour-goer brandishing a camera.

"Hey, hey, man, just be a little more discreet about taking pictures of that corner," he said. "They don't like that, man."

Then Seymour resumed his spiel.

"The drug dealers are commuters," he said. "People don't know that. They come in from Antioch, Fairfield, Vallejo, Richmond. One day, BART broke down and nobody was out here selling."

Most of the violence stems from drug deals gone bad, like the time in February 2009 when six people were shot outside Grand Liquor.

"You'd come out here and step over the bodies," Seymour said. "It's getting better, but still our biggest problem, right here."

Seymour opened the heavy oaken doors of St. Boniface Catholic Church on Golden Gate Avenue, took a few steps into a darkened alcove, then stopped. All you could hear was the light snoring coming from the 76 pews—every single one of them occupied by a homeless man or woman hunched under blankets.

It was a stark and vivid image—rootless individuals, their worldly possessions often stuffed into a plastic garbage bag, amid the stained-glass splendor, marble columns and ornate gilt facades.

"This is Project Gubbio," Seymour said. "It gives the homeless a place to sleep after the shelters close in the morning."

Each day, from 6 a.m. to 1 p.m., the church doors are opened. No one has to sign in or check names. They can just rest for a few hours, the nonprofit providing blankets and use of bathrooms.

"Our mission is twofold," said Laura Slattery, director of Project Gubbio. "One is to provide a safe, quiet space for the guests. The other is to bridge the gap not just with the worshipping community but with the neighbors and the schools and people in the Tenderloin, to re-envision how we view the people living on the streets. They are our brothers and sisters, not just faceless people."

Such charity extends across the street to St. Anthony's, which provides free meals, free computer classes and use in a state-of-the-art tech lab, and a free medical clinic.

The midday cafeteria serves 2,500 meals a day, according to dining room manager Charles Sommer. It was packed on this particular lunch hour (turkey in gravy was the entree), but Sommer said a new, larger facility is being built at a vacant lot across the street.

Up on the second floor, Seymour led his group to the medical clinic, which was as empty as the cafeteria was full.

"You can walk right in and see a doctor within 10 minutes," he said. "You go to S.F. General (Hospital) on a Monday and still be there on Tuesday. I'm serious. I did that. But this is a top-of-the-line place."

You wouldn't think an SRO hotel, one of scores that dot the Tenderloin, would be a place of distinction. SROs are notorious for crime among transients. Shell out $50 a night for a roof over your head, but watch your back, buddy.

But this one on Eddy Street, near Leavenworth, isn't named the Cadillac Hotel for nothing. Built in 1907 and a city landmark, the Cadillac exudes charm. The lobby features original wood floors and artwork, even a Steinway piano. Its grand ballroom once was a boxing rink called Newman's Gym.

"Back in Jim Crow days, a lot of jazz musicians, artists and athletes, when they came to town, couldn't stay downtown, so this was the luxury hotel for Negroes in the '30s through the '50s," Seymour said. "Louis Armstrong, Muhammad Ali and (Joe) Frazier—anyone black and famous—stayed here.

"Then (in the mid-1970s), Leroy Looper bought the Cadillac and turned it into the best (supportive) housing in the city. You gotta behave yourself to live in here, man. You come in drunk or drugging, you're out on the street."

A block or two over on Taylor, Seymour stopped in front of what looked like a gray, nondescript building. A plaque on the sidewalk marks it as the site of the 1966 Compton's Cafeteria Riot. The cafeteria was one of the few places where transgendered people could safely congregate during an era in which cross-dressing was illegal. A police raid led to a violent uprising.

"That predated Stonewall (in New York)," Seymour said. "Lot of history here."

What is the building now?

"It's a transition house," Seymour said. "You get out of San Quentin, you go to the top floor, then move to next floor next and eventually out the door. If you're on work release, they'll breathalize and urine-test you. You fail, you'll be back in San Quentin in an hour. I've seen them hauled away."

Many of the historical sites on the walking tour no longer serve their original purpose.

Seymour showed off the Hibernia Bank Building, built in 1906, at McAllister and Jones, a classic example of Beaux Arts design from architect Albert Pissis. It fell into disrepair, became a police substation in the 1990s and, since 2000, has been vacant. As Seymour shuffled by, pigeons scattered on the steps and fluttered up into the granite columns.

"They keep talking about developing it," Seymour said. "You see how far they've gotten."

Two blocks up on Jones is another noteworthy Tenderloin spot: the site of the Screening Room, where a plaque reads that "the first full length adult oriented hardcore feature (was) legally shown in the U.S. (in 1970)."

"See what's here now?" he asked. "A swingers club (the Power Exchange)."

Seymour laughed. Couldn't help himself.

"Some things don't change, man."

From Military Munitions to Fetish Porn

July 2015
City sector: Mission District
Population: 47,234
Square miles: 1.8 miles

My, such a lovely building anchored at 14th and Mission streets. So stately and, yes, regal is the former National Guard Armory, built in 1914, with its burnished brick facade and moody Moorish castle design, classical wainscoting and elegant stone portico. Its look connotes nothing less than solidity and forthright authority, unquestioned probity.

Wonder what they are doing with it now?

They give tours, I soon learned.

Great. Sign me up.

A few days later, I went online at work and—uh-oh—I got this stern message: "Content blocked by your organization."

Turns out, the Armory now is the corporate headquarters and primary shooting location for Cybernet Entertainment, LLC (aka, kink.com), the world's largest conglomeration of BDSM websites. Upon further research, I discovered that BDSM does not stand for "Battle Depot for Service Materials"; rather, it's "Bondage, Discipline, Sadism and Masochism."

Now, isn't that just so San Francisco, the clash between two worlds: the disciplined, regimented and no-bullshit ethos of the Army, and the tightly wound, handcuffed and whip-cracking, bottom-bruising milieu that is the hard-core online porn industry.

Rather than clashing, the online literature for the Armory tour promised "historic" information about the building, how its 200,000 square feet housed six decades of National Guardsmen and equipment until its closure in 1976; how it "served as both a barricade and safety point for officers during rioting in San Francisco in 1934"; how, during its dormancy post-Guard, George Lucas used its facilities in *Star Wars*; and how part of Mission Creek flows through the building's subbasement.

So, there is considerable nonprurient interest in the tour. But, caveat emptor, there's a lot of porn on this 90-minute tour. Dildos galore, fetishistic implements that will make your skin either crawl or tingle, depending on your proclivities. You won't actually get to see how the sausage is made—that is, no actual porn taping will be shot while you gawk—but it does provide a behind-the-scenes look at the bare-bones, rather unsexy sets, props and elaborate studios that service 29 pornographic websites.

Some of the docent-led narration—"models" (euphemism for "porn stars") moonlight as docents—is a little salty, language-wise, but except for a few in flagrante delicto oil paintings lining the staircases between floors, the tour could be rated a solid PG-13. OK, maybe R. But seriously, you'll see much more flesh at, say, an afternoon Giants game, and certainly more cleavage on stage at the San Francisco War Memorial Opera House, than at the Armory. That's because the tours are held in early evening, once the "talent" has long since left the building after a hard day at the office.

Only on rare occasion, say "docents" Dusty and Piper (first-names only is an industry mandate), have people innocently entered the Armory not knowing its current incarnation. That can be a little startling. And, in fact, sometimes it can lead to hilarity, because kink.com rents out the huge, fieldhouse-size gymnasium on the building's west flank to nonporn organizations. Serious plays have been performed there, fundraising dinners held, as well as concerts, raves and community celebrations.

A month before I took a tour, Dusty said a group came by and was gobsmacked to learn that filming of fetish porn took place within its walls.

The group?

California Gov. Jerry Brown's advance security detail.

Seems the governor was planning to attend a San Francisco Film Society event at the Armory's public space, alongside such luminaries as Rep. Nancy Pelosi, director Francis Ford Coppola and actor Richard Gere. Brown's bodyguards apparently inspected the site and, well, let Dusty describe the scene:

"They are like, 'What's that?'" she said, pointing to chains dangling from the ceiling in one room, "and I explained what it was and then I'm like, 'Do you guys even know where you are?' They're like, 'No, where are we?' I said, 'Well, it's the original Armory for the National Guard, but now it's a BDSM porn palace.' They honestly did not know. This (gym) was the area they were in so, obviously, nothing in here is kink-based. That's on purpose. But they needed to inspect the whole building, because, like, the governor and these big names were coming in."

Were Brown's functionaries OK with the site?

"No, not really," she said. "It was really awkward. But also really funny."

Nearly everyone else, though, goes into the building with eyes wide open.

"Definitely," concurred Piper. "That's the first thing we say on the tour."

Beyond the whole *Fifty Shades* (and then some) *of Grey* stuff, you get a fascinating look at the interior of a historic San Francisco building, where the walls, when not lined with images of sex acts, are adorned with cool black-and-white photos of the Armory in its heyday. It hosted boxing matches and other sporting events in the gymnasium, first as an outdoor structure and later enclosed.

You also get a brief bio of owner Peter Acworth, who, Piper recited with genuine enthusiasm, "was studying for his Ph.D. in finance at Columbia, and he read a newspaper article about a firefighter making his own porn and selling it online. Peter had this great idea to use his lifelong love of roped bondage to launch his own website, hogtied.com. So, Peter moved to San Francisco and met a bunch of perverted people . . ."

The rest is adult-entertainment industry history. Acworth became incredibly wealthy, so much so that he could easily afford to pay $14.5 million to buy the Armory, which had been abandoned after the Guard left in 1976 and was crumbling. Over the years, there had been talk of using the Armory for high-end housing, low-income housing, a shopping mall, a nonprofit center. But nothing ever came of it. When Acworth bought it in 2007, some city activists howled in anger, but the site was zoned for "industrial" use, so, voilà, the SoMa/Mission corridor had a new corporate neighbor.

Acworth poured millions more into retrofitting and refurbishing the nearly acre-length interior, fashioning former offices and storage facilities into dens of lascivious iniquity. The only room he left the same was the subbasement, the erstwhile Guard drill court, where water from what's believed to be Mission Creek still flows under the cracked concrete.

"You can still see the bullet holes from target practice," Piper said. "At night, it really gets creepy down here, guys. It's the creepiest place at the Armory."

And that's saying something. Piper and Dusty showed our group all three sets that kink.com fans know oh-so-well: the Gimp Room, where such sweet torture takes place with all manner of Turkish-prison-type chains and racks; the Hog Set, where getting hog tied is only the start of the fun; the padded cell, where some crazy sexual shenanigans take place; the

Abattoir, whose activities between (we assume) consenting adults draws blood, sweat and other forms of bodily fluids. There's a Speakeasy and a crushed-red-velvet-wallpaper parlor called the Lounge, faux fancy sets to play out period fantasies. My tour's big hit was the opportunity to take selfies inside while on a rack inside iron cages.

What struck me most is that each room, or set, was exceedingly, almost OCD-like clean. You could eat off the floor—and, in some videos, I'm sure actors in dog collars certainly did—and there was the heady aroma of Lysol and Febreze being circulated through the vents.

One unexpected highlight, a vision that will stay with me for years, was seeing a row of industrial-size vats of gel lubricant, 450 pounds worth. The expiration date on one read "10/2016," but Piper assured us with a confidence that comes with first-hand knowledge that it would be used up well before then.

Ditto the industrial barrels of dildos and related sex toys. Good to know that these tools of the trade are not reused. They are, under OSHA regulations, treated almost like a biohazard and either whisked off to a recycling center or taken home for employees' personal enjoyment.

Dusty, the senior docent, said afterward that the tours, held several days a week, are popular and abide by kink.com's mission statement: "to demystify BDSM and alternative sexuality through transparency."

But I was mystified that, even in San Francisco, angry, repressed, Church Lady–types haven't protested this use of the once patriotic Armory. I mean, Mission Dolores, a Catholic Church icon, is only a few blocks away. Turns out, it's the city politicians who make Kink folks show their wares to the public. Seems that part of Acworth's contractual agreement when he bought the Armory building was to allow public access, via tours, because of the Armory's "federal historic landmark designation."

"We're happy to do it," Dusty said. "The tours might be kind of edgy for someone who isn't into anything like this. But, maybe afterward, they might be."

Then she winked.

Mission District: A Portrait of Change

March 2012

Stroll, do not power walk, down Balmy Alley in the Mission District. Slow your overcaffeinated pulse from too many espressos in neighborhood cafés, quell your fired-up metabolism from super burritos scarfed in corner taquerias, empty your mind of the thrift store bargains beckoning on the boulevard. *Tranquilo, amigo.*

Take it easy and allow the brilliant colors of this block-long gantlet of murals, located in the less-trendy and -trod part of the district, to wash over you with sensations both visual and visceral. Let the walls tell their tales: the images of life in the Mission in times past and the ever-evolving present, from Spanish cathedrals to turn-of-century horse stables; from poverty to AIDS; from lowriders to low-rent flophouses; from the Central American struggles that made immigrants leave the homeland to the struggle by those same immigrants to stay rooted in a neighborhood transformed by gentrification.

Linger at one particular work, titled *Victorion: El Defensor de la Mission.* Get in close, nearly nose to wall, to catch the subtlety of the fine details. Muralist Sirron Norris, using what he terms "cartoon literalism," paints a cityscape at war between tradition and progress. Billboards sardonically extol "New Organic Fair-Trade Condos." Storefront windows tout "Tattoos and 10-Speeds" under an awning with the sign "Hipsters Unique Together." A skinny-jeaned skateboarder careens down the street, holding a Scooby-Doo-like dog, while below, so tiny as to be inconsequential, a brown-skinned mother holds a child's hand at a bus stop. At the center, a looming presence, is a robot dubbed "Victorion," whose mission is nothing less than to preserve the stately Victorian homes lining the avenues.

"There's a lot of tension in this one," Patricia Rose, who leads tours of Balmy Alley for the community arts store Precita Eyes, told a cluster of sightseers one recent rainy afternoon. "A lot of people in the Mission feel they're being pushed out. They can't afford to buy a Victorian and afford to live here anymore."

Her tour group dutifully pointed iPhones and clicked to capture images. Then they moved to the next wall, and the next, documenting works not only about mid-20th-century Latino immigrants, but also stretching back to when the newcomers were Italian or Irish. By the time they reached the tour's end at 24th Street, near Harrison, tourists could make a choice that was all about old and new: bopping over to the renowned designer ice cream boutique Humphry Slocombe for a chocolate with smoked sea salt scoop ($3.25); or stopping at a vendor pushing a sticker- covered ice cream cart selling Fudgsicles ($1).

It's all about gentrification, a word fraught with sociological baggage. New lofts and restored Victorians have infused the neighborhood with money to spend on local businesses, yet the escalating cost of living has resulted in a 20 percent drop in Latino population in the past decade, according to census figures. In 2010, the hyperlocal website Mission Loc@l illustrated this dichotomy with an ingenious "Gangs and Cupcakes" grid map, showing 20 bakeries selling cupcakes in either Sureño or Norteño gang territory, using as a pull quote an excerpt from a Yelp review: "This quaint little spot is in a slightly unsavory part of town."

So, do we celebrate the Mission as it was, grit and drugs and crime and all? Or do we applaud efforts, initially fueled by dot-com money in the '00s and now sustained by artists and free spirits, to launch new businesses and restaurants, to boldly challenge the city's other sectors for the tourist dollar?

There is no easy answer. Surely even those muralists who decry the supposed soulless sanitization of the Mission certainly don't want Balmy Alley to return to what it was in the early '70s, a shooting gallery strewn with needles and empty bottles and no real art.

But what to make of $20 artisan grilled cheese sandwiches or $40 shaves or $24 infant onesies made of organic Egyptian cotton, all of which now are available on a chic stretch of Valencia Street?

"It's a definite gray area," Norris said of the "G-question" in the Mission. "Gentrification is part of the Mission's history. It wouldn't have been called the Mission originally if it hadn't been gentrified. This has been a curse laid on the Mission long ago. People have been totally displaced (by the growth), but it's not black-and-white. I have friends who earned college degrees, got good jobs and bought a condo in the Mission. Is that a bad thing?

"Back in the day, you could get a super burrito on the street for five bucks. Now, you can't get one for under 10. But, you know, you used to never be able to go get a burrito at night without stepping maybe into a sketchy situation. That's changed, too."

Burrito inflation notwithstanding, the Mission District is one of San Francisco's most intriguing places to visit because, as writ large in Norris' mural, it perfectly encapsulates the cultural contrasts at play in many major cities. For that alone, it's well worth spending a day—and, yes, even a night—exploring. The Mission may not be the most obvious tourist haunt in a city fueled by tourism. It lacks the guidebook cache of a Union Square, North Beach, Chinatown, Golden Gate Park or Nob Hill. Nor does it possess the campiness of the Castro, the cutting-edge trendiness of South of Market, the unapologetic commercialism of Fisherman's Wharf.

But the quirkiness quotient of this 1.9-square-mile neighborhood south of downtown trumps the others. Perhaps you need to embrace the contrasts and treat the incongruities as splendid diversity, not stark, alienating contrasts.

Take breakfast, for instance. On a weekday morning in a less-gussied-up block well east of Mission Street, commuters in a rush could choose to stop at Dynamo Donut & Coffee or Panaderia La Mexicana Bakery.

Dynamo opened in 2008 and has a loyal following for its designer doughnuts, including a glazed maple bacon and spiced chocolate, which mixes cinnamon and sugar with chipotle and chili powders and adds a dash of potato in the dough.

On this morning, with the line out front five deep, the Belinda Carlisle channel on Pandora Internet Radio played Bonnie Tyler's "Total Eclipse of the Heart" on an iPod speaker by the cash register, and counter worker Walter Chumley sang the refrain "Turn around, bright eyes" with full-throated vigor between taking orders. He tried to get people to try the maple bacon instead of playing it safe with something chocolate.

"I was a vegetarian for five months when I started working here," Chumley said. "But the maple bacon is persuasive, even for a vegetarian. Eventually, the curiosity got to me and I tried one. I just giggled and giggled. Every month or so, I get the same urge to have one."

Harrison Pollock, a new Mission resident, is addicted to the chocolate spice.

"All the ones here that sound a little weird on paper, when you actually try them, make a lot of sense, taste-wise," he said. "Nothing feels strange to put in a doughnut. And I also come here because it's the closest place to my house."

A block away, presumably also near Pollock's residence, is Panaderia La Mexicana. No music blares, but the scent of anise and pineapple waft as several Latino customers, armed with tongs, peruse a dazzling array of pan dulce (sweet bread). Customer Marcos Ortiz takes a BART train from downtown, where he lives, just to stock his breakfast shelves at home.

"I've tried other (panaderias)," he said. "Nothing tastes as good as here."

Asked if he's tried Dynamo Donut, Ortiz shook his head.

Food, perhaps even more than art, binds the Mission. What the district is most known for, and rightly so, is its taquerias. There has yet to be a definitive count, but there are at least two dozen in the vicinity. And everyone—Latino and Anglo, Asian or African American—has his favorite stop for a burrito the size of a football. At the tail end of the dinner-hour rush at Pancho Villa, on 16th Street, Derek Hanson and Carlene Cotter bowed their heads into massive burritos. Former Mission denizens, they had come from Oakland, where they live now, for a pilgrimage. This was their place, back in the day. They've tried other Mission taquerias; none measured up.

"I never liked Mexican food, any Mexican food, until I moved to the Mission," Hanson said. He laughed, then added, "I don't think it's required or anything, but I learned to like it."

Based on sheer customer volume, Taqueria Cancun on Mission Street might be the most popular taqueria. At the prick of noon, the place was packed. Four fresh-scrubbed, pinstriped-suited businessmen doffed coats, carefully rolled up sleeves to mid-wrist and tucked paper napkins in their buttoned collars before each diving into the Mojado ("The Big One"), while someone punched up some mariachi music from the jukebox.

Diner Barbara Fried, a Cancun fan, said she likes the burritos there because "they don't fall apart, and it's important to have the right proportion of meat to everything else." Finished, she came over to offer a bit of advice: "You know, if you're going to write about taquerias, you really should talk to a Mexican."

Talk to a Mexican? Not a problem here. Despite gentrification, the most populous ethnic group in the district remains Latinos. Many of Latino ancestry, it turned out, were lunching at La Taqueria. There was plenty of time to chat up customers, because the line was 15 deep. Linda Montoya and friend Carlos Arteaga said they were ordering tacos, not burritos, and they chose this taqueria because, as Linda said, "This is as close as you're going to get to authentic Mexican as you'll get in the Mission." Arteaga, who speaks limited English, touched Montoya's arm and asked her to translate his opinions: "This is real Mexican food. The other places add too much stuff."

The Anglo influence is felt by another Mission food fetish—ice cream, highlighted by the Bi-Rite Creamery and Humphry Slocombe. Bi-Rite, at 18th and Dolores, is more traditional but gives a nod to hipness in its use of organic ingredients and a few vegan offerings.

Humphry Slocombe, however, has become a phenomenon in the food world since opening its tiny shop under an unassuming blue awning saying, all in lowercase, "ice cream" in 2008. The *New York Times Magazine*, in 2010, devoted 3,569 words to Humphry Slocombe, detailing not only its odd flavors (Boccalone prosciutto) but explaining the origin of the establishment's name (taken from two characters in the low-brow English TV show *Are You Being Served?*).

Each day, the Humphry's 303,837 Twitter followers eagerly await the posting of a snapshot of the flavor board, pining for their favorite concoction. Amanda Szakats and Margaret Wooliever were tasting free samples under prints of Warholian Campbell Soup cans tweaked to feature its ice cream flavors. The friends mulled the Jesus Juice (red wine and Coke), Harvey Milk & Honey Graham Cracker and Apple Coded Bacon. Szakats chose a dissolute favorite, the Secret Breakfast, made of Jim Beam bourbon and cornflakes.

"I think I'll be OK to drive back across the bridge," Szakats cracked.

The friends were holding shopping bags and sharing the scoop as they sauntered (not stumbled, Bukowski-like) back to the 24th Street BART station.

Shopping has long been an integral part of the Mission District, with its bodegas selling fresh produce and Central American delicacies. Thrift stores abound, because they cater to both low-income residents in search of bargains and vintage-clothes divas looking for that just-right retro look. Several of the long-closed theaters, whose facades blessedly remain intact, now house 99-cent-type discount stores. Same-day, check-cashing and money-wiring services, often with adjoining travel agencies for trips to Mexico or Central America, seem to be on every other block down Mission Street.

Upscale shopping? Not so much. But that began to change a few years ago, when younger residents with more disposable incomes and eclectic tastes arrived. Valencia Street now has become the nexus of quirky boutiques, none more so than the pirate store that fronts author Dave Eggers' nonprofit literacy project, 826 Valencia, and the odd bones, stones and freaky taxidermy home design shop, Paxton Gate, next door at 824 Valencia.

At Paxton Gate, customers can construct their own terrariums from materials such as Mexican river stones ($1.75 a pound) and black lichen ($3 an ounce). Or they can purchase the skeletal remains of animals ranging from a cat's spine to a coyote bone. Want a freeze-dried frog encased in acrylic? Of course you do. Fork over $59. All manner of stuffed and mounted critters stare down at you, from a snarling hyena to a pouncing bobcat.

"We get some unusual, really specific requests," said Francesca Giuliani, working the checkout stand. "Somebody once asked if we had lemmings (dead and stuffed, presumably). Most customers know what they want. They're that eccentric."

No doubt, those same customers will check in next door at 826 Valencia, a tongue-in-cheek "pirate store" whose proceeds help fund Eggers' youth-tutoring and -writing programs. Darkly lit with faux wooden warped shelving, with dirgelike organ music wafting, the interior of the store is made to look like a ship's galley. Much of the merchandise does not rise above upscale gag gifts like Can of Blood ($14.99), Mermaid Bait or Repellent ($4) or Glass Eye Drops ($15).

Plopped in the center of the store is a tub of lard, displayed as if it were in a bulk food section of a grocery store. What gives?

"Oh, see that bottle of hair clippings behind me?" worker Iris Alden said, slyly.

"We actually trade lard for some (locks) of people's hair. For me, this store serves more purposes than just being a store. It's a store where people bring their out-of-town friends and family members. It's like an attraction."

The Mission teems with unexpected attractions. Look up into a window of a Victorian on 18th Street, a few hundred feet east from Valencia, and you have found the Troll Window (http://sftrollwindow.blogspot.com), which each week or so features gussied-up troll dolls festooned in an idyllic scene. On this day: pink- and green-haired trolls cavorting amid rainbow bunting. Elsewhere, a vacant lot on Mission Street features an impromptu mixed-media installation about love hung on chain-link fencing. Sometimes, the art is mobile, such as the man dressed in tight gold lamé pants and Rick Santorum–issued red sweater vest, with an infant nestled in a Snugli. He loped down Mission Street strumming a ukulele; no one paid him any mind.

Another unexpected pleasure (at least for the customers, if not the proprietors) is finding four specialty bookstores housed above a discount paint store on Mission Street. To enter, you must find a call-buzzer intercom, state your intentions ("Uh, to, like, browse for books") and wait to get buzzed in. Then you climb two flights of stairs and get to Valhalla Books (first-edition fiction), then climb one more flight to the troika of Bolerium Books (radical politics), Meyer Boswell Books (collectible law tomes) and Libros Latinos (scholarly Latin American and Caribbean books).

As you enter Bolerium (motto: "Fighting Commodity Fetishism With Commodity Fetishism Since 1981"), co-owner John Durham looks at you with a mock stink-eye.

"Oh, you found us," he said, crestfallen. "We don't get many walk-ins."

No surprise there. These specialty bookstores cater mostly to dealers, scholars and university libraries. But there are gems to unearth on the shelves, especially at Bolerium, such as a section devoted to "The White Problem in America," meaning white supremacist groups, as well as another on the Spanish Civil War and random eyebrow-raising titles such as *The Romance of Proctology.*

Should you ever need it, Bolerium boasts the nation's largest collection of tracts on the Communist Party in California.

Bolerium's niche fits the Mission as snugly as a hemp muscle T-shirt. At least, if you're judging by the ubiquitous murals, most celebrating revolutionary causes. As muralist Norris says, "We're in the Mission; it's in our blood to protest."

Which brings us back, inevitably, to the mural alleys, this time to Clarion Alley near Valencia Street.

Late in the afternoon, Li Lightfoot, a photographer who catalogs street art, admired a flowing, swirling work representing the early '80s Nicaraguan war. He leaned in close, thinking that someone had "tagged" the work with graffiti.

"No," he said. "I think that's part of (the mural). I've found that taggers will not tag over a well-done mural. If it's not so well done, well . . ."

In the Mission, apparently, everyone's an art critic.

Just Your Typical Asian Country Music Yodeler

February 2013

You can expect to see most anything at stylized Mission District dive bars, known for their high quirk quotient. Habitués cultivate aggressive nonchalance and need something truly unusual, just short of cattle-prod shocking, to get them to look up from their PBRs and pay attention.

How about this: a 65-year-old Japanese man, barely 5-foot-4 and carrying a guitar that seems to weigh down his slender frame, walking onto a makeshift stage wearing a straw cowboy hat, red plaid shirt and wire-rimmed granny glasses, warbling old-timey Jimmie Rodgers songs, yodel and all?

Yeah, that'll do it.

A crowd of about 30—which also seemed about the average age—at the Rite Spot, a red-walled watering hole at 17th and Folsom, was entranced, totally captivated, on a recent Tuesday night by the song stylings of one Toshio Hirano, the least likely country singer you could imagine.

For the better part of an hour, Hirano, backed by stand-up bass sideman Kenan O'Brien, dipped deep into the Rodgers songbook, extracting gems that were popular in the late '20s and early '30s when most of this crowd's grandparents were young and no doubt affecting hipster attitudes (unless they were standing in bread lines).

Hirano's voice, an alluring mix of his clipped Japanese accent and affected Southern twang, rose and fell, dipped and quavered and, at the songs' finales, erupted into high-pitch yodeling that would prick dogs' ears several blocks away.

He sang about the romance of the prairie, roaming the range with guns hanging proud, riding the rails, losing it all in a gambler's hall, winning the hearts of rodeo sweethearts, putting in hard time in the Appalachia coal mines and, most of all, expressing the ethos of the high lonesome life.

That such a polished, yet heartfelt, performance comes from an unassuming man who immigrated to the United States in the mid-'70s could be dismissed as mere gimmickry, something the Coen brothers might dream up for a movie. Likewise, the crowd's appreciation could be perceived as being steeped in too-cool irony.

But it's not. There's no rule, after all, saying you have to be American to sing Americana. And Hirano is as earnest as they come, a true Rodgers disciple and bluegrass aficionado, and the audience responds in kind. People seem as enamored with Hirano's between-song patter about the Cowboy Way as they are about his yodeling.

"I don't think it's ironic at all," said fan Eric Suesz, sitting at a table in the back with two buddies. "Some might think it's ironic because he's Japanese and doing roots music. But it's genuine. He has a genuine love for Jimmie Rodgers and songs from the '30s. I've seen him many times."

Word has gotten out, clearly. Hirano does monthly gigs at Amnesia, a trendy Mission nightclub on Valencia Street, and at the Rite Spot, as well as occasional sets at the Lucky Horseshoe in Bernal Heights.

This night, the Rite Spot was dotted with uninitiated Hirano listeners, including young couple Kate Goldstein and Conor Doyle.

"This is our first time," Goldstein said. "Somebody told me he's a Japanese Jimmie Rodgers. That sounds pretty awesome. It's what got us out on a Tuesday night."

What young 'uns may not know is Hirano's backstory.

It's a doozy: how he first put a needle to vinyl on an album called *The Best of Legendary Jimmie Rodgers* as a Waseda University student in Tokyo in 1968 and how it changed his life; how he finagled a four-month tourist visa in the mid-'70s into a full-fledged green card; how he later made pilgrimages to Nashville and Austin, Texas, to scare up a few gigs, opening for Townes Van Zandt and Robert Earl Keen; how he gave it all up in the late '80s when he married, moved to San Francisco and became a father; how he rediscovered his yen for performing Rodgers' songs in the mid-2000s and hit Bay Area stages once more.

Hirano, who works days as a teaching assistant in San Mateo, spins out his tale in rapid-fire fits and starts, skipping decades and then circling back. But when asked how he was introduced to Rodgers' music at a time when other college students in Tokyo were grooving to the Stones and the Beatles and musing over Bob Dylan, Hirano slows down and speaks in reverential tones. Notice, too, how he always refers to Rodgers by his full name, a sign of respect, perhaps.

"When I listened to that first song, 'Peach Pickin' Time Down in Georgia,' that blew my brain off," he said. "That first line, with that voice and melody and everything, that became everything to me. I had been listening to Hank Williams and Bill Monroe, but this took me to another space.

"Oh, and then, the yodeling comes along at the (song's) end and that added another dimension. That blew my brain, too. The only yodeling I had heard was the original Swiss Alpine yodeling, that high-pitched beautiful, clean-cut sound. But Jimmie Rodgers' yodeling has a dusty, creaky, muddy element. Wow."

The sound is what hooked Hirano, but as a child he had been intrigued by cowboys he had seen while watching American Westerns in Tokyo movie theaters.

"I wanted to become Shane," he said. "I said, 'When I come to America, I can put on that costume.'"

When Hirano finally did come to America, he spent a month on a Greyhound bus touring southern Appalachia, and two more months bicycling through the Blue Ridge Mountains.

"I was expecting to run into a lot of people who knew Jimmie Rodgers," he said. "I didn't find too many. I was disappointed, to be honest. Depressed. Then I thought, 'OK, I'll play Jimmie Rodgers' music. That's good enough.'"

Hirano has no delusions of stardom. He's played at San Francisco's annual Hardly Strictly Bluegrass Festival and clubs such as Odeon and the Blue Lamp. But most gigs are intimate affairs at dives like the Rite Spot.

"The best thing," he said, "(is) I now meet young people who before didn't even know Hank Williams. I get to teach them about Jimmie Rodgers.

"After a (recent) show, a young man walks up to me and says, 'You sang something about trains. Who wrote that?' I tell him, 'Go to Amoeba Records. They have Jimmie Rodgers records.' The young man comes back a month later, and now he's a big Jimmie Rodgers fan. That makes me happy."

A Theater Where Irony Overflows Like Popcorn

March 2013

This city's oddest "movie theater"—and the reason for the quotation marks will become clear shortly—sure isn't easy to find. Then again, you wouldn't expect a place called Oddball Film+Video to have a glowing marquee and an expansive parking structure. And it's in the Mission District, where oddity is the norm and grunginess a way of life.

Oh, and did we mention the evening's feature presentation is *Oral Exam: You Can't Handle the Tooth*, a compilation of silent films and early talkies, industrial and educational shorts and classic commercials, all espousing the virtues of dental hygiene?

No wonder it's not playing at the multiplex.

Anyway, finding the place is a challenge. The address is 275 Capp St., somewhere between 18th and Mission, one of those less-traveled roads that used to be sketchy before gentrification. But when you get to the appointed spot, all you see is a sign reading "Sutter Furniture."

The door is open, though, so you walk in. In the vestibule, a smaller sign leads you down two hallways, then up a flight of rickety stairs.

You know you're in the right place when you reach a warehouse space with row-upon-row of floor-to-ceiling film cannisters, made more homey by a retro interior design featuring old black-and-white TV sets, a jukebox and vintage signs.

This is what Oddball's day job entails, rescuing, preserving and licensing stock footage and then licensing it to feature films, documentary and TV projects and advertising. It boasts, at last count, more than 50,000 odd films and videos, feature-length, shorts and lots of B-roll.

Kat Shuchter, one of Oddball's curators, takes your $10, hands you a blue stub and points you to a room around back.

There resides the "theater," illuminated by a glowing disco ball and Christmas lights, and surrounded by a '70s-era wet bar used to prop up film projectors.

A dozen movie buffs lounge on couches and chairs in front of a 20-foot screen. Once the lights dim, you get "coming attractions" that focus on the evening's theme—in this case, close-up shots of beavers devouring wood, cows chewing their cud, dogs gnawing of sticks and a redheaded girl in braces lustily biting into a carrot.

The soundtrack: the Undisputed Truth singing "Smiling Faces Sometimes."

In an ironic twist, Oddball has placed a bowl of candy—Smarties and Lik-M-Aid Fun Dips—for people to munch on, gratis, while their tooth decay hastens.

Eschewing the candy but soaking in the scene are Oddball regulars Brandon Carter Meixel and Brenda Berys.

"Coming here's like watching *Curb Your Enthusiasm*, like seeing how, historically, uncomfortable topics were explained to people, things that are commonplace to us," Carter Meixel says. "You sort of cringe, but also laugh, at how history treated what used to be taboo."

Scoping out the sparse crowd, Carter Meixel smiles knowingly, as if clued in to a hip event for the cool kids.

"It's definitely one of the secrets of the Mission, for sure," he says. "The first time we came in, we were like, 'Oh no, we're going into somebody's house and we're going to see something on a projector in the living room.' Then we walked in and it was like this is a legitimate film archive."

Before the real show begins, the lights come up and Stephen Parr, wearing a jaunty felt fedora and trench coat, makes his appearance to introduce the evening's fare. He's the founder, chief curator and visionary of Oddball Film+Video, the result of 30 years of collecting.

"When we're not screening about 100 films a year, we license them," he says. "We just did one today about a soul singer called Eddie Kendricks and (recently) worked on a project for a (Steven) Soderbergh film about Liberace and a movie that just ran at Sundance called *Lovelace*.

"That's why people call us. They need footage that nobody else has. This scene (in the Liberace biopic) apparently takes place in an adult bookstore, and (they needed) appropriate (period) footage being played in the background."

Last month, reels of Parr's stock footage from the 1960s was featured in a more wholesome film, the PBS documentary *American Experience: Silicon Valley*.

But on this night, it's all about teeth. There's Charlie Chaplin's *Laughing Gas* (1914), W.C. Fields' *The Dentist* (1932) and little-known gems such as *Lancelot Link, Secret Chimp: To Tell the Tooth* (1971), a claymation educational oral opera called *The Munchers* (1973) and a Cesar Romero mock-horror flick called *The Haunted Mouth* (1974), the latter made as propaganda by the American Dental Association. There are '50s ads, too, including a particularly cheesy spot for a toothpaste called Cue, "with Floracton."

"It's good to be able to screen these in the original format because, (with) about 70 percent of the films you see now, you're actually not looking at film, you're looking at a digital copy," Parr says. "You might notice some of the films are beat up. That's a good thing. That means people have watched them before."

As the evening unfolds, the crowd guffaws at comical overacting in the education spots, the comedic brilliance of Chaplin and Fields, and the weirdness of shorts in which adults try too hard to be hip in appealing to kids while inculcating them with brushing-and-flossing dogma.

The presentation does not go without a hitch, nor would you expect it given the dated stock. Shuchter occasionally has to wrestle with the shaking horizontal hold, and the images get a little grainy. But that's part of the charm. Baby boomers with a sentimental bent can relish the click-click-click of the clattering projector, a reminder of school days.

And, just like in school days, I take the educational films' messages to heart.

First thing I do when I get back home? Floss.

Mapping S.F. History in North Beach

October 2015
City sector: North Beach
Population: 18,915
Square miles: 0.49

Beyond the iron gates at 1435 Grant Ave., in the heart of North Beach, worlds await. Or, more precisely, intricate and painstaking charting of the world as we have known it, fluid and ever evolving. More than just paper-and-ink renderings, really, you'll find nothing less than the story of our physical and emotional landscapes, writ both large and very, very tiny.

To call it merely an antique map and print shop fails to capture the scope of its breadth and appeal. What spouses Jimmie and Marti Schein sell are history and memories, guides to where we came from and, perhaps, where we're going.

As soon as you cross the threshold, you feel transported.

It's not just the burnished floor-to-ceiling shelves crammed with oversize atlases that can be plucked from on high only by way of ladders set on tracks and rollers. Nor is it the muted overhead lighting, augmented by a few laser-focused spotlights, that gives the setting an almost sepia tinge. Nor is it the air of orderly chaos—maps and vintage photos in protective sleeves sprouting from old produce crates, or rolled into tubes or placed in thin-drawered desks with hand-scrawled cards denoting regions and period.

Jimmie Schein, of Schein & Schein map shop, knows that people use smart phones and GPS, not printed maps, to get around. Yet his shop endures as a part of San Francisco history.

There's simply an air of reverence and preservation—nothing musty or sepulchral here, despite some cracked bindings and weathered pages that must be turned with utmost care—that permeates the place, personified by the hyperintense, fast-talking infectious zeal of Jimmie, 52, who found his way in life through the collection, study and ultimately sale of maps.

Here's a guy with an interesting backstory—as manager of a music logistics company, he toured for years with rock and jazz artists, doing everything from tuning instruments to driving a truck—who'd much rather enthuse about German lithographers Charles C. Kuchel and Emil Dresel than tell stories about hanging with Metallica and Miles Davis. No rock star excesses, even by proxy, for Jimmie. He spent his $800-a-week per diem hunting down vintage maps at antiquarian bookstores from Auckland to Zurich and many a middling American town. When, 12 years ago, he decided the romance of the road was waning, he took a buyout from his company and donned his rectangular spectacles to peer hard at lines on grids and share his passion with the public.

And the public, he and Marti say, has responded. The couple doesn't make a killing, no expansion of Schein & Schein is in the offing, but, yeah, they do OK.

Even in this era when digital trumps analog in all things, there apparently is still interest in poring over the physical and tactile details of streets and landmarks, either still around or long since plowed under. The mutability of borderlines, be it cities, states or countries, tell a story that travels far beyond pixels on a screen showing you the best route to San Mateo.

"Without getting too existential . . . ," said Jimmie, who then proceeded to wax existential, "maps are hard-wired into who and what we are. We are maps. We differentiate ourselves through language. What were the first things we discussed? Where we were. Where was danger. How we got there. How we got here. This is mapping. This is, in technical terms, the use of the hippocampus, the part of the brain that in fact is spatial memory and memory that allows us to recall both through the directional as well as the olfactory. All these tangential associations support mapping.

"That's the lizard-brain stuff. We're talking way back in our evolutionary chain. With that, then, we have a love of maps. Maps provide security. Maps provide perspective. Maps provide a sense of place. . . . Besides, everybody wants a map of their own backyard. It shows them who they are."

Quite a soliloquy for an ex-roadie, you might think. But Jimmie lifts with his head as well as his knees. He grew up the son of academics. One brother, Richard, is the chairman of the geography department at the University of Kentucky. His other brother, Chris, is a landscape architect in Baltimore. Jimmie is a proud, roll-up-your-sleeves autodidact.

"They did the hard grind of 10 or 15 years writing doctoral theses and all that," he said, smiling slyly. "Me? I toured."

And collected maps—mostly maps of California and the United States, though his stash also encompasses vast swaths of Europe, Asia, Africa and even the polar regions. But it's San Francisco, Sacramento and the Sierra regions that drive sales and engross Jimmie the most. He can deliver disquisitions, mainly from memory, on most of what's charted on the hundreds of maps filling cabinets, boxes and shelves lining the walls. Prices range from $5 to $50,000, but Jimmie doesn't like to dwell on monetary concerns. That cheapens the intrinsic value of each map, though there are a few that, he says, "really belong in the Bancroft" (Library, at the University of California, Berkeley).

Two such maps, framed, hang over the cash register. One depicts a faded drawing of Sausalito from 1868, with the cursive quill annotations by Navy Adm. George F. Emmons, who signed the surveyor map a few months after witnessing the Alaska Purchase signing on his ship. The other is the first map of Mission San Jose (in what is now Fremont), drawn in 1868 by Bay Area surveyor W.F. Boardman, whom Jimmie speaks of almost in reverence.

Marti has her favorites, too. One is James Whistler's—yes, he of *Whistler's Mother* artistic fame—depiction of Anacapa, one of the Channel Islands, made for the government in 1854. Etched into the otherwise straightforward steel-engraving was a tiny flight of birds. Turned out, his employer wasn't thrilled with the artistic flourish and fired Whistler, who fled to England and became established as an artist.

"I could just picture him saying to the government, 'You're stifling my creativity,'" Marti said.

The Scheins consider maps a legitimate art form. Jimmie, in fact, holds many so dear to his heart that he sometimes has a hard time letting go, though he jokes that some customers give him visitation rights.

"Now, he just hides some things away, but in the beginning, people would say, 'OK, I want to buy this,' and Jimmie'd say, 'Oh, yeah, that's not for sale,'" Marti said. "I'm taking him aside and going, 'I know it's hard, but you've got to part with it.' This is a business."

It is a business that survives, but for how long? Jimmie wistfully recalled the days when "in every city, there were two or three places like this," to scavenge for maps. He does not despair, though, when looking ahead.

"The youthful population is looking for the unique and the individualized in a mass-produced world of the trite and the digital," he said. "They use maps more than you and I ever did—on their phone. But that's ephemeral and not worthy of the paper you'd print it on. But I do find they're interested in conceptual mapping, geospatial mapping, or statistical overlays, like where the sewer lines run, or three-dimensional paradigms. Maps won't go away. They'll just change."

A Sensory Tour of San Francisco

April 2016

They always say San Francisco is a feast for the senses. By that, I'm sure they mean the scent of sourdough mingling in the briny breeze at Fisherman's Wharf and that screen-saver view from Coit Tower, not the uremic reek on Mission Street and the cacophonous capitalistic hum of the Financial District.

But they don't know the half of it. If you're seeking to really delve into the realm of the senses, by both deprivation and heightened awareness, then this is the city for you.

Hewing to the ethos of addition by subtraction, you can spend a good part of a day in San Francisco in the dark, literally. Not crepuscular dimness; I'm talking blackout dark. The blackness of nullity. All to give you a greater understanding and, perhaps, appreciation of one's seemingly less employed senses.

You will sacrifice sight at a restaurant called Opaque to focus on taste, that most difficult to describe but truly piquant sense, aided and abetted by its sensory partner, smell. You will be plunged into pupil-expanding darkness at a concert venue called Audium, where 176 speakers send something of an aural tsunami swirling about, sounds so sharp and penetrating it's as if you're hearing viscerally, not merely by stimulation of the stereocilia inside the cochlea. And you will venture to the dark side once more at the Exploratorium, where you step inside a blacked-out geodesic dome, called the Tactile Dome, and navigate through a crazy maze purely by touch, perhaps our most underused sense but the only means to suss out how to crawl, slide, climb and stumble your way toward the light.

Senses are something we are constantly told to "come to," as if it is, as Kant famously posited, where all knowledge begins. But we tend to rely too much on sight, the Gladys Knight to the other senses' Pips, to guide the way. It is a visionary concept, then, to temporarily blot out this dominant sense and let these understudy senses take a star turn in the spotless spotlight.

Remember that our senses are constantly, if often obliviously, at work. Senses take in 11 million pieces of information at any given moment, psychologist Timothy D. Wilson writes in his book, *Strangers to Ourselves*, but the mind can only consciously process 40 pieces of information per second. Take away sight, and processing gets even more difficult. Like typing with only two fingers, it can be done, but it sure takes longer and can get a bit messy. That's because the so-called lesser senses (hearing, touch, taste, smell) are like muscles that can atrophy from lack of use.

So it might do you good to take touch out for a stroll, give hearing a full hearing in a concert space, let taste and smell do the heavy lifting at mealtime.

Opaque

We formed something of a conga line at the thick black velvet curtain separating the pitch-dark dining room of Opaque, near Civic Center square, from the lit bar and reception area.

Per the instructions of Jennifer, our visually impaired waitress, I stood directly behind her and put my hands upon her shoulders. Behind me, hands resting on my shoulders, was my dining companion, a gastronomic savant known as The Palate. We took tiny steps, almost shuffling along, parted several curtains until the last sliver of light faded. I couldn't help but think of that most politically incorrect of expressions, "the blind leading the blind," but didn't dare say it.

Navigating the dark is no problem for her. She's worked at Opaque for five years, knows the layout by memory and, with a firm hand and kind words, has helped hundreds of disoriented sighted people through this sensory chamber. We were her latest. She seated us with care, guided our hands to the cutlery and linen napkin, explained entrees on the prix fixe menu ($100 a head) and then vanished to bring us water. (Kim, our hostess out front, said the restaurant employs only visually impaired servers, serving as sherpas for the sighted, because "once you get in there, your eyes will never adjust.")

The Palate and I, being the first reservation of the night, then sat there in silence staring at each other across the table after she left. Well, I presumed he was looking at me, or in my general direction, because, actually, it was like staring into a void. That's how dark it was. I fumbled around, grabbed my salad fork and brought it millimeters away from my face. Couldn't see it. The room was black, all right, but not devoid of color. Those phosphenes— you know, bright floating dots you see when you close your eyes—were there even with eyes open.

I brought The Palate to this dinner not just because he's one of my best buds, but because his taste buds are famously refined. He often can name-that-ingredient in one bite, so his purpose was to serve as guinea pig and order the "mystery menu"—essentially forking into a surprise with every bite. Me? I chickened out and ordered the roast chicken, salad and banana-almond cake for dessert.

The Palate's only concern was ordering a wine that would pair with his mystery meat. Not to worry, Kim the hostess said, "We can do mystery wine for you, too. We take into account any allergies with mystery food."

I would not get off easily, though. The first two courses would be a mystery appetizer and a mystery soup. Even before that challenge, there was the problem of orientation. Jennifer instructed us that she would place my plates on the table's corner, near my right elbow, for me to move to the center. For The Palate, it would be on the left.

Our first foray was the basket of bread. We were told that the butter dish was nestled inside the wicker (at least it felt like wicker) container. I reached to the center, patted the basket's lip before plunging my fingers into a cool, creamy concoction.

"I found the butter," I told The Palate, discreetly wiping my hand on the linen napkin under the table.

(I caught myself: Why was I being so furtive? No one could see me, anyway.)

The adventure was just beginning. When the mystery appetizer came, I nearly knocked it off the plate. It was rounded, slick, thumbnail-size with something sticky on top. I bit in first.

"Is it a . . . grape? . . . with frosting?" I asked.

The Palate snorted, ate his in one bite.

"Cherry tomato," he said, a bit bored, "with goat cheese."

The Palate would surely be more challenged in the next course, salad for me, a "mystery" for him. I stabbed at the balsamic-drenched lettuce leaves; it was hit or miss whether my fork would emerge with any produce impaled on the tines. The Palate took one bite and declared, "Easy. Calamari with, hmm, I think on a bed of . . . peas?"

Upon Jennifer's return, she broke the news to The Palate that those were mushrooms, not peas. I couldn't see The Palate's face, of course, but his audible exhalation told me he was frustrated his taste buds had betrayed him.

The soup course, thankfully, came in tiny pitchers with spouts and handles, lest one's dry-cleaning bill skyrocket by trying to spoon out the viscous liquid. And viscous it was. The Palate, tentative now, seemed stumped and gave a guess: "Squash soup?" When Jennifer returned, I took a sip and had no clue, but it felt grainy on my tongue, vaguely sweet, certainly something plant-based.

"Split pea?" I ventured.

"You're correct!" she exclaimed.

By this point, at least two other parties had been seated somewhere near us. It sounded like a table of three was to my left and fairly close at that, given their high decibel level. Do people talk louder in the dark or something?

No time to muse on that. Jennifer brought the entree, including the "mystery wine," and I could hear The Palate sniff at the plate. Then he sipped the wine. "Red," he said. I could hear his knife sawing away—"Hey, they already put it in bite-size pieces, that's nice"—and then the grinding of his molars. "Oh, it's some type of steak," he said. "Definitely steak." I, meanwhile, was chasing my chicken in roasted garlic cream around the plate, trying to cut the darn thing.

Jennifer laughed at The Palate's guess of steak, saying, "I'll whisper it in your ear so other tables won't hear."

"No way," The Palate gasped.

(It was pork.)

Fortunately for The Palate's self-esteem, he was dead-on with his dessert prediction: espresso panna cotta, with chocolate sauce.

At meal's end, Jennifer helped us to our feet and we repeated the conga line back to daylight. You know how people use the phrase "blinding light"? Well, it was like that. It took a good five minutes for my eyes to readjust. By that time, I had already signed the bill, $268, with tip, a tad extravagant but worth the experience. The Palate, however, said they robbed me, well, blind.

Audium

That nondescript building on Bush Street, the one with the wood-paneled facade? You know, that place that used to be a bakery and doughnut shop?

Some serious sound experimentation goes on there under the cover of darkness every Friday and Saturday nights.

For more than 40 years, musician and "sound choreographer" Stan Shaff has been experimenting with the aural vicissitudes of music and sounds, from sweeping and soaring to dissonant and atonal. It's Philip Glass mini-

147

malism meets radio sound effects, with a dash of Hans Zimmer sonic bombast thrown in.

No, it's more than that. Its effects depend greatly on where within the space itself you are hearing it. With 176 speakers, white on black and arranged around, above and below the circular space that seats 49, you feel like you are aboard a spacecraft about to lift off. This was even before the lights were extinguished. Dave Shaff, son of Stan, warned the sellout audience that if they suffer some any "anxiety" in the dark, "follow the illuminated arrows along the floor." A few in the crowd chuckled but, later, Stan will say that in Audium's early years, he'd always see a couple of people bolt for the doors in the first five minutes of the hour-long program.

"There are some deep reasons for the reactions people have, having to do with dreams, memories and fantasies," Dave said in the preamble. "Some people liken it to an audio waking dream. But you can draw your own conclusions. Oh, and cell phones: Turn them off. We need total darkness."

Darkness did not fall all at once, as at Opaque. Rather, it was a gradual dimming until blackness prevailed.

Our sonic journey began subtly, almost noiselessly. Plops, like drops in a water bucket, coming at you from all directions. I, instinctively, turned my head toward the sound, a futile gesture. I eventually just let the soothing sound seep into me.

But then it built quickly, with percussive force, drums like horses hooves in mid-stampede. You felt it as much as heard it. But before the piece could devolve into an aural assault, the tone softened once more, caesuras filling spaces. Back once more, sounds perhaps meant to represent a rainstorm. But, no, it must be waves, because the singsong voices of toddlers at play chimed in from your right, then seemed to swoosh across the room and hit from above. And what was it now, horns from the floor? Playing a dirgelike melody?

I looked at the man next to me. Hard to make out, but I thought his eyes were closed. No way he could've been sleeping, given the booms, blips and arpeggiated chords. At odd intervals, those children's voices returned, eerily dreamlike, followed at times by ominous synthesizers. It was unsettling bordering on creepy. Near the piece's end, though, a tonal pattern emerged and the sound seemed to bring you back into a contented sense of self.

When the lights incrementally came back on, the crowd shuffled out. A few exited quietly, some looking shell-shocked. In the lobby sat Shaff, 87, sipping coffee and offering to debrief anyone who'd listen.

"We literally play the space," said Shaff, who composed and recorded this particular piece five years ago. What changes from performance to performance is the way Shaff, from an elevated console, manipulates different instrumentation and sound through different speakers placed throughout the venue.

"The space itself, like melody and harmony and rhythm, has a very important notion to add to performance, sound composition and whatever you call it," he added.

But why play in it darkness?

"The darkness is a very important part," he said. "That immersive quality. The funny thing is, darkness, one of the first elements of Audium, is beginning to sneak into performance spaces of other musicians. Other groups are beginning to see—or, rather, I should say, hear—that the nuance that our hearing potentially captures in darkness helps. You get inside the sound and find subtlety, the coloration you miss normally. Some people really get into it. Some can't wait to leave."

Back on the street, the Friday night hubbub of nearby Van Ness Avenue— the revved engines, blaring horns, heavy-bass throbbing lowrider cars— didn't seem nearly so sonically dissonant. Close your eyes, and you could even detect a certain rhythm.

Tactile Dome

Jake Spund wanted us to know he'd be watching. Well, not in the literal sense, since the Tactile Dome exhibit inside the Exploratorium science museum at Pier 15 is shrouded in darkness. But Jake's been working here long enough to know that some people freak out inside the domed maze where a keen sense of touch provides the only way out, so he takes pains to reassure beforehand.

"If you have any issues, which is not likely, but if you feel nervous or claustrophobic or feel like you need to come out, I'm listening in to make sure things go smoothly. Just give me a holler and say, 'Jake I want to come out,' and I'll get you out. I've got you covered."

The five of us—Boston couple David Bamforth and Giuliana O'Connell; Fort Worth, Texas, mother and daughter Mary Katheryn and Christina

Kelley; and your correspondent—have shed our shoes and fears. Spund has given us the dome's thumbnail history, how designer August Coppola (brother of Francis Ford and father of Nic Cage) built it in 1971 as a sensory experiment. Finally, I let the two other groups go first in a staggered start. Meanwhile, I chatted up Spund.

I asked, skeptically, if people really have freaked out on the five- to seven-minute maze journey.

"From time to time, yeah. Part of the job," he said. "It usually happens within the first 5 feet. That sudden realization they'll be going through a confining space in darkness is shocking to them."

He wished me luck and sent me off.

Plunged into darkness, I turned right, stretched out my arm, feel nubbly plastic. Turned left, spongy fabric. Reached above me, dangling strings of either beads or small chains. Finally, I reached down and to my left and felt . . . nothing. An opening. I crouched and scuttled through. Then I was on hands and knees, padding on all sides. It felt as if I was heading through a tunnel, and this disturbing Freudian thought struck me: I'm in the womb reliving the birth experience. I really felt it upon reaching the point where I slid down a chute and landed on a springy, trampoline-like surface. You walked, crustacean-like, until gamely straightening up. But, of course, I proceeded to hit my head on a padded wall or something.

Onward I trudged, feeling all different surfaces: corrugated grating, fishing nets, computer mouse-type rollers, ridges like slatted fencing. Who knows? I kept moving forward, one arm outstretched like a football player stiff-arming a tackler. I climbed until I reached an LED sign on the floor saying "OUT." I slid down into what feels like pebbles or marbles and poked my head out into the lobby, prairie dog–like, to see what was up.

Spund arched an eyebrow in my direction, checking to see how I survived the journey. I hesitated bringing up my Freudian theory, but, what the heck, I have no filters.

"You may be crazy," Spund said, "but not because of that. That was the artist's interpretation. It was meant to be a rebirthing experience, starting in the 'womb' when you feel helpless except by touch and then bringing it to fruition into the light."

Yes, the light. The glorious light. But I also found, after these experiences, I was no longer cursing the darkness, once I'd been enveloped by it.

Enveloped by "the Wave"

April 2012

This city, so justifiably smitten with its historic landmarks and tourist haunts, likes to go for the grand gesture, the bold statement, the self-consciously arty design that trumpets, "Woo-hoo, look at us."

And true, as with any object of beauty, you cannot help but gawk in admiration. From the sweep of the Golden Gate Bridge to the cloud-piercing jut of Coit Tower, from curvaceous Lombard Street to the asymmetrical perforated copper facade of the de Young Museum, San Francisco is a visual splendor.

But why don't we check out a lesser-known San Francisco landmark, one that has only recently gained recognition in tourist guidebooks after languishing for decades in relative fog-shrouded obscurity. This edifice is subtle and stealthy—indeed, most of it is submerged—yet no less grand in its own way, no less a sensory delight, and no doubt a must-stop for both stressed-out city folk and overstimulated tourists seeking a respite.

The objet d'art is the Wave Organ, and the problem is finding it. Actually, that's not a problem; that's part of the whole Wave Organ's experience. This art installation-cum-public space is meant to be a contemplative refuge. So, naturally, they aren't going to erect a neon arrow pointing the way or, even, a sign.

It sits on a spit of land at the very tip of the Marina District, with the Golden Gate Bridge to the left and Alcatraz to the right. Just drive as far out in the Marina District as you can go, until Yacht Drive dead-ends, then park and just start walking down the windswept promontory until you run out of land and see a jagged heap of discarded granite tombstones from a Victorian cemetery intermingled with jagged jetty rocks and contorted PVC pipe.

Yup, you've found it.

Designed in the mid-1980s by Peter Richards, artist in residence at the nearby Exploratorium, and constructed by stone-mason artist George Gonzales, the Wave Organ is precisely what its name implies.

"It's exposed to dynamic waters and it's neither land nor water, but something in between," Richard says. "It's this tiny sliver of solid ground that puts you out and away from the normal hubbub of life, which is why it's so peaceful. You can shed the daily grind and attach yourself to other things, and pay attention to other things.

"We wanted it to blend in. We wanted people to feel like they'd discovered it on their own, make them think it was theirs."

Sit atop the granite slabs, or nestle into the coveted quadraphonic alcove, tilt your head toward one of the 25 exposed, periscope-like tubes that snake into the lapping water below, and listen. I mean it: Put away all electronic devices, exhale and just listen.

Plop.

Gurgle.

Kerplunk.

Whoosh.

Splat.

It is, undeniably, a percussive force, changing in pitch and tempo according to the dictates of that celebrated conductor, Mother Nature.

It is best, Richards says, to go at high tide and full moon, when tidal forces are at their most creative.

What you'll make of the aural arrangement will speak volumes about your sensibilities.

You'll either:

- Be dismissive and compare the "noise" coming out of the tubes with the sound your stomach makes after eating some sketchy seafood at Fisherman's Wharf, or perhaps the gurgle of bad bathroom plumbing.

Or

- Be transported and experience it as something akin to a John Cage aleatoric symphony, the waves themselves responsible for the composition and texture, the dissonant notes it emits part of a greater body of work.

Me?

I interpreted it both ways. Let's be honest: Some of the sound does strike you as more epiglottal than elegiac.

But the longer you stay, the more your mind lets go of the literal, and you gain an appreciation of nature's artistry. You forget this is merely the reverberation from waves sloshing in and out of PVC piping and start imagining underwater timpani and xylophones jamming with a concussive djembe in some aquatic drum circle.

A mix of pulsing sensations and repetition would make Philip Glass nod in appreciation.

And, in fact, Richards says musicians have used the wave organ for accompaniment. Then again, others have used the Wave Organ as a cozy corner for picnics, a tucked-away late-night make-out spot, a place to contemplate life's existential questions.

"Weddings have happened there," Richards says. "Any way that people behave, they behave out there. It's a true public place—a source of inspiration, celebration and meditation."

At high tide one recent morning, I felt a noticeable slowing of my blood pressure. The Wave Organ: nature's Inderal.

I stood, ear-height to a tall tube, and for a good 45 minutes listened to the symphony as the morning sun rapidly turned to fog, enveloping the Golden Gate and Alcatraz until all I had left was the sound. It was, truly, golden.

4

Baring Souls and More

We are at any given moment living the totality of everything. . . . The vibrational oscillation of nature is quickening. . . . Just remember that you are God, and act accordingly.
—Shirley MacLaine

Coherence is a constant. It can be difficult to know where to begin. Have you found your myth?
—"New Age Bullshit Generator," at sebpearce.com

Retreating into Silence

July 2013
City: Nevada City
County: Nevada
Population: 3,068
Elevation: 2,477 feet
New Age Vibes: High

Sometimes—no, often—I get tired of hearing myself talk, especially all those voices in my head. So, I can just imagine what others must make of my logorrheic tendencies. I needed to get away for a weekend to a place where I would not feel the compulsion to chat, chew the fat, make small talk and pass the time with a story or three.

So, at the request of my wife, my boss and my sanity, I chose to hole up and shut up. That I picked the summer solstice, the longest day of the year, to do it made me feel as if I might achieve prolonged illumination, both seasonal and personal. Or, at least, that's what the New Age nondogmatic dogma promised.

I am embarking on a 48-hour vow of silence. I am secluding myself deep in the Sierra foothills 20 miles northwest of here for a weekend getaway at a meditation retreat for which the selling points are no external stimulation, no outside contact with the wider world (either wired or human) and no inane chatter.

Lest you consider it an act of harsh asceticism rather than a valid vacation option, my two-night stay at the Ananda Meditation Retreat on San Juan Ridge in California's Gold Country also promised the possibility of a deep connection with myself and the divine, the chance to commune with nature and the nature of my being, and to both unplug and recharge amid stately oak, pine and alder trees.

That I'm neither a yogi nor an Eastern-religion "seeker" matters little. For decades, people of all faiths—and maybe even a few with none at all— have repaired to Ananda's verdant 70-acre spread to meditate and rejuvenate and, most of all, contemplate the meaning of life and their place in it.

Long-standing silent retreats such as Ananda, Esalen in Big Sur and Green Gulch in Marin County lie at the forefront of what some say is a growing phenomenon in personal travel. Before I signed up, I had it that no less an arbiter than *Travel + Leisure* magazine has proclaimed silent retreats "a top trend." The Huffington Post called them a "perfect antidote to work-driven lives," and ABC News gushed "you can find peace and quiet for days on end!"

All over California, from the nondenominational Silent Stay in Vacaville to a Benedictine monastery called the New Camaldoli Hermitage in Big Sur, retreats have taken root and sprouted in recent years. Supriya, who manages Ananda along with her partner, Chaitanya, isn't at all surprised.

"Retreats like this are badly needed because it's so hard for people to unplug from phone and Internet," she said. "It's gotten so we're just constantly bombarded with information. People expect you to be at their beck and call all the time. Here, you can slow down."

And relax. And mull. Engage in stock-taking and priority-evaluating. All without the distracting chatter of Twitter and Facebook, Reddit and Instagram, YouTube and Yelp.

Sounds easy. Sounds blissful. Sounds great—until you actually have to unplug and deal with the residual sounds, voices and stray pinging noises searing around your brainpan from "real" life. Calming down, you soon find, takes hard work, which does not defeat the purpose of the exercise; it only makes it more rewarding once it's achieved.

Or so I'm told.

There I sat on a Friday night, solstice night, on a bench in a circular spot of Ananda's vast garden called the vortex, because it's said to funnel energy within. This is a prime spot for "secluders," gardener Charles Evans said, to reintroduce themselves to the outer world and to summon their inner world, as well.

So I stared at the sun, still shimmering through branches of heritage oaks far past 8 o'clock, and felt only slightly bereft without my smartphone or my watch. I tried to envelop my senses in the clean smell of the pines above me, the loam of the mulched oak leaves at my feet, the chirp of birds darting shrub to shrub, the rustle of branches and hum of bees.

But the high-pitched whine of mosquitoes dive-bombing me negated potential reveries. All I could think as I slapped away the mosquitoes was the karmic blow-back I would face from smooshing the little pests.

I wondered what Paramahansa Yogananda, on whose yogic teachings this center's precepts are based, would think of my mass mosquito slaughter.

Then again, I thought, let the mosquitoes serve as allegorical stand-ins for the tweets and texts and status updates that inundate my life. I was thinking that while I was supposed to be thinking nothing at all, merely being, my brain didn't have an on-off switch, or even a dimmer knob.

Clearly, I was suffering from an "interiority" complex. I should have just been sitting in the garden watching plants photosynthesize, deep inside myself, but these divergent, self-conscious thoughts intruded like the car radio set on scan.

"It's really tough, even for myself," Surpriya said, "and I've been doing it 22 years. I once made the analogy that I'm like an undisciplined puppy, sniffing around and not focusing long on anything. It takes training."

Supriya—that's her Sanskrit name; she was born Sheri Goldberg in the San Fernando Valley—told me this before my veil of silence fell.

She checks in guests like the kindly innkeeper she is, showing them their cabins or tent bungalows, the garden, the free-range chicken coop, the solar panels (the retreat is "off the grid") and the hiking trails. But she also tries to introduce them to the way of Ananda, Sanskrit for "joy."

Her final instructions before, well, silently retreating back to her domed office were for me to check the guest binder sitting on the counter. Inside was a blue laminated badge I was to wear, declaring "I AM IN SILENCE, Thank You," and an essay for neophytes on how to deal with the inevitable "what now?" feeling of vacationing without the crutch of structured activities.

Included along with the helpful hints in the binder's "Time Out for Seclusion" section—"bring spiritual books to read, hatha yoga tools, meditation devices"—was a warning that one might fear being alone and in silence because "many people are afraid to face their own demons."

But staring down demons, apparently by giving them the silent treatment, is part of what you signed up for. Great thinkers from Thoreau to Merton have alighted to the hinterlands to do battle with the ineffable, and no less a thinker than Blaise Pascal once mused, "All the problems in the world stem from man's inability to sit alone in a small room."

What are those sounds?

The sitting alone part I thought I could hack. What was vaguely unsettling was being silent around others.

At dinner that first night, I took my bowl of Czech mushroom soup and a plate of quinoa, broccoli and salad, and sat alone in the dining room. There are eight of us, alone together. I looked around: a woman in the back corner with two journals open; another woman staring into her bowl mouthing silent prayers; two couples at a circular table being sociable merely with occasional eye contact.

Never had I been so self-conscious while eating. The very act of mastication and peristalsis seemed hideously amplified. When I crunched a radish, the noise seemed as deafening as an explosive blast, the sharp snap of a carrot on my molars like a gunshot, the clink of metal utensils on ceramic flatware as intrusive as a tinny cellphone ringtone.

Yet, I also found I had never been more conscious about what I was eating. I noticed the gradations of texture in the mushroom soup, at once creamy and gritty, the subtle tang of the balsamic salad dressing, the truly cardboard-like components of the rice cakes that substituted for bread.

That night, in preparation for the morning meditation, I read from Yogananda's seminal 1946 book *Autobiography of a Yogi*, which Surpriya suggested would give a primer on the practice of Kriya yoga.

"The vast majority of people here, if not exactly on an Ananda path, are on some kind of Eastern yogic path," she had said. "Sometimes, it's hard for other people to stomach when (Yogananda) talks about miracles that occurred or things that are unfathomable to Western minds. They have a hard time finding it credible."

Surpriya had been, perhaps, preparing me for the section in which Yogananda writes about the immortal Indian saint Mahavatar Babaji who "retained his physical form for centuries" and apparently still lives in the northern Himalayas.

Only slightly less esoteric is Yogananda's explanation of Kriya yoga practices. In short, it's a breathing technique meant to induce a state of tranquility and renew life energy that travels the length of six spinal centers in the body that correspond to the 12 astral signs of the Zodiac.

The book also clued me in to the meditation mantra "Hong-Sau," which helps focus the mind on the task at hand. It's "hong" on the inhalation, "sau" on the exhalation. Repeat as necessary.

Early the next morning—I didn't hear the 5:30 gong but was up anyway, anxiety-ridden about meditating—I gingerly walked into the temple just as spiritual directors Nayaswami Dharmadas and Nayaswami Nirmala chanted to the stock-still adherents.

Supriya had told me this group of Kriyabans—practitioners who had gone through extensive training—had given the OK for guests to sit in on the last half of their three-hour meditation.

I took off my shoes, grabbed a blue yoga mat and found a spot near the back. I unfurled the mat, and staring at me was the familiar Facebook logo. It was as if the universe was laughing at me, saying, "Ha, you think you can turn off thoughts of social media so easily!"

Cross-legged on the mat—even though several Kriyabans were perched on chairs and looked much more comfy—I tried to stay still and empty my mind but not before glancing around the temple. At the altar were five portraits of spiritual leaders: Jesus Christ, Babaji, Lahiri Mahasaya, Yukteswar Giri and Yogananda. Below it was a larger photo of Yogananda and a smaller photo of the recently deceased Kriyananda (born James Donald Walters), Yogananda's disciple and founder of the Ananda Retreat in 1968.

Why Christ? I wondered. Were they just covering all the bases, or what?

Later, Supriya would tell me that Yogananda considered Christ "a great yogi who practiced meditations. I know some (Christians) might be up in arms about that, but . . ."

As at dinner previously, I was painfully self-conscious at the start of meditation. My slightest movement—nose-twitch or swallow—led me to think I was disrupting something sacred. A man in front put on noise-canceling headphones about 10 minutes after I arrived, and I hoped it wasn't because he could hear my breakfast-craving stomach rumbling.

Eventually, I got down to some serious hong-sauing. Eyes closed, I tried to will myself to banish invasive thoughts. For a moment, I felt a blankness, a pleasant absence—nothing intruding on the nothingness.

Then I thought, "Hey, I'm not thinking about anything," and the process began all over again.

I could not help it: Thoughts swirled in my brain, a Gertrude Steinian stream of trivial consciousness. I told myself, "This won't look good for the story," then scolded myself for thinking about the story when I should have been thinking about not thinking, about letting go.

After a good spell, my overheated mind calmed, my breathing—hong-sau—got shallower until I wasn't aware of breathing at all. I didn't know how much time had elapsed, but I was mildly surprised when Dharmadas intoned, "We'll end this meditation with a prayer."

I'd been sitting for an hour and 45 minutes.

A silent breakfast of oatmeal and a banana awaited me, like a karmic reward.

In the afternoon, after a two-hour nap, I took a hike on one of the retreat's trails, lined with manzanita, oak and pine. I was feeling calmer—or maybe just half asleep. Ambling along an overgrown fire road shaded by oak branches, I looked down at the trail at a fortuitous time: A rattlesnake lay stretched out sunning itself not 3 feet in front of me.

It was a standoff for a minute or two. I tried to slow my breathing—"Hong-sau, hong–freakin'-sau"—but the snake didn't budge. I stared at it and marveled at its clever camouflaged properties, how it almost seamlessly blended into the landscape. I forgot that its bite can be lethal. We had a moment there, the snake and I, maybe not of understanding but of détente. I gingerly stepped around it, exhaling a mighty "sau," believe you me.

After an evening kirtan (chanting concert) and cleansing fire ceremony, I had no problem sleeping. The snake incident had been recast in my mind from anxious encounter to profound meeting.

The next morning, a Sunday, upon breaking my silence, I told Supriya about all I had experienced. She nodded sagely, smiled when appropriate.

When I asked what a snake symbolizes in her faith, she brightened: "Oh, that's a good sign. Snake means 'transition.'"

It was time for me to transition back to the verbal world, the whole crazy, information-besotted spectacle of modern life. When I turned my phone back on in Nevada City, I heard the bing-bing-bing of incoming text messages accumulated over nearly three days, as rapid-fire as rounds from an AR-15 assault rifle.

Tempted to look, I instead turned the phone back off.

Just a little while longer.

Vibrational Recharge

April 2013
City: Landers
County: San Bernardino
Population: 2,606
Elevation: 3,100 feet
New Age Vibes: Otherworldly

So, apparently, my body, or "carbon unit," is running dangerously low at the cellular level. Unless I "change frequencies" in my electromagnetic field, I will die, someday.

You, too, of course.

The aliens, as well as some scientists, said so.

We all are like cellphones that get only one-bar reception—two, if we're particularly spry.

What's needed, I'm told, is to plug in and "distort the space-time continuum" by lying in a "rejuvenation machine" that essentially is something of a cosmic battery charger in a primo geologic and magnetic spot here in the high desert of Southern California.

As extraterrestrials once told a "connector" named George Van Tassel during a "visitation," if you build a conductor of negative ions at this precise location north of Joshua Tree and near a giant rock called, well, Giant Rock, people will plunk down $25 a shot to try to give their waning cells a little goose.

This is not New Agey, folks; it's otherworldly.

So, whattya say? You with me?

Are you ready to temporarily suspend disbelief and climb to the magical second floor of a huge, white parabolic edifice called the Integratron, to lie supine for the better part of an hour while listening to the reverberative echoes of music from quartz crystal "singing bowls" whose eerie notes correspond to our seven chakras?

I knew you'd be game.

About a dozen other "amoebic life group" members joined me for a "sound bath" on the handsome, impeccably polished Douglas fir floors, supported by mats, Navajo rugs and an open mind about such things as a higher consciousness, other life-forms and the healing properties of acoustic alchemy.

These must be people interested in aural sects, you're probably thinking.

But you'd be wrong.

These were nondenominational grandmothers in white tennis shoes, moms and dads with teenagers, the occasional 20-something. No one reeked of patchouli and there was nary a dreadlock in sight.

I spoke with visitor Tammy Ishibashi, husband Todd and teen son John before entering. They were hardly the crystal talisman types. Ishibashi said they saw the Integratron featured on the Travel Channel show *No Reservations* and thought, what the hey.

Not even our musician-docent-cosmic facilitator Drayton ("no last name, please") looked the part of seer; he wore jeans and parted his short hair on the side. It was only when he talked that things got a little metaphysical.

By the way, the above phrase bracketed by quotation marks came from Drayton's prefatory remarks before putting pestle to his singing bowls and making beautiful (and loud) music.

At times, his talk was a lot to wrap one's head around. But we seekers listened carefully as Drayton's soft-spokenness bounced off the curved wooden walls and swirled around us.

"The original intent of this building was to rejuvenate human cells, so that we could eventually live for maybe 50 more years," he said. "(Van Tassel) asked (his alien pals), 'Why in the world would you want to?' They said, 'You need to wise up and save your race.' I think that time is coming soon. All humans need to be happy again and eventually die with love in their heart and a smile on their face, or they miss the whole point.

"We're not spending any time in the out-of-body school of life and, subsequently, we're giving our solar system and our galaxy in this sector of the universe a headache."

Head nods, all around. But a little part of me could only think: 50 more years? Gee, and you think we've got a major headache funding Medicare and Social Security now? Just wait until baby boomers live to 140.

"So," Drayton continued, "your electromagnetic energy field is the same diameter as this acoustically perfect sound chamber, if you're a healthy adult. That would be 55 feet across, measurable by your electric footprint. This is truly an international power amplification point. These bowls get flying around and your (magnetic) field is having its way with it, raising the frequency of everything. You may have shown up stuck in your antennae, but (the sounds) are going to go through your body faster than you're hearing them because of the density properties of water."

Wait, he was losing me. I was an English major. Don't go throwing science at me.

Fortunately, I had boned up on the history of Mr. Van Tassel, his Integratron and the supposed magnetic properties of the area by checking out the website. Let me boil it down thusly: Van Tassel was an aeronautical engineer by trade who moved to Landers in 1947, became a leader in the UFO movement and had a visit from a saucer from the planet Venus in 1953. Shortly thereafter, on the advice of the aliens and inspired by the work of Nikola Tesla and other scientists, he devoted his life to building a "time and rejuvenation machine and an anti-gravity device."

Van Tassel died in 1978 at age 68 (just a wee bit short of 150, alas), but his dream of extending life and finding psychic harmony with the universe has lived on with a dedicated group of adherents, including the current owners, the three Karl sisters.

But back to Drayton. Just when he concluded the science portion, he started to brief us on what we'd experience, so as to quell any anxiety.

"You're going to float this way and that way to check out what's going on," he said. "And you'll realize you're filling your field up with your awareness and you're stabilized somewhere between awake and asleep, which gives you access to time-space where your little 6 or 7 ounces of spirit go flying out of your head at night when you rest these carbon units (sleep, I think he meant). We're not allowed to remember where we go when we get back. A flash here and a flash there, perhaps. So, that's kind of it."

One last thing, actually: It seems the body gets so relaxed and rejuvenated during a session that people tend to fall asleep. Snoring, however, is verboten. It kind of harshes the mellow of your fellow seekers. In fact, any noise in the Integratron is amplified way out of proportion, so try to not even sigh loudly.

OK, enough jaw-flapping. How about some sound?

For 23 minutes, Drayton played the bowls deftly and sublimely. Sound did, indeed, bounce off the walls and vibrate to my very core. It was the most visceral experience I've had since the time I ate bad clams at Fisherman's Wharf.

Seriously, though, it was a trip. A late-afternoon desert wind kicked up and, combined with the vibrations, truly made this an echo chamber. When the 23 minutes were up, Drayton encouraged us to spend the rest of the hour "bathing" in the lingering good vibes.

Afterward, I admitted to Drayton that I did, indeed, feel more relaxed.

"You feel like Jell-O, right?" he said.

Well, a bit.

As she left the Integratron, Tammy, too, was impressed but not ready to fully commit.

"This is why I'm never good at meditation," she said. "I can't turn my brain off."

Her disbelief, apparently, never was fully suspended.

But me? I can feel my dying cells perking right up.

Springing to Life

October 2012

Cities: Middletown, Wilbur, Calistoga, Ukiah

Counties: Lake, Colusa, Napa, Mendocino

New Age Vibes: Bubbling

I have lost all objectivity, abandoned all skepticism, don't even feel an iota of cynicism. I blame the waters. They say the lithium levels are miniscule, just enough to give you a mild feeling of well-being, but if I wasn't so blissed out, I'd question that assessment. As it is now, I really don't care. I'm as credulous as a toddler and make about as much sense as one, too.

This is what spending time under the influence of Northern California's mineral hot springs will do to a guy. My aggression, ambition and journalistic drive have seeped from my pores, my fingers look old-man wrinkled and my senses completely altered from three days of marinating in a heady sulfuric bouillabaisse.

Much as I might try to summon his well-cultivated snark and emotional detachment from my hardened core, it just ain't happening, folks. Among all the minerals—selenium, potassium, carbonic acid and, yes, even that touch of lithium—that have pierced my epidermis, I find himself strangely irony-deficient.

This is what a Tour de Hot Springs will do to a guy.

It is highly recommended.

Nothing renews spirits like being naked as the day you were born cradled in the all-embracing arms of a Hawaiian goddess helping a guy relive the birth experience in the healing waters, or being suspended, like a prehistoric bug in amber, in a vat of heated volcanic ash by a dude named Fernando, or being plopped like an Alka-Seltzer tablet into steaming waters crackling with carbon dioxide.

Stressed? Frustrated? Enervated?

Get thee to a hot springs, stat.

Scores of springs burble up from the restless mantle throughout Northern California, many located in the Napa wine country and surrounding environs. So finding one is not the problem. Finding the right one to fit your temperament, level of modesty and tolerance of healthy hedonism is another matter. Be it hippies or yuppies, new agers or old-timers, naturists or clotheshorses, choices abound.

The hottest and wildest of the Northern California hot springs trail is (or, rather, was) Harbin Hot Springs, which burned to the hot spring core during the 2015 fire season in a blaze that pretty much wiped out the neighboring town of Middletown. It had been a neo-hippie haven where clothing was not only optional but nearly uniform in its absence. Now, it sits on a denuded landscape where towering pine trees and nymphs and sprites and other unclothed Bay Areans once frolicked. Owners have vowed to rebuild, even if it costs them the nonexistent shirt off their backs.

Fortunately for the hot-spring aficionado, other choices are available. Wilbur Hot Springs in Colusa County, a place of near-monastic quiet, where clothing is optional in the baths but mandatory elsewhere. Indian

Springs in Calistoga, home of the volcanic ash mud bath and decidedly swimsuit-required at its Olympic-size mineral pool. And Vichy Hot Springs in Ukiah, one of only three spots in the world with carbonated mineral water in its sulfur-tinged, 150-year-old, swimsuit-required tubs.

One commonality: These springs may drain your worries, but not your bank account. Rooms range from $60 on the modest end to $250 at the top. The food ranges from a kitchen where guests make their own meals to restaurants replete with vegan, gluten-free, organic free-range options. Even the spa treatments—massage, mud baths and body peels—fall on the reasonable end of the pampering spectrum.

That's because these places are retreats, not resorts. Meaning, you don't necessarily have sycophantic workers at your beck and call, catering to every whim. Meaning, also, that it's not, despite reputation, the Club Med pickup scene.

Nudity, poolside, is accepted with a shrug of one's bare shoulders. There's little overtly sexual about going suitless in baths and, except for occasional canoodling by a few couples at Harbin, no touching or hassling, either. Yet, there was this low-level vibe, an erotic hum at Harbin, people checking out bodies via furtive glances. So much flesh in so many configurations. Skeletal men whose ribs could easily be counted; Rubenesque, hirsute older women who have been introduced to neither a razor nor a sense of modesty; gnarled, arthritic men with sagging guts and creepy leers who walk in such a swaying way that their manhood moves pendulum-like; lithe, athletic younger women, many in the odd combination of dreadlocks and Native American jewelry, whose breasts bobbed like buoys and whose physiques made everyone of any sex feel body-image deficient.

One thing everyone wears, though: a smile.

"It just feels so natural to be in a completely natural setting like this, looking up at the stars and feeling this hot water that comes from the earth," said Carly Giesen, who works at Wilbur and frequents hot springs from Sacramento to Mammoth Lakes. "It's an otherworldly experience you can experience every day."

I had heard Harbin was the place for hard-core hot spring action, so I swallowed hard and went there first. Pulling into the parking lot, you notice something unusual: People are clothed. Yes, in fact, they are carrying suitcases into the reception area. What kind of nudist colony needs porters to carry your bags? You'd think that this would be the one place that people really could travel light to.

Good thing I did bring some shirts and pants, because Harbin was clothing-mandatory at all areas (rooms, restaurants, movie theater, hiking trails) save the hot springs themselves. You experience a kind of *Wizard of Oz* moment—from black-and-white to Technicolor—once you wander over to the pools and see the stark transformation: everybody's starkers, as the Brits say.

At the front desk, I had signed up for what was Harbin's signature "experience," a private "Watsu" water massage. But that was still 45 minutes away. I had lots of time to shed my clothes and inhibitions and soak next to about 150 people on a warm early October weekend.

The locker rooms are coed. I undressed next to two high-tech workers— one female, one male—jabbering nonstop about some coding problem back at the office. The woman's bra flew out of her hand and landed at my bare feet, and her male friend thought nothing of reaching over me as I was removing my shirt. That gave me a, let's just say, clear view of his fat butt. Now I know why proctologists are said to be heavy drinkers. Before making my debutante-like debut in the nude, I gave a little tug to my shrinking manhood, which had retracted turtle-like in the breeze. Got to present, you know, something for the masses, after all. But I noticed that, for the most part, protocol was for bathers walking by to keep eyes at eye level. That is to say, eyes straight ahead. At least until initial eye contact is made, then, it seems you can feel free to scan downward, albeit briefly, without getting a scowl and bring silently marked as a "creeper."

Once escaping the changing area, I dipped a toe and then other digits into the medium-hot bath. I slithered in and looked around. Thin curls of steam rose from the water—I'm tempted to write, thin, pubic curls of steam, but that would be too obvious. Around me were couples entwined, the women sort of sitting in the men's laps, the men's backs up against the poolsides. I kind of suspected what they were furtively doing but, seriously, could detect not a quarter inch of vertical movement by either of the entwined. Several older gentlemen with forests of graying chest hair slicked against their D-cup breasts were doing some serious "manspreading," their arms akimbo and hooked around the edges of the pool, their legs taking up space for three people.

Nearly all the women and I'd say 70 percent of the men were not overt in showcasing their sexual genitalia, except for a redheaded woman in her late 20s whose blazing patch of pubic hair was front and center as she performed something of an Esther Williams water ballet routine. Several times, for at least a minute, she would plunge her head into the water, duck-like, then do a handstand underwater, her muscled calves and thighs scissoring and then opening and closing as if using one of those Thighmaster exercise machines. People of both sexes took it all in. Each time the redhead would resurface for air, she'd pop up, smooth her red tendrils back into place and flash a slightly naughty smile. Her smile was gap-toothed, which only made it more fetching.

Such a display was clearly meant to titillate, but, interestingly, I felt nothing stir below my waist. I had been worried about my bodily reaction at the sight of unclothed women, regardless of degrees of conventional attractiveness. But I was so self-conscious that you couldn't have gotten me up with a forklift and a bottle of Viagra.

This boded well for my tête-à-tête with the Watsu instructor, which would take place with both of us in our birthday suits and she cradling me to her breast, infant-like. (Signing up for the $100 session, you are given the choice of male or female instructor. This caused a dilemma. If I specifically asked for a woman, would the receptionist think, "Oh, another horny middle-aged guy out for his jollies?" But if I asked for a male, would the receptionist think, "Oh, another horny middle-aged gay guy out for his jollies?" A lose-lose proposition. For the record, I'm a straight middle-aged guy not out for jollies, just another "experience" to record. I hedged and told the receptionist, "Either is OK." This was rolling the dice, and I didn't know until I showed up at the hot springs up the hill near the geodesic domes that a woman instructor had been assigned.)

So there I was, plunged into the amniotic warmth of the private pool. Before my guide, massage therapist Sara Kealani Takahashi, cradled me into the crook of her shoulder, she looked me straight in the eye and intoned: "For some people, Watsu is like reliving (birth) and very nurturing. For others, it's just a water massage."

Did she mean that as a challenge? But I thought, even if I didn't get "reborn," a little nurturing could never hurt, right? Soon, I was floating to and fro, limbs stretched and palpitated in the swirling, in-utero buoyancy of the mineral bath.

"I tell people," Kealani added, soothing as a psychologist talking a man down from a ledge, "to let your body feel like seaweed floating in the ocean."

And then she stopped talking. For the next 45 minutes, safe in her embrace, I felt disconnected from gravity and reality. My body felt loose-limbed for the first time in decades: arm and leg tension palpitated into submission, back and neck knots loosened, emotions rising to a crescendo of, yes, near tears.

When it was over, swaddled once more in a towel, Kealani told me, "You definitely need some nurturing, dude."

Then she pocketed the cash and drove off in her Camry.

I was left to contemplate the appeal of a Watsu massage—a smashed-together term meaning "water shiatsu." It was developed at Harbin in 1980 by practitioner Harold Dull and today is a "modality" practiced worldwide. To come to Harbin and not experience Watsu is like visiting the Louvre and not seeing the *Mona Lisa*.

Harbin has been around for more than a century—it opened in 1870 as the Harbin Springs Health and Pleasure Resort—and since 1972, it has been owned and operated by the Heart Consciousness Church ("An embodiment and a manifestation of the New Age," according to its literature). So they have the means and tax advantages to fully rebuild after the fire.

Despite its affiliation, guests barely see evidence of any religious doctrine, save some ubiquitous Buddha statues, a few altars and a labyrinth. See, at Harbin, it's more about a separation of church and clothes. In fact, the one sure way to turn heads is to don a bathing suit.

The hottest of Harbin's springs are meditative places where talking is forbidden, but its heart-shaped warm-water pool is where guests soak and converse. In my post-Watsu bliss, I chatted with a couple, Madalyn Suozzo and Rick ("just Rick, please") and a young Quebecoise named Melissa, who showed off her Om symbol tattoo between her breasts and spun a fanciful story about how she had just returned from living two years in a cave in the Amazon.

No one believed her, but little mind. This seems a place where you can shed personas as easily as shedding clothes. Later, clothed and eating dinner, Suozzo said she loves Harbin for just such interesting people. "If you want to be social, Harbin is the place to go," she said. "I have friends of mine who hate this place. And they're not prudes. They just think men are stalking them and they don't feel safe. But I've come here a couple times a year for 20 years, both alone and with someone, and always felt safe. There's not sex everywhere, like you'd think. But it's a very, very spiritual place. Your average Joe will not go for it."

A half an hour northwest of Harbin sits a slightly more "Average Joe"-friendly hot springs, Wilbur Hot Springs, though you'll doff suits there as well. It's located in the agriculture-rich Capay Valley. Near the end of a 4-mile dirt road at Wilbur's gate, a large sign reads: "Time to Slow Down."

It is both a greeting and a friendly admonition. But, really, people have no choice. Wedged between oak-studded hillsides, Wilbur has no cell service, no guest Wi-Fi, no televisions.

"Right now," said manager Michael Van Hall, "even our (landline) phone service is down. But we're getting by. This is what you'd expect in nature. We're trying to create a place of healing, self-reflection. We're on the inner-contemplative end of the (hot springs) spectrum."

Like Harbin, Wilbur has had to deal with a devastating fire in recent years. Its structure-destroying blaze came a year before Harbin's 2015 fire. But Wilbur's owner, the avuncular Richard Louis Miller, never thought of closing what is his life's work.

As flames engulfed his building and smoke and chaos reigned, firefighters worked to douse the Wilbur blaze, which already had taken the second and third floors of the main building, west of the springs themselves, and threatened to spread. Distraught guests, their Saturday brunch interrupted, milled and fretted outside, fortunate to be safe, certainly, but saddened to see their possessions and peace of mind lost. And, wait, were two guests missing? They couldn't still be inside, could they? No, he soon learned, they were just out hiking in the nature preserve. A relief, a blessing.

Only then, on the bright, brisk morning of March 29, 2014, the occasion of his 75th birthday, did Miller decide to gather guests and staff, including his wife, Jolee, and daughter, Sarana, in a circle. They held hands. They looked to Miller for guidance.

"I remember," Jolee said, "that Richard had the presence of mind and heart to say, 'It's just a building. No life was lost, and it's still my birthday, so you know, let's just sing and be grateful.' It was a poignant moment, very bittersweet."

So that's what the group did. They serenaded Miller with "Happy Birthday," while the historic 1910 hotel he bought in 1972 and lovingly restored over the decades crackled and smoldered.

"Next time," Miller said at song's end, "not so many candles."

The blaze, which burned well into the evening and was believed to have been caused by a heater failure in a guest room, gutted the main building but mercifully spared the bubbling hot-spring pools and the 1,570 oak-studded, hilly acres where people have long flocked for rest, rejuvenation and refuge. That same day, Miller and family took stock. Losses were big, and they were uninsured. They figured out how much money they'd need to rebuild, and how much money they had in the bank. The figures, frankly, didn't pencil out. Little matter—they started rebuilding, almost immediately.

"There was never any doubt in my mind," Miller recalled. "I mortgaged my life."

Six weeks later, with no fewer than 180,000 pounds of debris hauled away, the wrought-iron gate to this Colusa County resort reopened, and guests once more could soak in the soothing springs, a natural mineral bouillabaisse of sulfate, chloride, sodium and mood-stabilizing lithium. But it wasn't until March 29, 2015—the symmetry entirely intentional—that construction was completed on the restored hotel and grounds and life, Wilbur-style, returned to normal.

There are noticeable changes, initially a shock to some longtime Wilburites who pretty much considered the place darn near perfect in its previous incarnation. The hotel is now one story, its library and reception area reconfigured. Replacing the rooms are stand-alone cabins a stone's throw away. Four private massage rooms, overlooking the creek next to the fluminarium (water flumes 20 feet long and 4 feet wide of increasing temperature, 98, 105 and 110 degrees), have been added. The kitchen, dining room and refrigeration area have greatly expanded to better suit the resort's popular Guest Chef's Weekends and give more room to guests who bring their own food to prepare.

One initially balking at the change turned out to be Miller himself. He is 6-foot-5, without his fedora, but comes off as avuncular rather than imposing. He was able to be swayed by those in favor of the reconfiguration, instead of identical restoration, of Wilbur.

"It was the right thing to do," Miller said. "It took me a while, but I like it."

Miller's wariness may have stemmed from the scores of letters and emails he said he received, more than 1,000, urging him to reopen, and quickly. People even sent in money, unbidden. Would they cotton to the change?

"Wilbur's a very unique place," said General Manager Andrea Speedie, who has held the managerial job for only four months. "I've found the guests to be fiercely loyal."

And vociferous in sharing their Wilbur stories. Weddings have taken place there, including Miller and Jolee's in 2013. Margo Miller and Jerry Eliaser, of Sebastopol, had a kosher, premarital mikvah (purification bath) at Wilbur. Several couples say they return each year on their anniversary.

The Rev. Ken Barnes, 76, a retired pastor at a church in the Bay Area town of Kensington, remembers visiting his grandfather, a cattle driver living near Cache Creek, and discovering the springs and ramshackle outbuildings in the 1940s. Later, he met Miller and started coming as a guest.

"My brother and I would swim, explore the mine entrances, catch turtles in the creek which flows past the hotel," he said. "We would go in what we called the Haunted House, which is now the restored hotel."

Joe Weatherby, of San Francisco, dates his Wilbur experience to Miller's early days, when rooms were lit by oil lamps. The compound is now entirely solar-powered, and its kitchen and facilities thoroughly modern, but Weatherby returns to Wilbur for its homey vibe and the tranquility he finds in the water. It fits him, temperamentally.

"As soon as I unpack and move (his) car, that first shower and dip into their miraculous water pulls the stress of driving from my neck and back instantly," he said. "It's a wonderful place for me to escape the city for a few days. It's only when my car hits the freeway on the way home does the stress resume its place in my neck."

Sacramento couple Gary Schiff and Danyelle Petersen, who have stressful jobs as an estate liquidator and a realtor, respectively, have visited four times a year for 15 years. It's their time to decompress.

"We have met people from all over the world while soaking in the waters," she said. "The nice thing is if you are looking for a quiet experience, it happens. If you are looking to meet people and talk, it happens."

For Renie and Jay Schober, of Santa Cruz, it's all about experiencing the blood pressure–calming Wilbur "vibe." Well, that and the water. The couple often will hop on the complimentary mountain bikes and explore the property, which includes a geyser and a Wishing Tree, where people leave notes.

Wilbur has a long history as a hot-springs retreat, dating to when the Wintun Nation used it as a healing ground. Legend has it that in 1863 Gen. John Bidwell had a man fall ill while mining for gold nearby, and the stricken worker was cured by soaking in the waters. Throughout the mid- to late 1800s, the area thrived as a resort, the first owner being Ezekiel

Wilbur in 1864. But by the turn of the century, Wilbur had seen better days and, by the time Miller entered the scene, the resort was run-down.

A doctor of clinical psychology, Miller in the mid-1960s left a teaching post at the University of Michigan to relocate to San Francisco and open a practice based on gestalt therapy. Along the way, he experienced hot springs on a trip to the Esalen Institute in Big Sur and became an avid student of the use of mineral baths for medicinal purposes. He searched for a hot springs of his own, venturing north from San Francisco, and found that Wilbur and Harbin were both for sale.

He chose Wilbur.

"Because of the water," he said. "In all the world, there's no waters like these. It may be the most medicinal water on the planet. The other places around are great, but they're basically just hot water."

According to U.S. Geological Survey reports, the water here is thus: 390 parts per million of sulfate, which has been used as an antibiotic; 9,810 ppm of sodium chloride, used by some to treat arthritis; and, of course, the 8 ppm of lithium, the powerful psychiatric compound long used to treat patients with bipolar disorder or depression. Wilbur's lithium levels may be low, but potent enough, Miller says, to serve as a mood stabilizer, entering the system transdermally (i.e., by soaking in the water).

Several studies gauging the therapeutic effects of balneotherapy have found that "balneotherapy may be truly associated with improvement in several rheumatological diseases. However, existing research is not sufficiently strong to draw firm conclusions."

Miller, however, tells those skeptical of the healing power of hot springs to look at his results, which he has presented at meetings of the American Psychological Association, among other groups. He offers compelling anecdotal evidence of Wilbur's healing properties.

In fact, during the height of recreational cocaine use in the early 1980s, Miller started a program called Cokenders Alcohol and Drug Program, treating addicted patients at Wilbur via talk therapy and the lithium-infused water. Miller said that in 10 years he successfully treated 1,500 patients addicted to cocaine, heroin and alcohol without a single one having to be hospitalized or placed in traditional drug rehabilitation facilities. (He still treats addicts, but at his private practice in Fort Bragg, not exclusively at Wilbur.)

Back then, it was an interesting time at the hot springs, especially that one week a month he'd close the resort to regular visitors in order to treat addicts from all walks of life.

"Doctors and lawyers, CIA, Navy SEALs, plumbers, electricians, garbage delivery guys, dealers—everybody," he said, voice rising. "I'm not exaggerating, OK? The dealers in those days, they'd show up in a $20,000 Rolex watch. You know those guys. None of our rooms had locks. Somebody could've come in and stole a Rolex. We never had one theft in 10 years from these addicts. I attribute that to the place. I had a guy show up here—no exaggeration—he showed up from Texas in a stretch limo. He had a trunk full of drugs. . . . Some of them were (initially) resistant, but within three days, four days, they were all different people. It's the water—and a lot of love. I come from a place of love in my treatment. This isn't phony love. This is the real McCoy."

He paused, finally, to take a breath, then spoke softer: "My life is about health. And Wilbur is an expression of my work. This is a health center. For me, Wilbur is a pioneering HMO. It's where people come for prevention and cure. So to not (rebuild) Wilbur would be like cutting off my arm. I couldn't not do it."

Sometimes, though, it's not so much the burbling water but its alchemic mixture (i.e., mud) that purported healing properties. Which is why I found myself at my third hot-springs stop, Indian Springs in Calistoga, staring into a black vat of bubbling sludge.

Fernando, the burly yet kindhearted mud bath attendant, helped ease me into the tub, which had the consistency of thick paste. Then he snapped on latex gloves, wiggled his fingers and started shoveling volcanic ash, heated with mineral water, onto my supine frame, first the chest, then the tender midsection, lastly the arms, legs, feet and neck.

Gradually, I sank deeper into the blackness, maybe 5 inches down. No steam rose, but the heat was intense and immediate. The mud felt as heavy on my chest as if wearing a lead X-ray vest. Rivulets of sweat poured from my face, the only unsubmerged part of my body. My heart beat with the frequency and ferocity of Charlie Watts banging away on "Paint It Black."

"We usually go 10 to 12 minutes," Fernando said. "I'll come back and check up."

Either five minutes or an eternity passed before Fernando reappeared, asking, "Would you like a cold washcloth on your brow?"

At the eight-minute mark, Fernando made another foray, as your correspondent breathed evenly through open mouth to quell his rising blood pressure.

"Want to get out?"

A curt nod, and I was back on my feet, a little wobbly and coated in tar-black mud like a vegetable having been dipped in a fondue pot. After showering, a rigorous exercise in itself, I was led by Fernando to a pleasantly warm mineral bath for a 15-minute soak. Fernando placed two cups of cucumber-infused ice water for me to sip. I drank one cup and poured the other over my head.

In no time, it was back to the intense heat: five minutes in the steam room, where my heart went on another long drum solo. That was followed by yet another cold shower. Finally, Fernando led me, now totally wrung out, into a private room. There, I was wrapped in high-thread-count sheets, had cucumber slices and a cold washcloth placed over my eyes and was left to nap for 15 minutes.

Rest was needed. Later, out at the pool, I compared volcanic mud bath battle stories with others lounging around.

"I did the mud bath last time I was here," said Greg Stemler of Oakland, honeymooning this time with his bride, Liza. "I was there until they forced me to get out of the mud. I was blissed out. I like mud."

But Bill Kirkham of Belmont said he was a one-time-only mud bather.

"I'm not claustrophobic, but it was not a pleasurable experience," he said.

Pleasure could be found in the Indian Springs pool, a gorgeous white Mission Revival–style structure built in 1913. The water, 92 degrees, was just right for mother and daughter Virginia and Katherine Houston of Falls Church, Va., and friend Mari Metcalf of Kensington.

"The sign here should say, 'Floating Only,'" said Virginia, "because that's all anyone does here."

"No one's doing laps, no one's even trying to move. You veg out," Katherine added.

Metcalf, who calls herself a "pool aficionado," rates Indian Springs among the best she's encountered.

"I love the vegetation (palm trees, cacti) and architecture (Mission) and the whole retro feel.

"And the water is swimming-pool nirvana."

Calistoga may be the place for monied Bay Area techies to visit and drop some major coin, but the neo-hippie burg of Ukiah features the hot springs that have lured the famous.

The billboard on Highway 101 heading into Ukiah features a photo of a raffish Jack London, posthumously endorsing the healing, carbonated "champagne" waters of Vichy Springs.

Jack, apparently, was not alone among celebrities drawn to Vichy, named after the original carbonated mineral spring in France. Everyone from Mark Twain to Teddy Roosevelt to Bo Derek to Clint Eastwood to Nancy Pelosi have "taken the waters" here. (All, presumably, wore swimsuits. I don't want to picture either Pelosi or Eastwood in the buff.)

Little wonder, then, why Vichy, 150 years old, has earned California Landmark status. While the landscaping and grounds have changed, the 90-degree mineral baths themselves remain the same as when they were built in the 1850s.

"You pull out the pipe (in the tub) at this end for the water to rush in and plug the pipe in on that end to keep it in," said a woman named Angela ("I never give my last name to anyone"), a Vichy employee. "They work exactly the same as they always have; they've only been repaired twice in 155 years."

Vichy has two pools—a mineral swimming pool at 72 degrees, a hot pool at 104 degrees—and a long line of mineral baths, some hidden behind walls, some exposed to the elements.

Guests Terry and Marie Kent of Redwood City had wanted to visit Vichy for a long time because its carbonated water makes it unique among California hot springs.

"We sat out and soaked and watched the full moon come up," Terry said. "It's pretty romantic, and we've been married 42 years."

Vichy, as with the other hot springs, offers massages and facials and features hiking trails. But its selling point, without question, is its bubbly baths.

I eased into the fizzing depths of the outdoor tub on an unusually warm early-October morning. As the bubbles coalesced around my newly pliant frame after three days submerged in four sites, I reflected on what Mark Twain might've quipped about taking the waters.

If ol' Sam Clemens had found golf "a good walk spoiled," perhaps he would've dubbed hot springs an "ordinary bath made delightful."

Flagellation for Fun and Health

July 2014
City: San Francisco
City sector: Bayview/Hunter's Point
New Age Vibes: Sprouting like tree branches

Sure, you can hie off to some bucolic locale for pampering body treatment at some woefully pricey spa. But if you live in the city and are hardened to an urban milieu, nothing perks you up like a little mortification of the flesh, a bout of flagellation using bundles of tree branches, administered by a guy named Alex from Belarus.

That is, if you're into that sort of thing.

I know what you're thinking: Oh, no, not another kinky, only-in-San Francisco "activity" undertaken by consenting adults and best kept private.

But it's not like that at all. Really.

Sure, I'm lying, naked and prone and sweating profusely, in a 185-degree Russian sauna, while Alex wails on my bloated carcass with oak twigs like the bass drummer in a marching band. (Check that: I am wearing something, a jaunty felt "banya" hat shaped somewhat like a Shriner's fez, sans tassel.) Sure, I'll be following up this Dantean circle of hell by taking a plunge into a vat of icy water, 45 degrees and dropping. Sure, I'm also being soaked to the tune of $60 for the privilege.

But this ritual is entirely for my health—strictly diagnostic, folks, akin to a 50,000-mile car tune-up—not something partaken for lascivious gratification. So get your mind out of the gutter, will you?

The procedure is called venik platza, a staple of Russian and East Slavic saunas (banyas) since about A.D. 900, and its health benefits have been touted by everyone from Ivan the Terrible to Vladimir Putin. Google it, people; this form of therapy is on the up-and-up.

Until 2012, San Francisco had been sadly banya-less, unconscionable for a city that prides itself on diversity—not to mention whipping people for fun and profit. But a Russian expat, Mikhail Brodsky, president and rector of Oakland's Lincoln University, finally ended the banya drought by opening Archimedes Banya in India Basin, making a bit of a splash in a milieu that embraces trendiness like a wool sock attracts static cling.

Initially, I shied from the banya, just as I have Westernized "spas," since sitting around naked and sweating in front of people is not exactly my idea of relaxation. But several friends, long-distance runners, have touted the effectiveness of the banya's venik platza therapy, saying their trail-weary legs felt revitalized after a session or two of being pounded by a bundle of oak, or birch, or eucalyptus—your choice. Their proselytizing reminded me of an old joke. Question: "Why do you hit yourself over the head with a hammer?" Answer: "Because it feels so good when I stop."

Now, runners often are attracted to quirky, quackish things (remember that whole Vibram FiveFingers craze?), but this sounded just strange enough that I had to bury my preconceptions and branch out, as it were.

So, there I sat on a bench outside the sauna at the appointed hour, wearing just a terry-cloth robe, waiting patiently to get beaten.

In came Alex, cradling two bunches of branches in the crook of his right arm. He was not at all the burly, hirsute "Borat"-type character I envisioned. Tall and wiry, with sympathetic brown eyes, he went to a basin and turned on steaming water into a tub, then immersed both venik bundles.

He then turned and gave me a quick appraisal.

"You sure you want to do platza?" he asked with a heavy Slavic accent.

I nodded.

"You sure?"

Three times he asked me that. Three times, I swallowed hard and said, "Yup."

Once assured I was game, he said that the venik needed to "steep" in the water for 20 minutes, "like tea for your whole body," and that I should do several intervals in the sauna room "for as long as you can stand it" to acclimate myself to the heat, since the treatment would last 15 steamy minutes.

Stupid me, I hustled over to the Finnish dry steam sauna, set at 220 degrees. The longest I could last in there was four minutes, sweat cascading off my body and my lungs feeling singed, before I exited and gulped water. I had no idea how I'd last 15 minutes of Alex's lashing and thrashing. It turned out, I was acclimating in the wrong sauna. I needed to be in the Russian sauna, a comparatively mild 185 degrees.

Once the leaves were thoroughly steeped, Alex led me to the banya, added some water to increase the steam and had me lie face-down.

"We start now," he said, sounding bored.

I could hear the shaking of leaves, like so much wind through a forest, then the steady drip-drip-drip of hot water on my shoulder, my back, my ass, my hamstrings and calves, even the bottom of my feet.

That was followed by a vigorous brushing of my skin—not swatting, more like pushing a whisk broom along a floor—with the softened oak leaves, starting this time at the arches of my feet and steadily rising until every exposed inch of my epidermis was exfoliated.

Then the intensity increased. The twigs came down harder but not painfully so. It was as if Alex was tenderizing a steak with syncopated thwacks, each stirring the hot air so that my pores were as wide open and flowing as the American River. That lasted all of a minute or two before he rested both venik bundles on my hamstrings and pressed down, hard, as if trying to drain every drop from a Lipton tea bag. That compression, radiating heat deep beneath my skin, moved to the small of my back then up to my shoulder blades.

"Turn over, please."

Like a burger being flipped on the grill, I turned, and Alex repeated the procedure. He didn't miss a patch of skin or a crevice, I'll have you know. I had been feeling a little light-headed throughout, but nothing serious, until Alex began the compression with the bundles around my clavicle and, yes, my throat. It loosened my shoulders, all right, but also briefly gave me the sensation of being strangled.

"Now we go to the cold plunge," he said.

I rose and followed him out. The wooden bench was strewn with shredded oak leaves and broken-off twigs. I put my banya hat on a peg and flung myself into the tub.

"Make sure you get head immersed," he added. "Very important to get your whole body in cold water."

Down I went, the transition from hot to cold bracing and eye-popping. My heart rate soared, my blood vessels constricted. I felt I had mainlined cocaine, with an epinephrine chaser.

When I emerged, Alex smiled.

"How do you feel?"

"G-g-good."

Later, I asked him to explain what he'd done.

"The treatment you got was oak branches," he said. "They are better at manipulating the skin. Thus, they are better for warming up particular parts of the body, like joints, muscles, back or whatever problem areas you have. The therapeutic effect is that it makes all the liquid in your body move and helps the joints. Also, if you work out and have lactic acid in your muscles, the hot temperature and the branches help dissolve or decrease that.

"So people who do a lot of sports come here for that. It reduces muscle pain and inflammation. Your joints wear out eventually, but this treatment allows you to heat them up and they expand a little and regain their natural shape."

I was too tired at this point to ask him about blind, peer-reviewed studies proving platza's benefits. I just nodded and kept listening.

"The other effect is on the cardiovascular system," he added. "The whole thing about warming up and then going in the cold water right away is for your cardio system. I tell people this is more like a skydiving experience than a 'spa' experience. It's intense but in a controlled environment."

Recovering a bit, I asked him about his wicked-fast wrist action with the venik.

"I kind of make a slightly beating motion," he said. "But not really beating. More like massage. A lot of Russians, actually, do the treatment wrong. They actually beat the hell out of you. Even though the treatment is Russian, many don't do it right. I'm from Belarus. I know the proper way with leaves."

I took my leave shortly thereafter. And I did feel better, invigorated. Why?

Because it felt so good when Alex stopped.

Perception Is Everything

May 2015
City: Jacumba Hot Springs
County: San Diego
New Age Vibes: Orgasmic

Sunlight glints off an object deep in the desert, brilliant in the stone-washed-denim hue of the afternoon sky in the border town of Jacumba. You are compelled to follow, lured by curiosity and some inchoate force moving you ever forward. When you reach the terminus of Railroad Street, literally the end of the road and the resumption of the vast and unforgiving high desert terrain, the object comes into clearer view. It is a pyramid, maybe 20 feet tall, and looks to be constructed of metal, maybe aluminum.

You can't get closer because a locked gate, adorned with wrought-iron sculptures, blocks the way. To your right is the abandoned husk of Jacumba's former train station, railroad cars in disrepair lined up with nowhere left to go. To your left is a caboose with a hand-painted sign hammered onto the wooden door. It reads: "Private Property. Institute of Perception."

This only heightens your curiosity. Poke your head around the caboose, and you see a sprawling, nicely appointed ranch house ringed by a few corrugated tin buildings and more railroad cars, painted with care by graffiti artists, petroglyphs for the 21st century.

Just then a tall, crane-like figure intrudes upon your blatant snooping. His long silver mane is harnessed in a brown bandana, which whips in the 15 mph wind. He is dressed in colors that hew to the landscape, pale green coat, black shirt, faded jeans. He is not smiling, but his facial hair—two ends of a mustache hanging like parentheses around his mouth, a soul patch segueing into a goatee with long gray tail—makes it seem as if he is.

"May I help you?"

A deep, rich voice. Welcoming, not intimidating.

You explain your attraction to the glint that is the pyramid and openly express interest behind the anointed "Institute of Perception," and here it comes now, a smile and a proffered hand.

"I'm Kirk," he said. "It's OK. We like visitors."

Kirk Roberts, aka Q, shows off the supposed sacred ground of the Institute of Perception, in Jacumba, a stone's throw from the Mexican border.

He is Kirk Roberts (aka Q), a musician, artist, philosopher (but then, some might argue, aren't we all?) and landowner. He and his partner, Noor, settled in Jacumba Hot Springs, the high desert oasis along the Mexican border in far eastern San Diego County, in the early 1990s, where the two along with like-minded artistic colleagues set about creating a "sacred" space for artists and seekers to ply their craft and commune with the ancient gods and goddesses whose spirits live in the very soil that Roberts says harbors a "power vortex" and mystical energy "ley lines" dating from neolithic times.

Think of the Institute of Perception as a permanent Burning Man installation, with a dash of Coachella grooving added. Kirk and Noor (they insist on first-name status) stage music and performance art festivals several times a year, the biggest being TeleMagica (30 bands, scores of artists) each spring.

You ask, again, about the pyramid and Kirk assures that will come, in time. He wants to show you the grounds. You walk three steps behind him up the prickly hillside.

Roberts has built a metallic pyramid in the supernatural vortex that he says dominates the terrain at the Institute of Perception In Jacumba.

"This goes all the way back to the Toltec days," he says, referring to the archaeological Mesoamerican culture, said to be a precursor to the Aztecs in Mexico. "We know of artifacts in the Carrizo Gorge (area around Jacumba) that are stone carvings, and the tribes that came here later did zero stone work. So they are Toltec. We protect these artifacts. I don't give out GPS coordinates.

"So, it's a sacred place. You know a guy named Wilhelm Reich? He was the originator of orgone energy and did studies of the mysteries of the orgasm. His last stop was in Jacumba. He came here because he believed the energy here was attracting flying saucers. We started the Perception center and people can walk around the grounds, a power vortex spot, and run into things like the pyramid and these hot springs tubs."

Jacumba is known for its geothermal activity, which leads to burbling mineral water hot springs, and Kirk and Noor designed a geometric alignment of hot tubs facing each direction.

"We call them dreaming tubs," Kirk says.

When he leads you to the pyramid, even shinier close up, Kirk pats his pocket. No key. He can't let you in to see the interior.

"People ask, did you do the pyramid at the exact angles and stuff? No, no, no, no. We actually put it in a place that was not a sacred node. . . . We put it in as a (psychic) weigh station, where there wasn't anything natural. It's a perceptual sculpture, first and foremost."

Near the pyramid stands a 6-foot block of concrete with a snake carved along its shaft. The Toltecs, Kirk says, believed snakes were sacred as the "guardians of the desert," and he says more than a few visiting artists here integrate shed snakeskins into works.

"One day there was (a rattler) in the pyramid and I was wondering why it was coiled right in the center in our concrete meditation area," he says. "I walked around it. It didn't care if I was there. The next day, all that was left was a perfect skin, which I then used for a piece of art."

Art pops up all over the desert hillside, ranging from works as simple as a stone circle of paintbrushes aligned like cacti with the corroded remains of a water tank that Kirk says has "amazing reverb and acoustics."

"In events such as Burning Man," he continues, "nothing endures. Here, they stay, and they make an impact."

Kirk and Noor's impact in their community of like-minded artists and mystical thinkers is huge. In addition to TeleMagica, which has drawn thousands, the couple is featured in Anthony Vega's book *Sex Dreaming: Esoteric Sexuality Revealed*, based on the teachings of philosopher Carlos Castaneda.

Monetary gains and widespread notoriety are of little concern to Kirk and Noor. They live simply on the land, consider the desert as "the place where all great spiritual seekers of the world" gravitate.

"This really is the last wild space in California," Kirk says. "When I came here, I thought, 'This is like a David Lynch town, the last place in the world to have a Starbucks.'"

Disregard, too, those "No Trespassing" signs. The locked gates, Kirk says, "are only to deal with the traffic, smugglers, dumpers and shooters preventing a peaceful area for the animals." He invites anyone to visit.

"It's a mystical experience," he says, leading you back to your car, back to prosaic civilization.

Dude, You're Fermenting in It

January 2016
City: Freestone
County: Sonoma
Population: 32
Elevation 220 feet
New Age Vibes: Steeped

Thin curls of steam rose from the tub of mulch, hovered for a moment in an ethereal mist before dissipating, yet leaving a lingering aroma. Fecund and yeasty—thankfully more redolent of a fragrant national park than an astringent taxicab air freshener—this biochemical bouillabaisse of finely milled cedar, Douglas fir, rice bran and 60 plant enzymes imported from Japan awaited my immersion.

Was I really planning to go through with this, doff my yukata robe and burrow into this vat of silage, this glorified compost heap?

You bet.

I mean, how often does a guy get to take part, intimately, in nature's fermentation process, experience its metabolic alchemy as it's happening rather than merely enjoying its result by quaffing craft beer and noshing cheese on sourdough?

Besides, I was paying $99 for Osmosis Day Spa Sanctuary's 20-minute session in the Cedar Enzyme Bath, found nowhere else in North America and considered the epitome of alternative, organic, medicinal treatments in an area, western Sonoma County, renowned for such things. So, yeah, there was no turning back.

At the pre-bath tea ceremony—an elixir of peppermint, yarrow, red clover, nettle and untold other beneficial herbs is served—my spa sherpa, Ariel Calistro, quelled my anxiety, which had been ratcheted up exponentially after filling out a three-page medical release form, by explaining the procedure and its therapeutic effects. Millions in Japan partake, apparently, to help them with everything from arthritis to lymphatic conditions, to purge one's corpus of toxins and infuse it with cedar-derived oils that baste one's short-circuited limbic system.

Or something like that. Yes, you sticklers, few peer-reviewed, double-blind, longitudinal, cohort academic studies have definitively proved the efficacy of cedar enzyme baths, but Osmosis' 30 years (300,000 served) in business attests to its popularity. A full explanation of the process and the molecular reactions, courtesy of owner Michael Stusser, would come later, post-steeping.

What I really needed from Calistro, at that moment, was reassurance. I'm no spa rookie, but I was coming off a rather unsettling bout of claus-trophobia during my last health adventure, a mud bath in Calistoga, a freak-out episode the attendants no doubt recall with hearty chortles. But Calistro poured me another cup of herbal tea and spoke soothingly.

"I've heard some negatives about the mud baths, that they are really too hot, stinky and heavy, and people feel like they're stuck," she said. "There's no actual liquid in our baths. We do add water to our material, but the material absorbs the water, and the heat is a by-product of that fermenta-tion. I'd say the heat is similar to a steam room. I've never had anyone faint on me. You can always, you know, get out early."

She left me in the tea ceremony room to mull and sip, while she prepared the bath. Placated, somewhat, I relaxed and took in the ornamental cherry and bonsai fir trees in the Zen garden.

Then she came for me. The closer we got to the door of the Cedar Enzyme Bath house, the more aromatic the air became. It reached full pungency— akin to being deep in a moist, fog-shrouded forest just after a rainfall, only more so—when you stepped in. But, by that time, other senses had taken over. I eyed the steaming pile of mulch warily but dutifully doffed the yukata and climbed the tub steps. I didn't lie so much as plopped down on the bed of russet-hued shavings, so finely ground that it could be bottled and put on a spice rack.

The mixture felt less pulpy than expected. Not exactly smooth on the skin, but not grainy, either, and there certainly was no chance of getting splinters in sensitive areas. I didn't sink into the sediment, à la the mud bath debacle, so much as hover, suspended in the stuff, like a pear wedge resting on a bed of lettuce. Calistro eschewed the rake and used her hands to spread swathes of mulch from toe to neck.

Only after she had me engulfed to just south of my Adam's apple did I notice the heat, far from oppressive but significant, and the curling wisps of steam emanating from below. I was, essentially, immobilized, my limbs encased but my digits still able to fidget, a nervous habit of mine.

When I mentioned the overpowering aroma of eau de Yosemite, Calistro's eyes widened.

"I know!" she exclaimed. "When it's fresh, like, brand new, it smells really good. You can smell it all the way in the lobby. The longer it stays in the tub, the less fragrant it becomes. But it also gets hotter. We change (the cedar) out every two weeks."

My batch, apparently, had been lying in state for just over a week, losing aroma but gaining heat. I tried to relax, as Calistro gently instructed, but I couldn't help but wonder about the buck-naked tub-goers who had preceded me, those adherents whose cleansing sweat had commingled (and, I feared, festered) with all of those plant enzymes. I calmed myself by thinking that, well, there probably were far more bacteria, fungi and bodily secretions on my hotel room bedspread than in here.

Calistro patted me down a final time, as if she had buried someone in sand on the beach, and gave me the once-over.

"Would you like more or less material anywhere?"

"No," I replied, jauntily, "I think you've got me covered."

When she didn't laugh at the pun, I added, "So to speak."

Still no reaction. Cedar Enzyme Baths are no time for levity, apparently.

"I'll be back to check on you in a few minutes."

With the requisite spa music playing, heavy on tinkling piano, muted strings and pan flute, I settled in. My brow beaded, but there was none of the flop sweat I experienced in the mud-bath-from-Hades. Though supine and staring at a wood-beamed ceiling perhaps made from the same kind of trees I was soaking in, I still could crane my neck and look at the rain beating down on the partially fogged-up window out to the Meditation Garden.

It was, in a word, soothing. More than that, the texture of the pulp friction on my body was sublime. At once rough and silky. And steamy. Really, really steamy. I closed my eyes and felt those life-giving enzymes seeping and absorbing, cell by cell, into me.

The door opened. Movement behind me. Then a cool, wet cloth daubed my unfurrowed brow, my cheekbones, my upper lip and chin. I hadn't been aware how much I'd been sweating until the sweat excreted in a wave after the water evaporated. Calistro offered sips of water—stainless-steel straw, a nice touch—but I, in a fit of misplaced machismo, waved it off. Well, not waved, since my arms were out of service, but shook my head.

At the halfway point of treatment, she returned. This time, she rang out the damp cloth and drizzled cool water over my head. I was so heated by that point that I was surprised my scalp didn't sizzle. This time, I accepted the water. She asked if I needed any adjustments, then slipped out once more.

I nearly fell asleep after that—and I am not a midday napper. That's a testament to the bath's Xanax-like effect.

Getting out of the tub, once the pan flutes went silent and my 20 minutes were up, was a trip in itself. I hoisted up my arms and legs, not unlike the world's most awkward butterfly emerging from a chrysalis, and looked with astonishment at my limbs and torso.

I had been breaded, like a veal cutlet!

A scrim of rutilant grit adorned every inch of me. Calistro was kind enough to take a whisk broom and wipe off my back, leaving the rest to me. Fortunately, the showerhead was the detachable kind, good for those hard-to-reach places. During the 30-minute decompression session on the "sound therapy" table, my mind pinged with questions about the Cedar Enzyme Bath, queries not silenced by more pan-flute music.

All would be revealed, in due time, when I would chat up Stusser.

An organic gardener and farmer by training—he helped start the organic farming course of study at UC Santa Cruz—Stusser said he "discovered" Cedar Enzyme Bath therapy on a trip to Japan more than 30 years ago. It helped ease his severe sciatica when "other healing modalities" had failed even to make a dent.

"It was a huge physiological change that relieved me from severe pain," he said. "But it was also a life-changing, if you will, spiritual experience."

When I asked about specific therapeutic benefits, he prefaced by saying: "I'm not a medical professional, but . . . first and foremost, it's relaxing. 'Relax' is a pretty simple word with a simple meaning, yet to really relax is not so easy, given what's going on in our culture right now."

As for specifics of the therapy?

"You get that profound level of relief because heat is generated biologically," he said. "It's warming up through this fundamental impulse in biology called fermentation. Fermentation is the mother of all enzymatic activity. What is known in science is that enzymes are the catalytic force in all change in living tissue. They are mostly known to help digestion, but they conduct a whole symphony of functions from the exchange of oxygen from the lining of the lungs into the bloodstream and the whole movement of energy through your nervous system.

"When you get immersed in a fermenting medium, there's a huge symbiotic effect of so many biological activities within the body. . . . There's also the benefit of heat therapy and aroma therapy, as well. Also, the (cedar mixture) releases fundamental oils used by aboriginal cultures for thousands of years for purification rites. This is like a full-body compress of an essential-oil treatment."

He was getting too science-y for my cedar-addled brain, so I asked where Osmosis gets its pulp.

"Oregon. The most fragrant cedar in the world," he said. "From a special mill. This is a type of cedar that only grows in one small area of Oregon (Port Orford). We had to look high and low to find it. It's almost identical to the type of wood they use in Japan called hinoki. We have a warehouse, and we get shipments once a quarter. We have an industrial facility where we regrind all the wood fibers down to a softer texture and use an industrial food mixer to blend the material together."

Stusser said the "biological catalyst" enzyme to propel the fermentation of the mixture—akin to the "starter" culture for sourdough bread—comes from Japan.

Stusser would like to say that people flock to Freestone primarily for the Cedar Enzyme Bath, but he admitted the essentially one-street town sort of specializes in a certain biologic process. There's the wildly popular Wild Flour Bread Bakery, Freestone Artisan Cheese and Joseph Phelps Vineyards.

"We're actually a kind of a fermentation village," Stusser said. "We've got the wine, bread, cheese and the Cedar Enzyme (Bath). You could call Freestone the fermentation destination."

Ojai: Valley of the Shadow of Depth

January 2016
City: Ojai
County: Ventura
Population: 7,461
Elevation: 745 feet
New Age Vibe: Saturated

Smitten scribes come to this valley bearing the same handy toolbox brimming with snazzy participles (nestled, carved, tucked), nifty adjectives (verdant, fecund, efflorescent), vague New Agey precepts (centering, balancing, energy vortex) and sparkly Hollywood name-checks (John and Yoko, Channing Tatum, Emily Blunt), and think, OK, good enough, they've got Ojai pegged.

And maybe they do. Who am I, a nascent truth seeker making a first foray into this valley of the shadow of depth, to judge? Maybe Ojai is the one place that truly transcends all hackneyed tropes, where the populace really is as warm as the summer temperature, the vibe as chill as a winter morning, the intense spiritual aura a balm to troubled consciousness. Maybe all that's been penned about—writers also are seemingly required to note that the valley was cinematically used as Shangri-La in Frank Capra's 1937 film, *Lost Horizon*—not only makes for a good story but is dead-on accurate.

To find out, perhaps I would have to shed my well-worn satchel of "isms" (skepticism, cynicism, hard-nosed journalism) at the city limits and open myself to the full Ojai experience, submit to its particular set of "isms" (esotericism, utopianism, veganism), supplicate myself humbly before the altar of crystalline goodness.

I vowed to embrace what's been called the Ojai gestalt—even though I thought "gestalt" was something you said after a person sneezed—and edify myself to the dogmatically undogmatic teachings of early 20th-century thinker Krishnamurti, who encamped on an Ojai hillside that now houses the Pepper Tree Retreat ("an oasis for the mind") and nonprofit center that includes a library, a medicinal herb garden and a meeting space for the Krishnamurti Foundation of America.

Ojai, in the hills north west of Southern California, has a reputation as a New Age mecca, and thousands annually flock to the Krishnamurti Foundation of America retreat.

I promised to put my overheated brainpan on simmer and partake in a group meditation at the aptly named Meditation Mount, a 32-acre "sacred place in service to humanity" that affords even more mind-blowing views of the stitched citrus orchards and oak-studded hills in the valley below.

I would call upon the better angels of my nature, literally, by getting an Angel Reading from one of the area's most renowned and respected clairvoyants (yes, their numbers rank in the low tens), who, channeling one's personal guardian angels, offers insight into the big, existential questions of life and also helps one find parking spaces in crowded lots.

I pledged to lie on a padded table and experience the "laying on of hands" that is Chakra Clearing, which, like some uber-powerful USB cable, would recharge my system, clear all seven of my misaligned chakras and leave me full of energy, if empty of wallet.

I would experience, if only in my mind (or third eye), the uniquely Ojaiian "Pink Moment"—what locals call the sunset over the Topatopa Mountains—even though January clouds enshrouded the hilltops and the forecast called for flash floods.

I would dine at Yelp-popular temples of organic, locally sourced, shade-grown, free-range veganism, Farmer and the Cook and the aptly named Hip Vegan Cafe. I would shop at the multitude of artisan boutiques selling wares such as Energy Muse Jewelry and Voodoo candles ranging from Recover Lost Money to Jinx Remover. I would learn about Ojai's evolution—from a sacred site to 19th-century writer/huckster/entrepreneur's health-spa gambit to the city's present incarnation as soul-nurturing oasis of calm—at the history museum downtown.

And I professed to keep an open mind and let the ethereal Ojai-ness of it all envelop my senses. That last piece of advice came from Ojai native Barbara Wahl, chatting amiably in the aisles of Soul Centered: Metaphysical Shoppe & Event Center.

"People are drawn to Ojai without even realizing why," Wahl said. "There's a calmness in the valley. A friendliness. What I call an old energy. It's hard to explain."

Explanations were forthcoming from Sandy Jones, proprietor of Celestial Song Mystical Emporium and author of *Barefoot at Heart: The Alchemy of Love and the Power of Light*.

"They say that there's a sort of vortex," she said. "Somebody told me that this is the only valley in California—now, I don't know if it's true, but I feel it could be—that runs east to west, not north to south. That has to mean something."

Don't know. Could be. One way to find out.

I girded myself for the Ojai Experience.

The Krishnamurti Dialogues

I want to be alone.
—Greta Garbo

Yeah, Garbo stayed at the sprawling 11 acres of the Krishnamurti center—so did such diverse luminaries as Jackson Pollock, Igor Stravinsky, Jonas Salk and Aldous Huxley—and, given her famous movie line, doesn't it serve as the perfect blurb for a retreat?

Me? I chose the D.H. Lawrence room at the Pepper Tree. And even after caretaker Anat Dagan shot down my illusions by telling me that Lawrence never slept in this actual room, with Lady Chatterley or anyone else for that matter, I still was impressed by the spartan twin bed and spare wooden writing desk. The room was right off the main salon, which had shelves lined with Krishnamurti's writings and DVDs of his lectures. I made the mistake of asking Dagan if many of Krishnamurti adherents come to the retreat as a pilgrimage.

"With Krishnamurti, there are no adherents or teachers; we all learn together," she said. "But it is my belief—and that doesn't make anyone else's less valid—but my belief this is the most peaceful, sacred place in Ojai. You just feel it."

I arrived too late to visit the Krishnamurti Library, but Dagan told me I was in luck, that the weekly two-hour "Krishnamurti Dialogue" would be held in the office at 7 p.m. "There's no guarantee how it'll go because it's, like, dynamic," Dagan said. "But I'm sure they'll accept you."

That gave me an hour to bone up on the anti-philosophic philosophy of a man, native of India, once heralded as the "World Teacher" by the Theosophical Society before renouncing all allegiance to religiosity and shedding material desires. From the 1920s to his death in 1986, he repaired to his mountaintop in Ojai—ironically, undeniably desirable real estate now—and devoted himself to his emerging philosophy that "truth is a pathless land" free of any creed other than this "emptiness" that must be cultivated within.

I cracked the spine of one Krishnamurti tome found in the salon, flipped to Chapter III, "Understanding the Self," and read this: "All human problems arise from this extraordinary complex living center which is the 'me,' and a man who would uncover its subtle ways has to be negatively aware, choicelessly observant."

Oh, I would observe, all right, at this dialogue. Don't know what I expected—maybe a room full of ascetics draped in dun-colored linen tunics, handing out paper poppies—but I was greeted warmly by 10 nonadherents around a conference table. One guy wore a San Diego Chargers hat. One woman slurped from a Nalgene bottle. Several sported bifocals. A few dressed spiffily, as if fresh from the office. One teenager rocked black high-top sneakers.

The moderator, Ivan (last names are so egocentric), passed out a passage of Krishnamurti's concerning the problem of desire, how desire inevitably leads to dissatisfaction and spiritual rot, how such constant yearning imprisons the self and turns one's mind into a "stagnant pool of the past."

Whoa. Heavy stuff. And it only got heavier. Two hours later, the conversational ball was still at full serve-and-volley, my head swiveling back and forth as at a tennis match. The briefest of excerpts:

Woman fingering necklace: "How can we survive without desire. To eat. To breathe. There has to be some kind of desire."

Ivan: "One thing David Bohm (theoretical physicist and Krishnamurti pal) said is, 'What we want out of desire is not the object itself but the state of consciousness that emerges in getting that object.'"

Man in glasses: "Do we know another way to live? It's like, I desire not to desire. Isn't that desire?"

At times, the dialogue resembled a sinsemilla-induced, college-dorm-room bull session; at other times a profound examination of the self. It finally broke up when a man in a green sweater cracked, "I desire to go home."

Meditation Mount

In retrospect, I made two rookie mistakes before I ascended to the mountaintop for my first group meditation. I drank copious quantities of caffeine—it was dawn, after all—and failed to eat breakfast.

This led to no little amount of self-consciousness and embarrassment during the 30 minutes of what was supposed to be mind-emptying peaceful, meditative mulling. I was content in the first 10 minutes, when our leader, Ron (last names are so limiting), explained how "we send out our light and love in the service to humanity" and then led us in a "quick survey" through our body and emotional makeup to get primed for relaxation and openness and compassion.

"Calm any annoyances and upsets," Ron said, "perhaps visualize a clear pool of deep water, calm on the surface, running free . . ."

No, not that. My caffeine intake was taking an inventory of my bladder at that moment, and visualizing flowing streams wasn't helping matters. Neither did the pop and sizzle of rain pounding on the roof. I had renounced desire the night before at Krishnamurti, but I would've given anything to leave the healing circle and find a bathroom, or even a bush, stat.

Then, during the 10-minute silent meditation, my stomach made itself known, and I feared its percolating gurgles would break the mellow, mind-emptying vibe. I could only hope that the rain on the roof drowned it out.

At finish, I couldn't say those three "Omms" fast enough and drive down the mountain to the Bohemia Coffee House ("Coffee, Art, Music, Enlightenment") for a bathroom and a blueberry muffin, in that order. My hunger—who knew mindful thought burned so many calories?—

didn't abate until after a hearty, if slightly cardboard-tasting, vegan burrito at Farmer and the Cook, the city's best healthy-dining option. Nothing like Swiss chard, fermented cabbage and cashew cheese to make you say, "Omm," if not "Yum."

Me and my angels

I sat face-to-face with Jenny (surname: Cothran, but, really, last names are so patriarchal), owner of Angel Touch Day Spa, in a room with crystals wedged in each corner to "keep the place grounded." She was about to rub a metal object dear to me—my wedding ring—and tell me all about my own personal angels. But I felt like a fraud, so I blurted out, "Do you have to be part of an organized religion, because I'm not religious?"

She smiled—and I have to admit the appropriate adverb was "beatifically."

"No," she said. "Me neither, on religion. Those prayers I gave you . . . you can use more like affirmations than a down-on-your-knees church thing."

She closed her eyes and fingered my gold band, rubbed it in first one palm, then the other. She spoke: "Archangel Michael, we are here today to do a reading for Sam. I ask we get clear, uninterrupted guidance and if there are any entities here that are not for our highest and best good that they are escorted from the room."

Her eyes popped open.

"Did you have questions, Sam?"

"Who are, you know, my guardian angels?"

"They hang out in a horseshoe shape around you, just behind your shoulders and sometimes up around the head. I don't actually see them, but I can get information on who they are. . . . Angels are androgynous, but they appear to humans in either male or female form because that's all we understand. I'm getting real strongly a female (angel). She says she's been with you the longest, since you were born. What is her name? She's very, um, flamboyant in a way and a little on the obnoxious side. She's telling me, 'It's not obnoxious; it's my brighter side.' I'm getting that her name is Deborah . . .

"Deborah tells me like she watched over you because there was so much craziness at home. . . . Now, I'm getting that one of your other guardian angels is Paul. Deborah seems so dominant he's in the background. He's doing this (arm wave) to get my attention. He's more a straitlaced angel, by the book, likes things done properly. Deborah seems like, she's all, 'Ta-da, I'm here, fly-by-the-seat-of-your-pants type of angel.'"

Jenny then told me about my personal relationships (none of your business, reader, but she was wrong), about my career prospects (again, none of your business, but perhaps . . .) and predicted, "I see you someday living by the water."

As a last bit of advice, she said: "You have to ask the angels for their help. They can hear your thoughts at all times. It doesn't have to be big things. I call on the parking angels all the time when I go to Santa Barbara. It's amazing. It works."

Chakra clearing

Before I stretched out on the table for my first Reiki massage and Chakra clearing, Linnea (last names are so last decade) offered reassurance in the soothing tone of a preschool teacher.

"Don't worry," she said, "you're not stealing energy from me. It's energy drawn down from the universe. Some people worry about that. I'm just the, you know . . ."

"The conductive force?" I added.

"Yes."

She explained the Seven Chakras, those spinning, internal life-force wheels in each level of your aura that affect all aspects of your being. She pointed at the crown of the head (denoting spirituality and inner beauty), then forehead (wisdom, the famous "third eye"), throat (communication), heart (love, naturally), solar plexus (self-esteem), sacrum and lower abdomen (well-being and pleasure) and pubic bone (financial and foundational independence, the "root").

I was thinking, but not saying, Wait, my "root" determines my finances? Let's just say I'm a little short on assets.

She added that if I started feeling intense heat at any of these chakra points, it's completely natural. It means the energy is flowing, is all.

I lay under a sheet to my chin, not unlike a slab in the morgue, wondering if there's a special iTunes store category for massage therapy instrumental music. Linnea sensed my restlessness and had me take deep breaths—the third time that day I'd been told to breathe deeply. She cupped her hands on my head for nearly 10 minutes and I felt a strange medicated-shampoo tingling. She moved on to my neck, but I felt—nothing. My heart—nothing. My solar plexus—slow rising heat, like a tea kettle on simmer.

When she got to the lower abdomen, my sacral chakra, I felt no heat but a rising dread that I might experience an acute state. By the time she ventured to the root chakra . . . sorry, I dissociated.

Afterward, be-robed and upright once more, I was asked if I had experienced any heat. I told Linnea of the scalp tingling ("That's the Reiki!" she exclaimed) but not so much heat elsewhere, except on my lower chest. "That's interesting because I felt it really strong," she said. "But that doesn't mean anything. I'm very sensitive to it."

I apologized. She shook her head. "That's OK because it is . . . well, life is what it is. No judgment." My judgment: They might consider inscribing that on Ojai's city limit sign.

5

California as Canvas

Art teaches us to see into things. Folk art and kitsch allow us to see outward from within things.
—Walter Benjamin

—*Kitsch is the inability to admit that shit exists.*
—Milan Kundera

Home Is Where the Art Is

November 2015
City: San Francisco
City sector: Mission District
Address: 500 Capp Street

Art and life, often barely distinguishable among those who toil in the conceptual realm, meld completely inside the lacquered walls of 500 Capp Street, where the late artist David Ireland lived and created, and created by just living.

Is that a chair, or an objet d'art? Yes.

Would that bare bulb dangling on a copper umbilical cord be an artistic statement, or a source of light? Absolutely.

Those gouges in the walls and stains from erstwhile wallpaper, do they represent an overarching theme, or just remnants from adventures in home repair? Sure.

Do the Mason jars filled with dust signify man's existential ephemerality, or are they merely examples a hoarder's pathology? You bet.

When encountering late-19th-century Edwardian-Italianate row house anchoring 20th and Capp streets, where Ireland resided from 1975 until a few years before his death in 2009, it's best to suspend judgment and slough off assumptions. Just enjoy the delicious ambiguity and inherent quirkiness from the imagination of a man who possessed both a finely cultivated aesthetic and a humorous penchant for elevating the mundane. So rare, after all, to be able to see the space of an artist just as it was during the height of creation, exquisite in its shabbiness, chic in its minimalistic design, its narrative revealed in a plenitude of small details.

At times, it almost feels downright voyeuristic, as if the viewer were intruding on something personal. Yet that's precisely the premise behind the recent opening of 500 Capp Street, to reintroduce the life and work of Ireland, whose reputation as one of the country's most renowned conceptual artists has only risen since his death, by featuring his very house as the definitive installation and distillation of his vision.

If nothing else, the David Ireland House should be celebrated as an act of preservation in the fast-changing, dot-com-fueled gentrification of San Francisco's Mission District. Mere days before the building was scheduled to go to auction in 2008—condo developers and retail owners no doubt queuing up—philanthropist and arts patron Carlie Wilmans bought it for $895,000 with the intent to conserve and restore the aging, crumbling structure to the exact way Ireland had it before he was forced to move in 2005.

Years of exacting renovation ensued—decades of grime was wiped away, shaky support beams secured, painstaking restoration of the mustard-hued walls Ireland had famously stripped of wallpaper and slathered with coats of clear polyurethane—with the goal of someday opening 500 Capp Street as a testament to Ireland's work, as well as a space to stage rotating exhibits of the 3,000 pieces he produced and, on the lower, modernized level, to feature an education center and garage gallery.

That day came in winter 2016. Tours at 500 Capp Street have drawn hundreds. It's been so popular, in fact, that tickets are sold out six months in advance. And this was just the introductory exhibit, a housewarming, if you will, showcasing the way Ireland lived and worked. A deeper delving into Ireland's oeuvre will come in the next few years, when artists, curators and Ireland's friends, such as San Francisco native Rebecca Goldfarb, present work showing his penchant for creating objects depicting flux.

What will remain on permanent display, of course, will be the house itself, where even the arrangement of furniture and placement of bookends became an artistic choice to be mulled, where Ireland's personal quirks (scrawling names and phone numbers on the walls, making plaques to "commemorate" scratches in the floorboards) inform an understanding of his work.

Far from being exploitative, this exposure of Ireland's personal space honors an artist who occasionally flung open his doors to the public and his dining room to friends in the arts, maintains Wilmans and members of the 500 Capp Street Foundation.

He believed, after all, in transparency—and not just when it comes to those lacquered walls. One of Ireland's role models was Marcel Duchamp, the so-called grandfather of conceptualism, whose portrait sits propped on a chair in Ireland's upstairs study. And it was Duchamp who once famously said, "The most interesting thing about artists is how they live."

Goldfarb, who knew Ireland well, doesn't hesitate when asked if her friend would've liked visitors tramping through his house.

"He'd be so honored, because it affirms his work," she said. "David was very mindful of how intimate this space was, so much so that some people not familiar with his work might be confused as to where the art was. But there really isn't any separation between work and life. The house is very diaristic. It's like walking into somebody's recorded events of their life."

Jessica Roux, the foundation's director of operations, flicked through her social-media feed to find a recent affirmative post that Ireland's daughter made: "He would've loved the sound of people (in the house)."

That's true, Goldfarb said. She recalled the first time she met Ireland at 500 Capp. Ireland excused himself to go to the kitchen ostensibly to make tea and stayed there a long while.

"He'd often do that," Goldfarb said, "to give people time to wander."

Docents from the San Francisco Art Institute, where Ireland earned a graduate degree, give visitors a grounding into the history of the building. It dates to 1886 and was the home and storefront for an accordion maker ("Accordions P. Greub," it still reads in gold leaf on the front window) before Ireland bought it for $50,000 in 1975.

The place, apparently, was in shambles, and Ireland methodically cleaned and rubbed and buffed. He stripped the wallpaper and paint off most walls until only the original plaster remained, then slathered on polyurethane, giving the space a distinctive glow. He wouldn't throw away much—for an artist, everything is material—and often chose to repurpose mundane objects in imaginative ways.

So a smattering of brooms the accordion maker left behind became Ireland's *Broom Collection with Boom*, in which the straw whisk brooms are arranged in a circular, tilted swirl, as if sweeping by their own accord. An island of misfit chairs became a trope throughout the house—a gravity-defying, three-legged one in a hallway; a seatless one with bound *San Francisco Chronicle* newspapers circa the Jimmy Carter era as the backing in the bedroom; and several hanging, seat-toward-wall sprouting wires or holding bare bulbs.

Common household objects served new purposes, most strikingly a pair of gas torches dangling from copper wires in the living room that, when lit, converge and retreat in a swirl of flames. The walls themselves have a stark beauty, some of the cracks so elaborate that they look almost marbleized or like ice breaking.

"The whole thing started off like any other simple home improvement project," Roux said, though noting that, with artists, nothing is ever simple. "There was this hideous brown wallpaper, really dark, when he got there. And he just started stripping. He seemed to have found more satisfaction in this process than in anything else. That's where this all started. Look here, where the backing of the wallpaper bled into the plaster. The company logo's on the back, exposing where the door had been. He liked that kind of thing."

It quickly became evident, Roux noted, that Ireland was not just cleaning; he was creating. A photo of Ireland from the late 1970s shows the stork-like 6-foot-4 artist in jeans and sneakers, donning a painter's hat on a stepladder, a tool belt around his waist, hammer dangling like a six-shooter off his hip. But what normal handyman-type of homeowner thinks to bottle and save dirt from window frames? One with an artistic sensibility, that's who.

The question must be asked, though: Was Ireland a hoarder?

Roux shook her head but conceded, "He definitely was sentimental for things. Like, he had an amazing collection of newspapers."

In the dining room cabinet sits a Mason jar bearing the remains of a birthday cake Ireland made nearly four decades ago for a friend's 90th birthday party. All that is discernible is a goopy, black blob.

"Here's a photo of Mr. Gordon blowing out the candles," Roux said, smiling. "You can see it was not a chocolate cake. I can confirm that it was a white sheet cake."

Not anymore. Ireland, the definition of eccentric, was nothing if not playful. He liked to work with industrial materials, cement being a particular favorite. He would form scoops of cement, put them in ice cream goblets and give them to dinner guests as parting gifts. Other concrete objets d'art: bookends, lamp bases, candleholders, washtubs.

Then there are his signature works, "dumbballs." Donning gloves, he would toss cement from hand-to-hand for hours until it hardened into softball-size concrete objects. They are scattered through the house, as if the artist were a kid who hadn't put away his toys.

Every household disfigurement became an opportunity for whimsy. Every wall smudge is preserved, bare footprints not sanded away. Wall gouges are seen not as mistakes to be spackled over but rather as happy accidents to be celebrated—or, at least, dutifully acknowledged.

"A safe was upstairs when David first got here," Roux said. "He tied a rope to it and tried to lower it down the stairs. It escaped once on the landing here and once on this wall. He decided to mark it with plaques: 'The safe gets away the first time, November 5, 1975' and 'The safe gets away for the second time, November 5, 1975.'"

Most pieces are not mere happenstance. Ireland thought long and hard about installations, Roux said.

When a windowpane in the upstairs living room shattered, instead of replacing it, Ireland installed a copper plate used for etching. It shut off the view, of course, but Ireland took a late-1970s-era cassette tape deck and recorded what he saw out the window for posterity. In a fast-talking voice more suitable for a TV pitchman, Ireland ran through the litany of neighborhood sights (". . . two trees, three-story apartment house, white with green trimming, red house, St. Charles Church, Bank of America, yellow house with gray roof . . ."). The tape deck sits on a table facing the blotted-out window.

Wilmans has said that she was moved to purchase the house and restore it after first encountering that installation, thinking that it would lose all context if it was crated and shipped to a museum.

Evocative as the copper window may be, Ireland seemed more interested in revealing than concealing. Yet, the more Ireland revealed, the more questions he raised.

Like, what's the deal with those names and phone numbers on the walls, forever preserved now in lacquer?

One recent day, in the midst of a tour, publicist Wendy Norris called over Roux to a wall near the dueling torch chandelier.

Norris, pointing to the name "Walter Chandler" and the date "1870" in Ireland's chicken-scratch handwriting: "You ever seen this before?"

Roux: "I missed that one!"

Norris: "I just Googled who Walter Chandler was. He was born somewhere in Portland, Maine, or maybe Mississippi. Why would David . . . ? You know anything about this?"

Roux: "No idea."

She turned to a visitor, said, "I've been here five years and emptied the house top to bottom and there's always something new I see. Never gets dull."

One Man's Castle on a Hill

July 2013
City: Cambria
County: San Luis Obispo
Population: 6,032
Elevation: 43 feet

Dynastic pretensions reside 15 miles up the coast at Hearst Castle, where that monument to capitalistic excess stands proudly amid the coastal mountain range.

Down here, where the proles dwell, lies a curious sight that many believe was constructed decades ago by the town crank as a snarky answer to the opulence on display at the mansion of newspaper magnate William Randolph Hearst.

It, too, is on a hill.

It, too, has a fancy name.

It, too, is a state landmark.

. Even without those official brown state landmark road signs to serve as a guide, you can't miss Nitt Witt Ridge, which is either Cambria's contribution to the nation's underappreciated folk-art movement or merely one man's junk-heap folly.

The man, Arthur Harold Beal, may have long since passed, but his enduring symbol of—well, no one's exactly sure what—lives on.

Nitt Witt Ridge is a four-story architectural marvel slapped together from driftwood, creek stones, metal tire rims, abalone shells, toilet seats and too many Busch beer cans to count, all held together by a concrete foundation and sheer force of will.

Beal, the town garbage man, began the project in the 1930s and still was working on it, at least conceptually, in 1992 when he died at age 96.

If it appears as though one big gust of wind—or maybe a minor temblor—would reduce Nitt Witt Ridge back to the garbage heap it once was, think again.

"It's stronger than it looks," said Michael O'Malley, standing in what passes as Nitt Witt Ridge's living room. "Eleven years ago, I had two people up here on a tour and we were inside this second level when a quake hit. Nothing happened. It surprised me. Nothing even got knocked down."

O'Malley, along with his wife, Stacey, are the proud owners of Nitt Witt Ridge—though Michael prefers the spelling "Nit Wit" but doesn't press the issue because the landmark sports the extra T's—and has since 1999. They bought the place in 1999 from a group of locals that formed the Art Beal Foundation to keep the place from getting razed.

A plumber who lives in town, O'Malley has spent years spiffing up the place, being careful not to make it too tidy lest the spirit of Beal's "vision" be tainted.

The purchase price was $42,000, and O'Malley figured he could turn the place into something of a tourist stop on Highway 1. That $42,000 did not include water rights, so the castle is uninhabitable. Still, O'Malley envisioned tourist buses stopping by to gawk at and walk amid the ruins.

"I thought of it as an anti–Hearst Castle," O'Malley said. "I paid 600 bucks to have people from the county up here. They walked through and said, 'You can make it a gallery.' But I got nothing in writing. Turns out, I couldn't. It's a residential-zoned lot."

So when O'Malley set up a table out front and started selling "Nit Wit" T-shirts, Cambria put the kibosh on the operation.

"What I am allowed to do," O'Malley said, "is give tours for 'donations,' but I can't advertise or anything. I'm OK with that. At this point, I'm not doing it for the money."

Several times a week, more often on summer weekends, curious tourists call O'Malley and ask for private tours after finding the information on the Internet. He gladly obliges.

Wearing a "Nit Wit" T-shirt he no longer can sell, O'Malley ambles through the house, marveling at the eccentricities of its builder. He shows how chrome tire rims and PVC pipe were used as pillars, rubs his palm over glimmering abalone shells and shakes his head at the sheer number of beer cans that serve as ballast for the foundation.

O'Malley never met Beal, but he's become a de facto historian as well as a curator. He says there are multiple versions of Beal's exploits, most apocryphal, but he passes along both fact and fiction and lets the visitor decide what to believe.

"He'd tell people he'd get wood out of the ocean. After big storms, planks come washing up," O'Malley said. "But look at the wood. It's nice. I think he may have collected some of it at night from the local construction sites.

"He'd told people (Hearst Castle builders) hired him to haul away stuff in this truck the first couple of years when they were building the place, and he kept the stuff for himself. Some people joked that when he was the town's garbage man, he'd pick up people's trash but never take it to the dump."

Everything had a use for Beal. He had a fondness for toilet seats. Used them as picture frames. Beer cans were used as everything from insulation to decorative wainscoting.

"While he was building the place, he'd take a coffee break every 15 minutes," O'Malley said.

But the "coffee" was really Busch beer, "which became building material," O'Malley said. "You'd think this (canopy made of cans) would collapse, but it's still here."

It's sort of eerie how O'Malley has left the dwelling almost exactly as it was when Beal lived there. Beal's clothes still hang in the closet, jars of preserves and canned goods still line the kitchen walls. Unpaid bills from the 1960s remain in drawers.

A major attraction of O'Malley's tour is Beal's ratty blue bathrobe. Word is that in his final years, Beal would wear the bathrobe—with nothing on underneath—around town. Many days, Beal would sit on a toilet seat he nailed to the balcony, and let the wind flap open the bathrobe.

"He'd size people up," O'Malley said. "If he liked you, he'd let you in. The ones he didn't, he'd start shaking his fist at them, yelling 'Move along, small change.' He built a woman's room, a guest room all pink. But that's funny: He never married and wasn't known to have a girlfriend. I don't know if any woman would be brave enough to live in this place."

Because Nitt Witt has been preserved in mid-decay, it almost seems as if Beal just went out to buy a case of Busch and will return shortly.

In fact, his voice still echoes along the hallway. O'Malley has unearthed a VHS tape of an episode of the TV show *Real People* that featured Beal in 1981. He was 81 years old at the time and sported a long beard and a walking staff. He looked a little like John Muir mixed with Dennis Hopper.

In the video, he's asked what the neighbors think of his castle. He growls, "If I'm such a nut and this is such an eyesore, why did Mrs. Rich Bitch and Mr. Stoopnagle come and move up here next to me? I was here first."

True, neighbors have come and gone over the decades, but Nitt Witt Ridge endures.

Finding Salvation in Desolation

March 2013
City: Niland
County: Imperial
Population: 1,006
Elevation: –141 feet

Drive east, and a little south, through the badlands of the desert, well beyond the washed-out pastel comfort of Palm Springs and environs. Never mind about directions. You'll know you're getting close when the stench, the briny, noxious, mouth-breathing odor, of the Salton Sea starts to appear. And you'll know, too, that you've reached your destination, Salvation Mountain, the outsize outsider art installation next to an arid, forsaken Imperial Valley curiosity with the flattering sobriquet of Slab City, when the unrelenting brown on the landscape turns Technicolor.

Here you've found Salvation, or at least the mountain so named, a three-story-tall, 100-foot-wide hillock of hand-painted stucco that blurs the line between sculpture and shrine. It has been elevated to almost fetishistic touchstone status for the religious or those who religiously follow folk art.

Cultural observers, pop and high-brow alike, have referenced Salvation Mountain, seeing it as both a metaphor for and a manifestation of temporal and metaphysical desires. Kristen Stewart asked Emile Hirsch to take a walk there in a scene from the film *Into the Wild*. Novelists as wildly disparate as William T. Vollmann and Sue Grafton have used it as set pieces. PBS's Huell Howser once gushed over it, even more than normal for him.

Too, you've probably seen photos on your friends' Instagram accounts or caught one of several documentaries about the mountain's single-minded creator, Leonard Knight, now 82 and living off-site in a nursing home. You may even recall Vollmann's spot-on description of the pious sensuality of the mountainous installation in his novel *The Royal Family*, how the mountain is "gleaming whitely like a bunch of candle-wax" and how its "colored slogans (are) bulging like breasts."

Given Salvation Mountain's cultural ubiquity, you might think you needn't bother with the onerous trip 60 miles southeast of Palm Springs to see it for yourself.

Big mistake, this thinking.

To fully grasp its strange grandeur, to soak up this brilliant palette amid the monochromatic landscape, you must make a pilgrimage.

Besides, there's a nascent sense of urgency to seek Salvation now, while it still is in good condition and while its creator, said to be in poor health, is still alive. The harsh Imperial Valley elements and the usual ravages of time have had their way on the artwork. Some of the stucco structures have chipped and crumbled, patches of the painted hillsides peeling.

Though a nonprofit group has formed recently to preserve the site, and a rotating band of Knight's disciples live in a trailer to keep a close eye on things, early signs of decay are evident, like crow's feet on a once-flawless beauty.

And whereas at its peak of popularity—around 2007, when *Into the Wild* was released—the mountain drew about 100 visitors a day, the visitors' book these days is a little thinner. Still, on a blustery December afternoon, a half-dozen tourists made the trek.

Their reactions could best be summed up by this breathy response from Milton Candil, visiting from Seattle with his friend Luciana Bermello. "I knew it was big," he said, lowering his camera, "but when I got here, I didn't know it was that big."

Candil and Bermello represent the artistic type of visitor, one who may or may not share the religious sentiments spelled out in chapter and verse on the mountain but who really visit because of an abiding fascination with folk art.

Contrast Candil and Bermello with visitor Ken Bergstedt, who drove from Chandler, Ariz., after hearing his pastor preach about the persistence, dedication and overall righteousness of the mountain and its message.

"It's off the beaten path," Bergstedt said, "but I've been wanting to come for a long time."

That sentiment is repeated many times over in the guest book in a make-shift kiosk with pages flapping in the omnipresent desert wind. The devout praise Knight for his interpretation of the Bible, and the secular note his artistic "vision" and use of color and found objects to forge something altogether original. Others, such as those who stopped on this particular day, didn't bother to check out the guest book or any of the reading about Knight's background or work. They were just mesmerized by the site itself.

Knight, by the way, never considered himself an artist or a religious figure. The story goes that Knight, a Vermont native, came to San Diego in the late 1960s and suffered a "spiritual crisis" that sent him to the desert for answers. The mountain became his answer and his life's work. He left it to others to judge the work's artistic and theological merits. And the Folk Art Society of America has, in fact, recognized Salvation Mountain as a site "worthy of preservation and protection."

A first glance can tell you that. The main "mountain" rises starkly above the valley floor. Multihued rivers and waterfalls are depicted and verdant pastures with painted flowers call for closer inspection, but it's the message that demands immediate attention. Rising from the mountain face, letters at least 10 feet tall:

GOD

IS

LOVE

Below it, written in white inside a blood-red heart, "Say Jesus I'm a sinner please come upon my body and into my heart."

On both sides of the mountain, in the foothills, as it were, are more messages, everything from a red tree of compassion to a "Love is Universal" banner.

All along, Knight encouraged people to interact with the mountain. He painted a "yellow brick road" trail up to the "summit"—partly to lead visitors into enlightenment, partly to keep the damage to the adobe facade to a minimum.

What you don't experience from photos and video of the mountain is its hidden treasures. Knight's meticulous craftsmanship is evident throughout. There are alcoves embedded in the main mountain, which Knight's adherents call "the igloo." Inside, Knight painted the walls white with religious slogans and, curiously, some decidedly secular knickknacks such as a large trophy Knight received in 1998 for being the "Niland Tomato and Sportsman's Festival Sr. King."

In the 30 years since the igloo's construction—and, especially, after *Into the Wild*—people have left offerings of their own, some personal notes scratched out on lined note paper, many driver's licenses, Visa cards, business cards and seemingly important travel documents such as the "International Youth Card" from one Samuel Metcalfe, age 19, expiring in 2014.

Exploring the igloo and other caverns gives insight into Knight's craft. He used hay bales and adobe, sprinkled with glass, to bolster the walls and free-standing columns. Close inspection of one section, an almost-psychedelic sculpture of colorful tree limbs and vines stretching 20 feet to the ceiling, shows that tires, straw and adobe keep the edifice standing. And it has remained standing, even through the periodic earthquakes that rattle the Salton Sea area.

The current caretakers of the mountain, Lucinda and Kerry Ward, have come from their native Ohio to work on the mountain and spread the Gospel of Leonard.

"It's constant upkeep," Lucinda said. "When you get up higher, it's harder to fix those areas. The sand's really taken over in a lot of spots. It's so nice here, but I don't know about July. We're kind of dreading summer, but we figured, Leonard gave the mountain 28 years so we could give it one."

Ward is certain that even when the earthy Knight moves on to a "mountain even higher," Salvation Mountain will endure.

But just to make sure, a hand-painted sign near the makeshift parking lot proclaims, "God Never Fails Salvation Mountain—Got paint?"

Cool Sculptures Make Cool Neighbors

May 2013
City: Sebastopol
County: Sonoma
Population: 7,379
Elevation: 82 feet

Florence Avenue, smack in the middle of the quaint community of Sebastopol, is one of those lovely and modest, in the word's best sense, neighborhoods where anyone in his right mind would yearn to reside.

It spans no more than 550 yards, curving and undulating only slightly, with trees and gardens framing handsome houses, and nothing so gauche as a McMansion to spoil the understated aesthetic.

Normally, you would not peg a place like this as a lure for visiting art lovers.

Yet, there they are on a weekday afternoon, four people roaming the sidewalks on both sides of the street, cameras cocked to one eye, getting just the right angle to capture the sublime beauty and cultivated quirkiness of the 20 pieces of scrap-metal art statues gracing front yards up and down the blocks.

There's the brilliantly red-haired, 7-foot-long, 6-foot-high mermaid, whose scales were once applesauce lids, reclining on the grass at 444 Florence.

There's the rabbit at 432, running late and checking his pocket watch, while his feet, made from old Electrolux vacuum cleaner bodies, are in midstride.

And, slightly farther south at 382, there are myriad installations, most notably a motorcycle-riding oil drum moose, 20 feet tall if it's an inch, with antlers made from reclaimed shovel heads and a messenger bag crafted from a dented tin box. It bears a cryptic inscription: "The Legend of Kootney Joe."

This last piece adorns the front yard of the couple responsible for turning this neighborhood into a de facto art gallery.

Sixteen years ago, husband-and-wife artists Patrick Amiot and Brigitte Laurent, natives of Montreal, moved to Sonoma County's version of

Berkeley because it seemed to have the right sensibilities. At least, Amiot sure hoped so when, shortly after closing escrow and moving to Florence Avenue, he installed a 14-foot scrap-metal fisherman, painted with vibrant primary colors by Laurent, right in the middle of his front lawn. (Amiot does the sculpting; Laurent the painting.)

The reaction, he recalls, was immediate and vociferous. Not the NIMBY rant of the suburbs, it was more YIMFY—Yes In My Front Yard.

Neighbors loved the concept and, since Amiot was working like a maniac on numerous pieces at the time, trying to establish himself in the Northern California art scene, he gladly installed some of his pieces in neighboring yards.

"At first, it wasn't so obvious for all these people to put artwork in front of their house," said Amiot, who now works out of a studio on Highway 116 instead of at home.

"It was new and it wasn't a given everyone would approve. Their front yards would become exhibit areas, and if someone wanted to buy it I'd sell it and replace it."

Soon, though, the concept took on a life of its own. Amiot started sculpting pieces that fit the interest or personality of the Florence Avenue homeowner. This took considerable time and money, considering he was doing it gratis under the caveat that if some art collector wanted to buy the work, the neighbor would have to part with it.

Looking back, Amiot said, it was a great way to get to know his neighbors, something of a bonding experience.

"Each neighbor took a little work to find their soft spot," he said. "(One neighbor) is an A's fan, so I did a ballplayer for her. I did a little profile of each neighbor and eventually found the piece that was appropriate for them. Some of them had two or three until it was just the right one."

It didn't take long for people outside the neighborhood to take notice. Amiot's creations today grace more than 200 locations in Sebastopol and the larger Santa Rosa. Some are public-art commissions, some stand in front of businesses as eye-catchers, some just are there.

With renown came attention—and people. Soon, Florence Avenue became a roadside attraction, even if the road is hardly near any highway. Strangers routinely stroll the 'hood, guys like Tom Fulton of Truckee and his buddy Ed Grant of San Jose, who brought cameras and a sense of curiosity after watching a report of Florence Avenue on PBS.

"We were headed to the (Sonoma) coast, so we had to stop," Fulton said. "This is great that this is a city where people don't go to town hall to try to get you to take down your artwork because it's diminishing their property values. You've got that everywhere else in the world."

"I just hope we're not bothering the people," Grant added.

Since it was a weekday afternoon, when many were at work, probably not.

But the owner of the home with the rabbit, Anne Lowings, said she's proud to display art in her yard.

"Actually, we love the looky-loos," Lowings said. "I work a lot in the front yard, in the garden, and I'm happy to talk to anybody about the sculpture. It brings people together. It makes you smile."

The Lowingses actually inherited the rabbit when they moved in three years ago. It was one of Amiot's original pieces and was starting to show some weathering from years on display. Still, Anne was immediately smitten.

"My husband always likes to say that we bought the white rabbit and the house came with it," she said. "When we moved in, the paint wasn't holding up so well. So Patrick came by, introduced himself and he said he'd have it redone for us. We didn't ask or anything.

"And it was quite a job to move it, too, really something to see this big rabbit being wheeled down the street. We just love this neighborhood. Most people who move here never leave here. But, you know, some people don't want them, don't like them. I guess it's not for everyone's tastes."

True, there are a dozen or so houses sans sculptures. It could be because they don't want them or just that Amiot is so busy now with commissions, including building the world's first all-recycled, solar-powered merry-go-round for a city outside Toronto.

On both counts, Amiot is almost apologetic. He laments that because of his commissioned work, he hasn't paid enough attention to the Florence Avenue pieces, many of which are at least a decade old but most not showing much wear and tear. He also feels sheepishly responsible for the crowds that sometimes assemble on the street when residents would just like to go on with their lives unobserved.

For a few years, when his two daughters were teenagers, Amiot indulged in his artistic whimsy and hosted a rave-like Halloween spectacle in front of his house. One year, it drew more than 3,000 people. He's since put the kibosh on that. Even artistic-minded neighbors have limits, apparently. (Side note: None of the Florence sculptures has ever been vandalized, not even amid the Halloween revelry.)

"(Halloween) got out of control, for a few years," he said with a head shake. "Now, I try to skip town Halloween. It's horrible now. There's this reputation. I just take my car, barricade my house and pack up, so my neighbors can't point the finger at me for causing all these people. All of my neighbors ran out of candy by 6:30. One year I bought $1,000 worth of candy and shared it with my neighbors because I felt so responsible somehow."

So what caused the Halloween stir?

"I shouldn't be talking about this, but we used to do this giant event where my house had this giant sculpture of Elvis. It was completely over the top. My kids were 14 and 15 then, and for them, having hundreds of people on the street with them cheering and dancing was an incredible rush."

Another way of making amends—even though Lowings said no one she knows on the street is irked—is that Amiot has now given all the pieces to the owners of the houses. No longer are they in jeopardy of being sold off to some smitten art browser. Amiot said that if people want one of the Florence Avenue pieces, he'll reproduce it using the same materials and Laurent's same color scheme.

"I mean, I should give it to them," he said. "Well, it's been 10 years."

He paused, laughed.

"Even if I wanted to take them away now, people'd probably get out their shotguns and stop me," he said jokingly. "I owe them a lot. It's really because of them that I've been able to make such a great living. I sell more than I can do. And if it wasn't for all these generous people who opened their front yards, that probably wouldn't have happened."

Joe Szuece, owner of Renga Arts, a studio space and sculpture gallery in Sebastopol, once told Laurent what a "brilliant marketing move it was to put pieces in people's yards."

Laurent's reply: "That wasn't a marketing move. That was desperation. They (the sculptures) were filling up our yard and house and I had to get them off the street."

"Patrick's brought the whole town together, in a way," Szuece said. "Florence Avenue was just the start."

But Florence may be finished as a space for new works. Amiot and Laurent have started working on bigger pieces, such as the merry-go-round, and have little time for more quirky characters such as the boat captain at 403, the four juggling Zucchini brothers made from trash cans at 348 or the firetruck at 413.

That's a shame for Celine Passage, who bought the house at 450 Florence two years ago. It is one of the dwellings sans sculpture, and Passage pines for one.

"I'm not optimistic," she said. "He is famous now, after all."

An Endless Backyard Art Project

February 2016
City: Palm Springs
County: Riverside
Population: 44,552
Elevation: 479 feet

Up close, you can really see the intricacy and exactitude of outsider artist Kenny Irwin Jr's work: the pink carousel made from toilets; the elephant-headed robot constructed from computer hard drives and flat-screen TVs; Clydesdales with computer monitors for hooves; the 500 ceramic John McCain gargoyle heads ringing a platform bearing a skulled Santa astride an exercise bike.

Yet, to appreciate the sweep of this art installation in a 2-acre backyard in this city's old-monied Movie Colony East neighborhood, to fully grasp the overpowering muchness of it all, you must see it from above.

So you follow the chest-length-bearded man in a gray shalwar kameez, whose pantaloons and body-length shirt billow in the breeze, up a series of wooden structures, stairs and platforms of varying heights and scale—the very works of art meant to be ogled. Irwin leads you beyond a model-train track ringing the space, higher than the hulking tonnage of looming robots constructed from all manner of found objects, climbing finally to sort of a gazebo maybe 50 feet from terra firma. Along the way, as he vaults over pillars and barriers, Irwin points out various works by name—*The Mongolian Easter Bunny's Mobile Throne, Alien Santa in a Space Sleigh With*

Ken Irwin gives a tour of his outsider art installation that has swallowed his father's backyard in Palm Springs.

Mother Goose's Shoe, Ferocious Toilet Bowl Deer, Microwav O Land—before stopping at the apex of this vision made real.

Here, from such great height, your jaw unhinges and your pupils dilate as you take in the scene in its totality.

Irwin, 41, has commandeered nearly every inch of the vast backyard of his father, Ken Irwin Sr.—save the swimming pool and a patch of grass on the west flank—for the ongoing work he calls *Robo Lights*, which draws upward of 30,000 visitors during the Christmas season, a good number around Easter and spring break and a trickle of curious types year-round.

What used to be a tennis court and a garden have long since been subsumed by robotic concoctions erected from recycled material ranging from ovens to junked cars to power tools and all manner of consumer electronics. And inside the sprawling custom home built by Ken *père*, 85, a retired real estate developer and resort owner, Kenny's more diminutive art is, piece by piece, taking over the large sunken living room with vaulted ceilings. There are resin skulls with materials such as watches, coins and

A section of the massive *Robo Lights* art installation that dominates Irwin's Palm Springs home.

costume jewelry, his ballpoint pen drawings melding Christian, Islamic and otherworldly imagery, even some conventional still lifes and ceramics.

Before descending, you take a gander at the surrounding neighborhood, dubbed the Movie Colony because, back in Hollywood's so-called golden years, the biggest stars in the business called Palm Springs home. And there, over your right shoulder, sits Twin Palms, the estate once occupied by Frank Sinatra and Ava Gardner. In fact, up and down the immaculate, palm-tree-lined streets, sprawling ranch houses sparkle in the early afternoon sun. You see two visored women stop their power walk to gaze at the artwork, and a van from the tour group Palm Springs Alive stops both in front of Sinatra's place and Kenny's.

That a display such as *Robo Lights* has alighted in Palm Springs, and not the more artistically bent Joshua Tree, may seem out of place. After all, Palm Springs is known for painting the town pastel, not red. Yet, for 30 years now, Irwin's life's work has coexisted nicely here. The city, of course, insisted on special permits, as city pencil pushers are wont. The neighbors hardly seem to mind and, in fact, they provide Kenny with materials, including a scorched paraglider once belonging to Paul Harrison, the guy across the street. Makes sense, really: Saves folks a trip to the dump.

Kenny, who still lives in his childhood bedroom (an overpowering art installation in itself), doesn't see any incongruity. He says he feels blessed that the overwhelming majority of Palm Springs citizens and tourists appreciate his efforts. Ken Sr., for his part, says he never had qualms about making his home so transformed, so public. It goes beyond just paternal love, he adds. Kenny's an artist—he's had exhibitions at the American Visionary Art Museum in Baltimore, had works displayed at the Palm Springs and Riverside art museums, made appearances on Conan O'Brien's and Oprah Winfrey's talk shows—and artists need patrons.

"He's one of the few people I've ever met, much less sired, that has that kind of incredible talent," Ken Sr. said. "I didn't 'give up' the backyard. We have a different priority. My priority was simply this: I was blessed with an exceptionally talented young man who had the energy and attitude to get it done. How could you not support that?"

"Eternally grateful" is how Kenny, not exactly the 9-to-5 working type, describes his father's support. "I mean, what would've happened if (patrons) didn't support Michelangelo or Da Vinci?" he asked.

An artistically inclined child, Kenny made elaborate drawings on the walls as a toddler, decorated his room at boarding school as a performance-art piece, and began work on *Robo Lights* at the tender age of 12. He received his formal training at the California College of the Arts in Oakland. He said he was never dissuaded by his father, never nudged to go into the family real estate business, and was always accepted for who he was.

Two decades ago, for instance, Kenny converted to Islam ("I like to say I 'reverted,' because it's always been with me"), though the rest of his family are Christian.

"Obviously, he has my blessing for his faith," the elder Irwin said. "He's one of the few people I believe has an understanding of the true meaning of that faith. We're a Christian family. I'm a Christian. But we've found Kenny personifies what I wish everyone was, whether Christian, Muslim, or whatever. He's very inclusive. He loves people."

Irwin's way of reaching people is through art. He is open and exceedingly polite, exudes an almost childlike air. Quiz him about unifying themes in his work, delve into his aesthetic, ask him to mention artistic influences, and he shakes his head. That's ascribing too much psychic baggage to his work. Mention that perhaps the world's most noted "outsider" artist, the late Noah Purifoy, has art historians and curators visiting his surviving installation about 45 minutes away outside Joshua Tree, and Irwin cocks his head in puzzlement.

"I was only recently told about Noah Purifoy," he said. "My art, really, has absolutely zero influence by other artists. There's so much force coming through me, there's no way to try to absorb what's coming through other artists. It's like, when the river is a gushing torrent, how do you put more water in it?"

What, then, informs his work? Why, for instance, his repeated use of skulls? What's up with the fixation on robots and extraterrestrials?

"Skulls?" he asks. "Who doesn't love skulls? Skulls are fun."

Irwin's main working principle is joy, to make real the vivid images that come to him unbidden in non-waking moments.

"Ever since I was born, I remembered every single dream I've had— every one," he said. "My dream memory is clearer than my daily memory. Through these dreams, I get a torrent of ideas, coupled with energy that powers my abilities to create the art on a massive scale. It's an unrelenting energy. It gives me a sense of purpose to share something wonderful with the world. My subjects deal with space exploration, sustainability, artificial intelligence and whimsical things.

"The ideas I get are crystal clear and three-dimensional—and then some—in many cases. Through the dreams, I perceive things that are impossible to perceive in this world."

In a review of his 2013 exhibition at Maryland's American Visionary Art Museum, a *Baltimore City Paper* critic called Irwin's *Sanmagnetron* Christmas sleigh featuring mounted guns and doves for ammunition "handsomely original even as they simultaneously mock and celebrate our winter holidays."

Any talk of social commentary in his works makes Irwin deftly deflect. He shows you an installation called *Microwav O Land*, in which microwave ovens cook up electronic gadgets such as iPhones, laptops and even other microwaves, and you ask if this is a commentary on mass consumption and capitalism run amok.

He scrunches his forehead and responds: "Commentary? It's a commentary about fun. The main focus is fun. There's enough of that (political) stuff in the world. I mean, look at the *Mongolian Easter Bunny's Throne* over there, or the slot-machine bot, or the *Iron Giant*, 54 feet tall and 50 tons. It brings happiness to people. I love to watch the people come by and spend time here. 'Better than Disneyland' is the most common comment I get from kids."

Still, you press. Several of the sculptures, you observe, prominently display guns.

"I take the ugly and the violent and transform it to something beautiful," he said.

If there's one overt message, it's ecological. Irwin decries waste and notes that much of our discarded electronic equipment will remain in landfills long, long, after we're gone.

"I used found objects because it helps mitigate the environmental damage caused by human waste," he said. "There are so many perfectly useful things being thrown away. The brunt of materials gets donated by neighbors, hundreds of neighbors over the years: TVs, toilets, furniture like sofas, electronics. Someone gave a broken gun to me. It ended up becoming the tail of Rudolph (the Red-Nosed Reindeer).

"I combine mediums to create installation art: painting, sculpting, drawing and carving. There's even a little welding, but the majority has been glued and screwed together. The only non-found objects I use are materials to support the structures."

Whereas many installation artists employ a team of workers to help construct, Irwin likes working solo. He does it all, from architectural mock-ups down to the gluing and painting.

"I just don't understand how other artists have other people build their art," he said. "I mean, it's my vision. Only I know how it's supposed to be."

Irwin may come across as almost an artistic-innocent, happy to create and let visitors enjoy it for free (he does ask for a small donation for electricity and upkeep during the holiday lights extravaganza), but he is not without ambition.

He envisions opening a "functional artistic" theme park, to be called Roboworld. He even has a site picked out in North Palm Springs. It's all still in the planning stages; he's not even started looking for investors.

"It'll be the next generation of amusement park," he said. "It takes the things not normally done in an amusement park and they'll, like, be done here. Like, how there's no photography. Here, I want people to photograph. I'll have cameras available to rent. When you go to amusement parks, why don't they ever have rides for the elderly or pets or the handicapped? This will have it all. Pets go tandem on rides of their own with their owners. I'll make all the rides myself. This takes a huge amount of money. It'll probably be decades before I could get it off the ground. Meanwhile, I'll still work here."

Irwin's grand plan is partly due to the fact he's running out of space in his dad's backyard. Even Michelangelo, after all, had only limited room at the Sistine Chapel. But an artist makes do with what he has, and Irwin presses on undaunted. He shakes your hand, goodbye, and returns to his work in progress, *The Tiki Ferris Wheel*, made from an old dryer and microwave ovens.

Outsider Art Master Inspires a Whole Town

April 2013
City: Joshua Tree
County: San Bernardino
Population: 7,414
Elevation: 2,700 feet

On a 7½–acre parcel about 5 miles north of Joshua Tree, where the roads cease to be paved and handsome houses give way to shacks that give way to trailers, one of Southern California's famous "outsider" artists has created a world unlike any you're bound to encounter.

It's called Noah Purifoy's Outdoor Desert Art Museum, and it's a trip. About 40 art pieces, some as small as a refrigerator, others as massive as a building, dot the landscape. From found metal, burned or decayed wood, old tires and pipes and discarded electronics, the late Purifoy built elaborate, often politically pointed, outdoor sculptures here from 1989 until his death in 2004.

His work has been exhibited at mainstream museums such as the Getty, Whitney, Oakland and California African American museums, but Purifoy had said the proper place for his sculptures is the desert, where the process of decay becomes part of the work.

Installations range from the silly to the sublime, often touching on social issues. One of his more famous works is *Kirby Express*, in which old vacuum cleaners, baby carriages, smudge pots and swamp coolers are affixed to bicycle wheels and placed upon railroad tracks. It represents, according to the Noah Purifoy Foundation, "a symbol of hope and progress for the well-to-do, built by the poor (symbolizing) lost hope and dreams."

Considering Purifoy's place in Outsider Art lore, his personal canvas is hardly venerated. If you weren't specifically looking for it, you might blow by on the highway, thinking it just another junk-filled yard along a dirt road that would just ravage your car's shock absorbers.

Stop, and you'll be disabused of such notions. You'll also be heartened that one of the late 20th century's most acclaimed artists, as set forth in his will, encourages people to tramp through what was his workspace and now is his gallery. The Noah Purifoy Foundation helps with upkeep but, really, the installations are supposed to dry and wither in the harsh desert clime. That's part of the message.

Purifoy made his name long before he decided to hole up in the Mojave Desert in the 1980s. In the 1960s, he started the Watts Tower Arts Center as a response to the Watts Riots on 1965. He moved east in order to have more room to create as well as to get away from the trendiness of the Los Angeles art scene. As Purifoy famously put it, "I do not wish to be an artist. I only wish that art enables me to be."

To that end, Purifoy's desert compound is dominated by acreage of what is called assemblage sculpture, art made from everyday, common objects—or not-so-common objects put to new, often ironic, use. The Los Angeles County Museum of Modern Art has taken notice, rotating some of Purifoy's pieces through its collection. And new pieces (well, old pieces rediscovered) make their way to the desert, as well. In 2016, a massive installation, *Unagi*, was assembled from freight train cars shaped into eels slithering across the landscape. Nothing if not an artist for the people, the foundation, per Purifoy's wishes, lets drifters squat in the freight trains for a spell.

Most of the people who visit the installation aren't looking for shelter; rather, for inspiration. Which makes it no surprise that while Purifoy's may be the most famous of the desert's art installations, it is far from the only one.

Among the pieces belonging under the umbrella organization called High Desert Test Sites is Sarah Vanderlip's piece that welded two aluminum discs together to shine like a crystal egg amid the boulders; Shari Elf's Art Queen gallery in town that features outdoor work; and the kitschy World Famous Crochet Museum inside an old Fotomat-type building.

Even some of the hotels are as much art projects as commercial dwellings. Two San Francisco exiles, Mindy Kaufman and Drew Reese, have turned a five-room motor lodge into a gorgeous throwback called Spin and Margie's Desert Hide-a-Way, with handmade tile floors and walls, as well as artwork in rooms and in the courtyard.

"We wanted it to be fun and reflect what we loved about road trips, which is fun and kind of quirky, like us," said Kaufman.

Quirkiness, it seems, blows through this town like a tumbleweed.

"Artists move here, well, maybe because it's not expensive," Elf said. "And a lot of us love having the freedom to do what we want with (our) property, do all sorts of crazy things."

Sometimes, the art pops up at you unexpectedly.

While I was driving on a dirt road way northwest of Joshua Tree, near the settlement of Pipes Canyon, my eye caught a glint in the desert. I pulled over and followed the shiny light. It was a giant orange arrow, at least 30 feet in height, pointing down into the sand. Next to it was this message, nailed to the post: "You Are Here."

Grandma's an Artist, Not a Hoarder

June 2015
City: Simi Valley
County: Ventura
Population: 126,871
Elevation: 768 feet

Can I be honest? Some outsider installations barely straddle that oh-so-thin line between art and junk. My interest, frankly, has more to do with the backstories of the artists than with any highly refined aesthetic consideration.

Which, in the case of Grandma Prisbrey's Bottle Village, is good, because, sad to say, the place is kind of a mess. Don't blame the artist, the late Tressa Prisbrey, or the devoted volunteer nonprofit foundation that maintains the grounds. It was the Northridge earthquake of 1994 that leveled many of the bottle-and-cement structures—augmented artistically and painstakingly by Grandma P. with found objects from the local dump—and reduced other works to mere shards of their former glory.

Seismic retrofitting, alas, was not in Grandma P.'s skill set.

What remains of this eccentric edifice, one woman's vision of . . . well, no one's really sure, is worth a stop in Simi Valley, best known for the Ronald Reagan Presidential Library. Tours are available by appointment and are led by a member of the nonprofit, which is fortunate, because you need context for what you're seeing. You need that backstory to fully appreciate what care and craft went into the decades-long construction, what flights of whimsy led a kindly, white-haired retiree to comb the refuse of her neighbors and to fashion elaborate mosaics and rooms from the detritus.

My guide was a board member of Preserve Bottle Village, Debbie Dennert, who unlocked the iron gate on the lot, which looks out of place sitting between a senior living center and a residential home. (Once, though, there was a turkey farm on one side of Grandma P., open space on the other.)

Dennert gladly filled me in on the backstory but acknowledged that some of the facts are in dispute. It seems that only Grandma P. really knew the motivation of her life's work, and she could be coquettish and cryptic.

Tressa Prisbrey, who died in 1988 at 92, came to California from her native Minnesota at 16 as a "child bride" to a man many decades her senior.

Grandma Tressa Prisbrey, the Simi Valley hermit who made art out of thousands of bottles at her home, may be gone, but her artwork endures.

She had six children and eventually divorced, "which was huge back then," Dennert says. She bought an empty lot at 4595 Cochran St., lived in a trailer on the property and systemically went about collecting bottles and other solid waste from the local dump to serve as ballast for her artistic vision, which would slowly emerge through her own spackle and sweat.

As you roam the grounds, try to ignore the crumbling walls and focus on the intact gems: the tile mosaics that look like playing cards; the "spring garden" made from reclaimed mattress springs; the wishing well made from deep-blue milk of magnesia bottles; the planter populated by bulbous car headlights rather than flower bulbs; the winding walkway embedded with all sorts of bric-a-brac, from automobile hood ornaments to shotgun shell casings, soda can pop-tops, a 1939 California license plate, a partially decomposed dishwasher cutlery rack and old TV tubes.

"She was totally ahead of her time in recycling, or upcycling," Dennert said. "We have people from all over the world coming here. They ask a lot of questions."

225

Most questions deal with Grandma P.'s artistic motivation. About that, several theories circulate:

1. Grandma built the first two structures just to house her ever-expanding collection of pencils—yes, pencils—and then got carried away.

2. Grandma collected all those beer bottles to, as the *Los Angeles Times* once put it, "remind the founder's husband how much he drank."

3. Grandma's affinity for gambling in Vegas inspired her work, as evidenced by sculptures of playing cards—heart, clubs, spades, diamonds.

4. Grandma's initial purpose was to build a concrete-and-bottle retaining wall to keep out the neighboring turkey smells.

5. Grandma often babysat her grandkids and needed some play structures.

All theories hold some validity, but Dennert cautions it's better just to appreciate the Bottle Village for what it is and to salute Prisbrey's octogenarian pluck in taking on such an ambitious project when many her age would've settled for a nice game of canasta while watching the afternoon soap operas.

"She once said, 'Anybody could make something with money—look at Walt Disney—but I did this without money,'" Dennert said. "I don't think she had any real (artistic plan). The dump was down here, close. And there was an auto place here where she got a lot of headlights. You can tell when she had more or less money by how thinned out she mixed the cement."

But Dennert lends credence to the theory that the turkey farm was a motivation.

"This place was really rural back then, the early '60s," she said. "It wasn't even Simi (Valley). It was Santa Susana. I do know that the very first thing she built was a bottled wall, which I think was 263 feet long and 6 feet high to keep all (the smells) out. Then she built one on the other side. But she also collected pencils. So she built her first house to store her pencil collection. She built more and more buildings, one for her doll collections and . . ."

. . . and then got carried away?

"Yes."

Before the earthquake, no fewer than 15 bottle-built structures stood. There was a "Round House," whose shape extended to the interior, with a round bed, round furniture and a pink glitter pole in the middle. There was a cabana with a palm-frond roof, and a "School House" where she entertained the grandkids while babysitting.

Much of that is rubble now—or free-standing walls with exposed bottles—but the nonprofit hopes to raise enough money via grants, school field trips, tours and donations from the folk-art community to either bolster the structures or rebuild.

"There's stuff I've never seen before every time I come here," Dennert said. "Those milk of magnesia bottles? She liked to joke around that Simi had a BM problem. She had a great sense of humor. I tell people to look her up on YouTube. There are a few videos of her from documentaries that are fascinating. She was quite a woman."

YouTube features several videos of Grandma, and she looks just the way I pictured her—fluffy, white Jiffy-Pop hair, thick, round glasses, blood-red slacks and a mischievous mien. She looked into the camera and said: "There was a man come in the other day from over there, and I was coming here about halfway and he says, 'Are you the crazy woman who built this place?' I said, 'I guess I am. I'm the only one here.'"

Tacos with a Side of Spicy Art

August 2014
City: Riverside
County: Riverside
Population: 319,504
Elevation: 827 feet

They call this vast, kiln-like stretch of Southern California the "Inland Empire," a kind of grand sobriquet for a sprawling land that snarky Los Angelenos say is "zoned for blight."

But the great thing about Riverside, the heart of the Inland Empire, is that you never know when you'll stumble upon something unexpectedly great—or, at least, interesting.

Take Tio's Tacos.

It's a family-owned restaurant in Riverside's not-as-bleak-as-you-might-think downtown, and the food itself is reason enough to exit that exhaust-choking parking lot known as the 91 Freeway. The bonus: Tio's boasts, on

Tucked away in an urban area of Riverside is Tio's Tacos, a Mexican restaurant that doubles as an art installation—the inspiration of owner Martin Sanchez.

its nearly block-long property that includes two patios and the owner's home, one of the largest and most impressive folk art assemblages this side of Joshua Tree.

Everywhere you look, there are towering figures of men and women, both anonymous and famous (Abraham Lincoln, Mother Teresa), made from found objects and topiary wire. Fountains from old pipes and tile pop up where you least expect them. Imitation palm trees rub bark with real ones. Figures made of wood, plaster, metal, tile, stone and whatever's handy loom over roofs. A Mayan temple and a chapel said to be consecrated by the Catholic Church formed from beer bottles and stucco are furnished with religious and secular totems in equal number.

From comical lucha libre mannequins to crazed Barbie dolls gone wild, from *Star Wars*–inspired robots to whacked-out unicorns that spill out into the parking lot, the whole thing is a glorious mess, a conglomeration of one man's vision and obsession. And that's just outside. The inside seating area is nearly covered with tile mosaics, fish and lobsters the dominant motif.

Wait, it gets better once you know the backstory. And, with something this lavish, there's always a backstory.

This is the work of one Martin Sanchez, 47, owner of Tio's and an immigrant success story. He grew up poor in Sahuayo, a speck of a town in the Mexican state of Michoacán, cleaning shoes as early as age 4. He came to the U.S. as a teenager, in 1984, and did whatever he could to get by, up to and including selling oranges at freeway off-ramps. He and wife Concepcion eventually started selling tacos out of a converted hot dog cart around town, hustling the lunch and dinner crowds downtown. He became a legal resident via the 1986 federal amnesty. By 1990, he opened Tio's about four blocks down Mission Inn Avenue from the Riverside Art Museum.

What adds a deeper layer to what is an inspiring tale of entrepreneurial success—poverty to prosperity, and all that—is that Sanchez embraced his artistic side and started constructing whimsical objets d'art from materials used and (ordinarily) discarded at a restaurant, detritus such as cleaning-supply cans, beer bottles, plastic cups, trays and broken plates, corks and cans and soda caps.

Call it extreme recycling, but it goes beyond just finding creative ways to avoid a hefty city trash fee. Any toys his three children outgrew or broke, any Barbie doll relegated to a shelf for too long, heck, even the clothing that could no longer be passed down, all finds its way into the art.

And it's arresting art, too, a little overpowering and lacking focus in places, but certainly a conversation piece for midweek businesspeople lunching on the front patio.

"I actually bring people here when they come to visit," said customer Lisa Erickson, of Riverside. "You gotta come on the weekends (on the back patio) and watch him work on new stuff, it's a lot of fun. Riverside is kind of known for being artsy, and this is an extension of the downtown art district. People know this place."

People beyond Riverside, too. Tio's Tacos has been featured on the MTV show *Extreme Cribs*, the late Huell Howser dropped by with his PBS crew, the Food Network taped a spot, and the big three of Spanish-language TV, Univision, Telemundo and TV Azteca, visited as well.

Sanchez's eldest daughter, Stephanie, 23, sort of the family spokesperson, said her father never expected such attention but obviously welcomes it.

She stressed, however, that her father's motivation had little to do with promoting the restaurant. The art is his way of making use of objects others might deem trash, since as one of 10 children whose father died young in Mexico, Sanchez lacked luxuries like toys and learned to make do with what he could scavenge.

"My father's vision was always to create a different unique place where people can feel out of the regular restaurant routine," she said. "The art has been popular because we believe it's very rare that someone is willing to create art with 'trash.' It's a new way to go green. . . . The attention it has been receiving, especially these past couple of years, has been a huge blessing that we are very grateful (for)."

Sanchez, in a 2007 *Press Enterprise* (Riverside) interview conducted in Spanish, said, "Sometimes, I think to myself, 'How can I throw this away when there are people in Mexico who don't even have anything?'"

For the Sanchez kids—Stephanie's two sisters, Kimberly, 19, Maiten, 8— this has meant growing up in something of a fishbowl, because the Sanchez home, resplendently painted pink, sits next to the restaurant. And, yes, the patriarch has adorned the roof and sides with all sorts of characters, including a person riding a bike (one of the girls' old bikes) off the front of the roof. People lurk with cameras snapping shots of their home as well as the grounds of the restaurant.

"It has been something that is hard to grasp for our family and friends, because we never have privacy, but we have grown up in this environment, so for my sisters and (me), that's all we know," Stephanie said.

"Many people are curious to see inside, and it's interesting because the back patio is our backyard, and many people don't know that this is our home, not just our restaurant. For that reason, we had to install a surveillance system due to people always trying to come in our house, not realizing that they were trespassing (in) our home. It's a blessing and a curse. Let's say that I have no excuse to be late to work."

A small price to pay for the sake of art, perhaps. Stephanie said the family encourages visitors and lets people pray and hold the occasional service in the chapel erected from beer and soda bottles.

"The chapel is a small way of being grateful for the things that we have been blessed to have," Stephanie said. "My mother always wanted a private place to worship in our own home, but since we live and work here, my father created that small chapel to honor her wish . . . creating it with his twist of art using nothing but recycled pieces—anything from twin bunk beds to benches (made of) broken glass."

A guest book, as at a museum or place of worship, allows people to sign and leave the Sanchezes a message. On the day I visited, the book was open to this missive from a Michelle Perez, of Puebla, Mexico: "*Me gusto este lugar. Que Dios me los bendiga.*"

Loose translation: "I like this place. God bless."

"Captain Marble": Dying Breed of Art Superhero

October 2015
City: Greenbrae
County: Marin
Population: 12,156
Elevation: 33 feet

The man's mise-en-scène may be weirder than the man, which, if you know Lee Greenberg, is saying something. His housing complex-cum-public art space he so lordly calls Rancho Shazam, located a spit wad's shot away from the Lucky Drive exit off Highway 101 in Marin County, is weirdness personified.

Scratch that. Call it eccentric, not weird.

As Greenberg eloquently points out, in this astringent New Yawka accent he hasn't shed four decades after leaving Queens, you graduate from weird to eccentric if you have a little money. I'm not certain where Greenberg got his money—impolite to ask, being a guest in his home and all—but he certainly qualifies as a Grade-A choice eccentric, a survivor of a once-flourishing breed of Bay Area junk-art artistes, now sadly shunted aside to society's margins as the region's housing market goes more upscale and its citizens more upstanding.

By whatever label, Rancho Shazam (more on the name in due time) is a head-turner and probably has been responsible for more than a few fender-benders on Highway 101. It's a two-story, two-building quasi-apartment complex made of glinting corrugated metal, set on a third of an acre crammed into a finger of land at the shore of the Corte Madera Inlet, the

Artist Lee Greenberg, aka "Captain Marble," has battled with the city of Greenbrae over his house/art project he dubs Rancho Shazam.

freeway crowding in from the west and Mount Tamalpais looming eastward. The buildings' industrial, longshoreman chic is offset by a whimsical, wacked-out array of ornamental oddities that have drawn the admiration of art lovers and the ire of the Marin County zoning department.

It would get a bit tedious to give a full accounting of the pieces that make up the oeuvre of 73-year-old Greenberg, aka Captain Marble (more on the name soon, promise), but here are some highlights:

The remnants of *Foam Henge*, a faux version of the famous druidical megalith that stood for years before county inspectors considered it a separate structure and violated code.

Mt. Pee Pee, a blushingly phallic foam tower crafted from said dismantled megalith, serving as something of a sentry leading to the 15 live-work studio apartments rented for a pittance to starving artists.

The Floating Bicycle, which, as its name implies, is a gold 10-speed strung along a wire 50 feet high between the two buildings, held aloft for a series of levers and pulleys.

The Tin Man, officially a mailbox but so much more: a junk-art version of Michelangelo's *David*, replete with a torso made from the original boiler Greenberg inherited when he moved in, a tiki-torch staff, ruby-slipper earrings, a yellow-caution-taped bandana, a heart from a See's Candies box and a sign proclaiming, "Directions: $ .05."

A *Yacht Club* on the water out back, including a deck with a fire pit, a wall where Greenberg projects movies on warm summer nights and an actual 40-foot yacht that fortunately remains forever anchored because it doesn't look at all seaworthy.

Oh, and did I mention the moat, the series of circular pool slides suspended from second-floor windows, the staircase to nowhere, the functioning hot tub on a roof, and several grappling hooks and a 12-foot wheel that, in a previous incarnation, served as a base for a boat crane?

It's all there. But Greenberg seems especially smitten with the moat, because he got into a tussle with Marin County inspectors over the addition.

"The county thought I needed a permit because they said it was taller than 18 inches," he said. "But look at it. It's sunken. It's minus-inches. They really need to read their own regulations more carefully."

But why a moat?

"You have to cross it to get to the property," he said.

But doesn't that seem too forbidding? Doesn't that go against the art-should-be-accessible ethos upon which Rancho Shazam was founded?

"No, not in the least," he said. "I just like moats. Anyone can come by and take a look at the art. I'll come out and show them around. That's one reason it's here."

To get at some of the other reasons, you need to step back from the scene and engage in a little biographic exploration.

Greenberg is happy to oblige that request, too, taking you into his inner sanctum, also known as his living room. There you are surrounded by more artistic imaginings, sandblasted whales and other marine mammals on marble and slate, paddles, propellers and wheels dangling from the ceiling, all manner of oil paintings and steel- and wood-cut sculptures, many in the form of lightning bolts. Follow him into his sleeping quarters, and on one side of his king-size bed are shelves of toy trains, ringed by a track, and on the other is a glass display of vintage toys, circa 1900.

But it's the lightning bolts that stick out. In fact, there's one dangling from Greenberg's left earlobe. It's an exact match to the bolt adorning the chest of the giant in an ornate gilt frame hanging prominently in the living room.

"You wanna know why I'm Captain Marble and this is Rancho Shazam?" he asked. "You wanna hear the genesis story? OK. I came here in 1970, left my Board of Education position in Manhattan to pursue the houseboat lifestyle in Sausalito. I was an artist working in marble and slate, so I called myself Captain Marble.

"In 1991, two years after the earthquake, this property was rubble," he continued. "It was all wet and ruined. I bought it. Built it all. By hand. I can call it a ranch because, due to a zoning anomaly, this is listed as A-2, B-2, limited agriculture. So I had chickens here. My favorite was called Shake 'n' Bake. Those chickens gave me the license to call this Rancho Shazam. Now, as you know, Shazam is what Captain Marvel uttered to change from a homeless newspaper boy to a superhero. That's my avatar."

Even getting the property dirt cheap, and even doing all the work himself, the construction of Rancho Shazam must have strained Greenberg's financial resources, especially since he says he rents out the live-work lofts below market value to promote the arts.

So you risk being impolite and ask him about money.

He beams: "People ask me, 'How'd you get to be a person of leisure?' I say, 'Well, I avoided most of the pitfalls. I never did drugs. I never got married. Never had children. Never had to give away half of anything in a divorce. I never had to send anybody to college.' The key: Don't have expensive baggage. Those drugs, they're costly. I may have been the only one I knew back then who never did drugs."

Which makes Rancho Shazam all the more remarkable.

Think about it: This surreal wonderland, this twisted Oz, was conceived and created without pharmaceutical enhancement.

6

Next Exit: The Unusual

We find after years of struggle that we don't take trips; a trip takes us.
—John Steinbeck

The worst thing about being a tourist is having other tourists recognize you as a tourist.
—Russell Banks

Flight to Nowhere

March 2015
City: Pacoima
County: Los Angeles
Population: 81,000
Elevation: 233 feet

I got to my flight with mere minutes to spare. Damn that Interstate 5 traffic; always bunches up in this part of the San Fernando Valley.

No worries, though. I wasn't at the airport. I wasn't subjected to invasive TSA body cavity searches. There were no delays or cancellations making those passengers milling around me grouse and gnash and bellow. No one charged me extra for every little thing, from baggage to the very ions in the air I breathed. Then again, I was traveling light.

From the moment I stepped into the terminal, on through the check-in process, boarding lounge wait, takeoff and cruising-altitude ascension all the way to touchdown four hours later (right on time, I might add), my every need and whim was assiduously catered to, every request indulged with a punctiliousness usually afforded only to those of royal lineage.

I'm talking hot towels, warm nuts, arctic vodka martinis, Sriracha-sizzling stewardesses whose royal blue uniforms showed off their gams, steaming Chateaubriand tenderloin carved seat-side, throat-burning Johnny Walker Red Label whiskey on overstocked libations carts, a super-cool captain whose epaulets glimmered as he glad-handed down the aisles, and just an out-and-out chill vibe.

Of course, we didn't actually go anywhere. Never even left the ground. Well, you can't have everything now, can you?

Wait, check that. We did go someplace. We were transported to the 1960s and '70s aboard a painstaking and lovingly recreated First Class and Clipper Class cabin of a Pan Am 747 that once graced the friendly skies but now sits anchored as kind of an exhumed time capsule on the lot of Air Hollywood, a sound stage in a business park in northern Los Angeles County.

Twice monthly, the Pan Am Experience takes about 30 "passengers" on a time-travel trip in which those of a certain age can relive the so-called Golden Age of air travel, and those too young to remember can see what they missed and pine for days they, alas, never experienced in the first place.

What's the appeal of dropping major coin ($345 for Clipper Class; $277 for First Class) for not moving an inch? I mean, you could actually fly, for real, from Los Angeles to Seattle for less money than four hours aboard a faux fuselage, so doesn't it qualify as a monetary extravagance, nay, an example of first-world decadence, to pay to be inert?

It's the inexorable pull of nostalgia, said Sandy Edelstein, 56, who made the two-hour drive from Palm Springs with his husband, Scott King, to relive Pan Am flights from his salad days (the airline "ceased operation," meaning it was swallowed up by United Airlines, in 1991). It also might be the prurient, *Mad Men*–type thrill of being politically incorrect and calling the faux flight attendants "stewardesses," or even the more lasciv-ious-sounding "stews," and using such archaic anatomical terms as "gams."

"Life and the world we live in today is so crazy and hurried that there's really a longing for days gone by," Edelstein said before settling into seat 1-H with a flute of champagne. "We're of an age, and we still remember it. So to have an opportunity to literally go back in time is not to be missed."

The conceptual visionary responsible, Anthony Toth, 47, he of the epaulets and brass-button captain's affectation, insists money was no motivator. Once you learn the anal-retentive extent to which Toth has gone to fabricate a Pan Am plane, circa 1971, fussing over every little detail, from the exact font for the boarding-pass envelopes to the color and texture of the fibers of the carpet, you understand his motives are purely aesthetic. The blue that pervades is not just royal blue. No, it's Pan Am Blue, he'll have you know.

"Look," said Toth, whose day job is working for an airline he prefers not to name, "this type of air travel doesn't exist anymore, and we could get into all the reasons it doesn't. But let's just say, back then, it was something really special."

(Pardon the parenthetical interruption, but a brief background digression about Toth is needed: His parents took him on a Pan Am flight to Europe at age 5 in 1971 and it "changed the entire course of my life." He admits to a lifelong obsession with aviation and its Golden Age mementos. Over the years, he bought every piece of Pan Am-branded merchandise he could find—let's just say he has industry connections—and even went to that airline graveyard in the Mojave Desert to purchase the last Pan Am 747-200 frame before it was stripped for scrap. He parked it at his home before teaming with Talaat Captan, founder of the Air Hollywood studio, and providing the "Experience.")

Even if you don't notice that the tricolored "wall carpet mural" of a clipper ship on the bulkhead is the exact design specification and synthetic blend as on a 1971 Pan Am 747 bulkhead, Toth does. And it matters. A lot.

"Every time I walked on a plane like this, I'd immediately run up to the wall and take up an entire roll of film shooting that wall," Toth said. "It just spoke to me. So when we were rebuilding this airplane, that was an absolutely 'must' to have. I took all the photos I had as a child and went to a custom carpet sculptor, and he made it for me exactly like it was."

I tried to put the next question tactfully, even though I was aboard a plane that transported me to a less politically correct era: "Are you a little obsessive-compulsive?"

"I am," he said, nodding.

"I'm just kidding," I backed off, feeling shamed.

"No," he smiled, "I *really* am."

Captan, whose vast, hangar-like studio has been used for cinematic airplane scenes ranging from *Bridesmaids* to *The Wolf of Wall Street* to the

TV show *Lost*, said he was happy to indulge Toth's vision. A preboarding "Clipper Club" lounge greets "passengers," with a check-in desk with props such as rotary phones and first-generation console desktop computers, and a wet bar featuring such '70s alcoholic mainstays as Tom Collins, Singapore Slings and Harvey Wallbangers.

"Anthony is very, very anal about every detail," Captan said, laughing. "He's a pain in the ass, actually. But in a great way. That's what makes this such a perfect experience."

Toth was gracious about the ribbing. But he turned serious, verging on misty-eyed, when expressing the joy he feels when he sees people segue into nostalgic-soaked reverie.

"My favorite moment is when people walk in and see the two steward-esses greeting them at the red carpet, to watch people's reaction, especially if they once worked for Pan Am," he said. "It's a special moment to see the brand come back to life."

Passengers are forewarned that they need to buy in to the gestalt, via an email detailing the dress code, prohibiting jeans, sneakers, T-shirts, etc., and mandating "dresses for the ladies and jackets and ties for the gentlemen." I felt right at home in the period-dress thing because the only dinner jacket I own (no exaggeration) was from 1987.

The surreality of the scene hit me crossing the threshold into the Pan Am "terminal." One minute I was walking through a parking lot in 2015 filled with Chevy Suburbans, Priuses and one Tesla toward a low-slung series of identical business-park warehouses, and the next I was greeted by a clean-cut, Up-With-People friendly young man in suit and tie standing behind the Pan Am Blue podium, adorned with the company's logo, a blue globe with parabolic curved lines. To the agent's left stood one of the six steward-esses, raven hair tucked primly under her jaunty Pan Am Blue bowler hat and white-gloved hands clasped demurely at waist level.

"Melorine will show you into the Clipper Club," he said, checking my ticket and not discernibly turning a nose up at me since I'm only First Class, not Clipper Class. She laid a gloved hand, oh so delicately, on my forearm and guided me into the darkened inner sanctum of the Clipper Club. She motioned left for check-in, right for the open bar in a fetching French accent, then turned on the 2-inch heel of her tan pumps and sashayed back to greet more arrivals.

Thirty minutes before boarding, and the drinks were flowing and the vibe felt much like an Updikean dinner-party scene, couples trolling with aggressive gaiety. I looked around for the key jar but couldn't find it. Not that kind of party, apparently. My eye was drawn to two elegant women and a distinguished-looking gentleman holding court, the nexus around which passengers orbited. All three, it turned out, were longtime Pan Am employees—Lynn Cook of Stockton and Saune Petersen of Manhattan Beach, former stewardesses; and Tom Hood, a sales executive.

I approached the women—Hood was preoccupied fumbling with his Marc Jacobs–designed iconic Pan Am tote bag—and asked about their careers as flight attendants.

"No," Petersen said. "You have to call us stewardesses. We only became flight attendants later."

I asked the gals (remember, it's a politically incorrect era) to compare and contrast air travel at present to yesteryear.

"The present is why I left," Petersen said. "It was a good run, you know, but . . . when they gave us barbecue tongs to serve with, I'm like, 'Oh, no.' We were used to spoon and fork serving (in the Golden Age). It was like, 'It's time.' I'm done."

Cook flew in from Stockton for the "flight" and groaned when commenting about the occasionally surliness and general lack of civility in today's air travel.

"That's because (airlines) pack them in tighter, and they charge for every-thing," she said. "There's nothing gracious about it anymore."

Their glance descended upon Adler, the professionally perky stew working the room while her colleagues prepped the plane for boarding.

"Look at that," Petersen said, with a sharp intake of breath. "Those are the exact same tan shoes we had!"

Passengers Phil and Anna Montejano, who drove in from Sacramento just for the flight, were chatting with Adler about her uniform. Anna asked, boldly, about whether Pan Am had a weight rule for stewardesses. Ask a flight attendant now about weight, and you're liable to get the imprint of a plastic tray across your face, but Adler merely chuckled.

"The food they serve is so good I understand why, back then, the girls were weighed all the time," said Adler, who, for the record, was petite and slim. "It's a five-course meal, and I'm sure they ate and they were flying all the time, so they might have worried about getting fat. . . . One of the girls (now) told me, 'I can't fit in my uniform anymore.' And I said, 'That's because you eat that meat all the time, you know.'"

Whoa, this really did seem a throwback conversation, to a time before body-image awareness took hold. Adler told me she is an actress, as are many of the "girls," and they really get into the part.

"In the beginning, wearing this outfit, we looked at each other and said, this is kind of funny," Adler said. "Then, we're like, 'OK, we're in the '70s, baby!' When we put the uniform on, we really believe it. We even . . ."

The passengers were called to board before Adler could finish. People boarded carrying their cocktails (to hell with that TSA-mandated 3.4-ounce maximum). Frank Sinatra was warbling "Fly Me to the Moon" as people found their spots, the uber-jet-setters taking the corkscrew staircase upstairs, the rest of us making do with wide "sleeperette" seats with manual footrests. The legroom was huge, ridiculously so, at least 3 feet. To reach the in-flight magazine (yes, period-specific) in the seat back in front of you, you had to scooch almost out of your seat.

All night, except when flight announcements were made or sound effects such as "turbulence" intervened, easy-listening muzak played: Mantovani's "Smoke Gets in Your Eyes"; "The Look of Love," by Dusty Springfield; "Strangers in the Night," Sinatra; Connie Francis' rendition of "Danke Schoen"; Sinatra again with "It's Nice To Go Travelin." This last song, seemingly played in a loop every 15 minutes, featured the lyrics, "It's very nice to just wander / The camel route to Iraq . . ." Oh, how we long for the days when we heard about Iraq only in terms of exotic travel adventures.

The food service, too, harkened to simpler times, back when few considered red meat an artery clogger, and passengers blithely powered down foods of gout-inducing richness. The high intake of alcohol consumption was offset, somewhat, by the five-course meal. Highlights: jumbo shrimp cocktail on endive, asparagus so fresh it could've been helivacced in from Bakersfield that very afternoon, chocolate cake that almost brought on sucrose toxicity. If this is the first-class fare, I wondered, what must they be dining on upstairs in Clipper Class, foie gras and beluga caviar?

All this pampering quickly went to my head. Maybe it was just that third shot of Claude Chatelier cognac, but I could've sworn there was a hint of flirtation evident when stewardess Tammy Munro lowered a basket of rolls toward me and asked, with a 400-watt smile, "Can I interest you in a hot bun, sir?"

It turned out, darn my luck, that Munro just had a wry sense of humor. When she was carving a generous slab of Chateaubriand for the man in front of me, she quipped, "That piece of beef is actually from one of our original Pan Am flights, too, sir." When, during the comical preflight instructions, she expressed mock mortification at having to wrap her lips around a nozzle and manually inflate the flotation device, laughter filled the cabin.

Only occasionally, and always sotto voce, would a stewardess break character. A woman two rows behind me asked Holly Gray, handing out hot towels, about her pouffy blond hairdo, a veritable tonsorial helmet with a cascading front bang that resembled nothing less than a wave breaking upon shore. "Takes lots of time and hairspray," she confided. "It'll stay this way for three or four days."

Alas, I knew the sedulous service had to end. As piped-in Dionne Warwick warbled the final chorus, "What the world needs now is love sweet love," the purser, Rachel Scorpio, cut in, "Ladies and gentlemen, we're just about to land at our destination in Pacoima. We hope you enjoyed . . ."

And then the passengers rose with great difficulty, bellies distended like 9-year-olds on Halloween night, and returned to 2015.

I cannot lie: It was a difficult landing.

The Force Awakens in Petaluma

March 2016
City: Petaluma
County: Sonoma
Population: 57,941
Elevation: 30 feet

Once you leave the exhaust-choked (except for all those pricy Teslas, their electric engines haughtily humming) stretch of Highway 101 that traverses uber-wealthy Marin County, the land opens up, rolling green hills replacing garish, boxy strip malls. You almost don't want to exit the freeway, but you know that a truly otherworldly roadside attraction awaits.

Problem is, it's not exactly along the side of the road. You have to traverse through charmingly quaint downtown Petaluma, beyond the chicken farms that dot the hillsides and depend on some dubious GPS directions to find a place of George Lucasian magic and wonder called Rancho Obi-Wan.

Yes, Obi-Wan, as in the oh-so-learned *Star Wars* character Obi-Wan Kenobi. Beyond the gates of what once was a chicken farm—and still

In a converted chicken farm in Petaluma, a man named Steve Sansweet has opened Rancho Obi-Wan, a tribute to *Star Wars* with more than 500,000 objects from the movie—and counting.

retains a dozen or so cluckers just for show—visitors are treated to (or is it assaulted by?) a vertiginous volume of *Star Wars*. Trust me, this isn't just some guy's collection spilling out of his closet. This is massive. This is jaw-dropping. This is *Star Wars* nirvana.

Where to begin. OK, how about this? What say I just list a few of the more than 500,000 items—and growing, ever growing, with 2,000 cubic feet of boxes yet to be sorted—belonging to uber–*Star Wars* fanatic Steve Sansweet, and leave the rest to you? Mind you, this will not even be the rare or especially valuable memorabilia, merely a glimpse (the deep cuts, as it were) into a collection seemingly as vast as a galaxy far, far, etc., etc.

Cue the soaring John Williams score, and here we go . . .

- Darth Vader toaster
- Lock of Chewbacca's hair
- Yoda toilet paper, with the instruction: "Wipe, you will"

- Action figure of Carrie Fisher's bulldog, Gary

- Wookie IPA, craft beer, from Denmark

- Cream of Jawa soup can

- R-2 Mr. T-2, replete with Mohawk and heavy gold rope chain

- Beavis & Butt-Head stormtroopers

- CoverGirl The Force Awakens lipstick, in colors such as Droid and Dark Apprentice

- Unintentionally phallic Jar Jar Binks Candy Lollipop

- Never-released (due to safety and liability issues) Rocket-Firing Boba Fett Action Figure

- A pregnant George Lucas cast in carbonite

I'm thinking that this list, brow-raising as it is, still doesn't do Rancho Obi-Wan justice.

Doesn't begin to depict the meticulousness care, the reverence and irreverence, afforded to the *Star Wars* franchise through these trinkets. Barely sheds any light, actually, on the psychosocial influence the movies have wrought, which comes through loud and clear at a three-hour Rancho pilgrimage. Fails to fully capture the effect, deep and visceral and spiritual, these sacred celluloid objects have on visitors willing—nay, eager—to shell out $100 (mandatory $40 member fee, then $60 for a tour) for viewings that take place maybe four times a month.

Believe me when I say that when Rancho Obi-Wan adherents first laid eyes on General (née Princess) Leia's costume, or point their smartphones at the animatronic band Figrin D'an and the Modal Nodes from the Mos Eisley Cantina, or nearly genuflect at the taller-than-life-size mannequin of Darth Vader (codpiece copped from the original costume) with red light saber aglow, the joy is palpable and the fellow feeling genuine. Sequel through prequel, this collection has no equal.

The entire complex is nothing less than a labor of love brought to life by Sansweet, a mere *Wall Street Journal* reporter when the franchise began in 1977, but soon so *Star Wars* struck that he parlayed his passion into a job at Lucasfilm, first as head of "fan relations," later adding licensing to his ken. And he hoardishly retained everything *Star Wars*–related, nothing too trivial, scavenged the sets for discards and trash cans for cast-off ephemera, even down to the lower leg cast—signed by the actors—that stuntman Paul Weston wore after breaking his leg jumping into the Sarlacc pit filming *Return of the Jedi*.

General manager Anne Neumann, who has the Sisyphean task of cataloging all that stuff, said Sansweet moved to Petaluma in 1998 for the express purpose of sharing his vast collection with fellow *Star Wars* appreciators. That, and he needed to be close to Lucas' Skywalker Ranch in Nicasio.

There is so much to see and experience that we don't want to get bogged down in Rancho Obi-Wan's lengthy origin story. Simply know that the man, from that fateful moment in 1977 when he fished out a *Star Wars* press packet from a trash can—placed there by a clueless *Wall Street Journal* colleague—felt a force so strong he had to share it far and wide in this galaxy. (He's also turned Rancho Obi-Wan into a nonprofit; it helps schools and community groups.)

Though Sansweet often gives the tour himself, the duties on this day fell to Lucas Seastrom, the Chewbacca to Sansweet's Han Solo. Named by his parents after a certain Jedi master with the surname Skywalker, Seastrom's knowledge and grasp of *Star Wars* lore belie his tender 23 years. Far from just pointing to various action figures and props and letting visitors gawk to their heart's content, which, frankly, would be enough for most people, Seastrom's presentation was an interactive, multimedia mélange of stories and skits.

You'll get a greeting from the wise and wizened sculpture of Obi-Wan Kenobi, with the voice of James Arnold Taylor, who played the part in the *Clone Wars* animated series. He intones, in part: "You'll be seeing things beyond your imagination, but your eyes can deceive you. Don't trust them. Stretch out with your feelings but not with your hands."

Later, at the entrance to the main gallery, Seastrom knocks on "John Williams' door," at which knock the *Star Wars* theme blazes to life and Seastrom dramatically flings open the door to a cornucopia of goodies. Finally, before entering the newest wing, where many of the really valuable mementos reside, visitors pass a re-creation of the corridor of the rebel blockade and finesse past a stormtrooper.

It's all great fun, and a little cheesy. OK, maybe cheesy to the casual *Star Wars* fan, but it was revelatory to those on the tour.

The Ruiz family seemingly smiled during the whole three hours. Friends Tyler Scott and Chris Roberts began the tour with sarcastic coolness intact

(Scott to Roberts: "Do ya think they'll actually have the bridge to the Starship Enterprise? I'm so psyched"). But by the end, Scott was enthusing with genuine admiration about the limited-edition, mint-conditioned *Return of the Jedi* speeder bike. (Scott: "Dude, I'm gonna make one of those for me right now. So cool!")

By far the most entertaining were Michael Koidin, a 66-year-old pediatric dentist from Lynn, Mass., and his son, Matthew, 38.

When Seastrom asked if anyone in the group was a collector of action figures, Koidin exhaled audibly. "Oh," he said, "I can tell stories."

Matthew: "Like how you got those Leias stolen."

Michael: "There were workmen at my house several years ago, and all they took was two Princess Leias. I hope he rots in hell, whoever he is."

Scott, smirking and looking mock-guiltily in Michael's direction: "All I'm sayin' is, I got two Princess Leias at my house . . ."

Michael: "Really pissed me off is all."

Matthew: "Dad!"

Father and son kept the banter going the entire tour, reminiscing in the manner other fathers and sons recall playing catch in the yard.

Matthew, to Seastrom, after Michael waxed nostalgic about trying, in vain, to collect the complete set of action figures from the original trilogy: "Hypothetically: Should a father buy a *Star Wars* toy for his son and then not give it to him and put it in the attic away from the son? Just asking."

Seastrom, perhaps sensing an Oedipal conflict as fraught as Vader and Luke's, wisely brushed off the question.

No need to go to the dark side, after all. Not when all those light sabers were casting such an otherworldly glow on all assembled.

Going Deep Underground in Fresno

July 2012
City: Fresno
County: Fresno
Population: 515,986
Elevation: 308 feet

What was I thinking? Fresno in the summer? To visit some cheesy roadside attraction? Might as well take a day trip to the surface of the sun.

When I opened my car door at the prick of noon on strip-mall-strewn Shaw Avenue and was greeted with a face full of oppressive heat, I thought about getting right back in, blasting the air conditioner and going through the drive-through window at the conveniently located Carl's Jr. for a tall iced tea before heading to the beach. Instead, I kept to my original plan, cursing myself as rivulets of sweat trickled down my back and as heat-wave shimmers made the asphalt appear liquefied.

Ironic, given that my express purpose for coming to this baking Central Valley metropolis was to escape the merciless heat, at least temporarily.

Was I mad, or is it just heatstroke that has caused this cognitive dissonance? Fresno seemingly is the last place, other than the surface of the sun, to go to avoid the summer swelter. Head to high-altitude hills or coastal climes, anywhere but to this bubbling crock pot of calefaction.

But then, I made a right turn on Shaw just after that tantalizing Carl's Jr. and followed a tree-canopied path down past Roman archways, down farther to a cool, blessedly cool, underground sanctuary, down to the architectural and horticultural wonder that is the Forestiere Underground Gardens.

I would gladly pay the $14 admission price simply to linger in the lobby, maybe 25 to 30 degrees cooler than the near-lava Fresnan mantle above ground. But there's much to see and admire during the 45-minute tour of the 10-acre subterranean oasis built by Sicilian immigrant Baldassare Forestiere more than a century ago.

The only bad part: The tour lasts only 45 minutes, meaning the oven that was my car awaited.

Whereas many Fresnans flee the Valley like refugees each summer, beach-bound or over yonder to Yosemite, some have lived here for decades and never set foot in the city's most notable roadside attraction.

"I live a mile away and have never been here," said Connie Seay, who brought her 4-year-old niece, Makenzie Wilcox. "We talk about it at my workplace all the time. 'Wonder what the underground is like?' It's right here and you know you can go at any time, so you don't. You know?"

In a way, summer is the best time to go underground. Visitors can get a full appreciation for the inspiration and desperation Forestiere must have experienced when he started digging to find relief from temperatures that must've seemed biblical.

What began in 1906 with the modest goal of sculpting a couple of cellars later blossomed into a lifelong endeavor that is an impressive display either of single-mindedness or of obsessive mania. That's because Forestiere just kept digging. Digging for the next 40 years.

The result is a singular space, a labyrinth of nooks and niches, full bedrooms and kitchens, courtyards and chapels, a wine cellar and underground citrus orchards.

As docent Latieshka Simmons wryly observed to a group of 15 sun-fleeing visitors, "After he built it, Forestiere couldn't understand why all people from Fresno didn't live underground. What is wrong with these people? It's so much cooler down here."

Until embarking on his quixotic downward dig, Forestiere was an aspiring citrus farmer down on his luck. He immigrated to the United States in 1901 and helped build the subway system in Boston. California and fruit trees beckoned, and Forestiere made a good choice for a relocation spot—Orange County.

"He loved it down there," Simmons said. "The only problem was, the cost of living was a little pricey. He couldn't afford the land. Then he heard about the Central Valley. The land was cheaper."

For good reason. When Forestiere first put spade to earth to plant trees in 1905, he soon hit solid hardpan. It can range from a foot to 5 feet under the initial topsoil, rendering the land useless. Good luck trying to get anything to grow here.

"In the summer, he gets another surprise," Simmons said. "It gets hot, 115 degrees maybe, every single day. This is before air conditioning, so

Forestiere is hot and miserable. So he starts brainstorming about how to get cooler."

After stewing in his wooden shack, oppressed by the heat and his situation, Forestiere hit upon a plan for his 80 acres.

"He knew from his experience building subways that it's cooler underground," she said. "He started digging out cellars. He moved his cot down there. Then his stove. Then he just moved in."

And kept digging, hand-excavating his own Middle Earth with only a pickax, a shovel and steely resolve.

Soon, Forestiere moved underground, carving out rooms and alcoves, boring funnel-shaped skylights to improve ventilation and visibility, adding Mediterranean flourishes.

Then came the planting. If Forestiere could not sow seeds for an orchard above ground, he knew the soil was rich enough 20 feet under to support growth. He started with ferns and herbs, which thrived, adding all manner of fruit trees (orange, grapefruit, lemon and grafted hybrids that resulted in one tree featuring seven types of fruit), grapevines, carob and date trees and roses.

What started as a whim became a consuming passion. Over time, Forestiere built 50 rooms, a wine cellar, a snaking tunnel made for automobiles, even a pond for fish to frolic (before they became dinner). Period photos of Forestiere show a man of lean and wiry build, with a furrowed brow and sculpted cheekbones and a winsome countenance. The modifier that pops into your head: "long-suffering."

At this point, a woman on the tour asked what everyone had been thinking: Did Forestiere ever marry?

Simmons smiled, seemingly prepared with the official Underground Gardens answer.

"No, never got married or had kids," she said. "People at the time were curious about Baldassare, and the *Fresno Bee* people came out to write about him and they were expecting a (she whistles and circles a finger around her head) crazy man. But he actually was a very brilliant man, a very friendly guy."

He built those 50 rooms, she said, in hopes of opening a resort for other heat-oppressed Fresnans. As the newspaper account quoted him as a saying, "The visions in my mind overwhelm me."

Alas, the resort never came to pass. He worked on expanding the underground manse until 1946, when he died of pneumonia after undergoing a hernia operation. He was 67.

Simmons repeatedly made the point that Forestiere was "not a hermit or recluse," despite his cave-dwelling penchant. When she shows the tourists the chapel, complete with a mission bell at ground level, where Forestiere would worship alone at day's end, some wise guy in the group muttered, "Yeah, and he wasn't a loner?"

"No, he really wasn't," Simmons said, voice rising in emphasis. "It's not like he was down here working and digging, 24-7. He loved people, built this for people to come visit. He was friends with a lot of the Japanese in Fresno. They shared that common immigrant bond and he'd bring them down here. His brother Giuseppe and (Giuseppe's) children would come down, too. So, again, he wasn't a recluse. I must reiterate that."

The Forestiere family still owns the gardens and they make sure Forestiere's character is not besmirched.

"According to Ric Forestiere (84, the property's owner and Forestiere's nephew), Forestiere did have a couple of lady friends who'd visit him often down here," Simmons said.

Even if Forestiere was not a recluse, it seems fair to say he, like many with an artistic temperament, had his quirks.

In one of his two bedrooms (one for summer, designed to keep heat out; one for winter, to keep heat in), Forestiere built a "peep hole" in order to espy visitors at his door. It consisted of a snaking tube running from his fireplace to outside the door, at ankle-level. If you wanted entrance into this sanctum, you had better pay attention to your footwear.

"He could look and figure out who you were by your shoes," Simmons said. "If you knocked at the door, if he knew your shoes, you could come in. If he didn't recognize your shoes, then he'd just let you stand there and knock.

"I imagine some of his friends saying, 'Don't shoot, Baldassare, I've got new shoes on . . .'"

What no one questioned was his dazzling engineering achievement using only hand tools and, later, a Fresno scraper, pulled by his beloved horses Dolly and Molly, to craft canals.

When it came to sustainable living, Forestiere was nearly a century ahead of his time. Self-taught, he not only devised natural air-conditioning of 70 on the second floor and low 60s on the third, but he funneled rainwater in to irrigate the subterranean trees and even fashioned solar-powered hot water for his bathtub.

"He kept a metal tank upstairs at ground level," Simmons said. "The sun would heat the water all day while he was working. At night, he'd drain it into his bath. How cool is that?"

Cool is several respects, actually. And the group, which was in no hurry to leave, seemed suitably impressed.

"He must've been a neat guy," said Marian Smith, visiting with her husband, John, from nearby Kingsburg. "At first, I thought he must've been a nerd. But he wasn't."

"I'd actually enjoy living in these temperatures all the time," John added.

True. Think what you want about Forestiere—eccentric or cuckoo—but grant him this: He was smart enough to escape the hellish Fresno heat.

Live Fast, Die Young, Leave . . . etc., etc. . . .

July 2012
City: Cholame
County: San Luis Obispo
Population: 1,295
Elevation: 1,157 feet

I am on a morbid mission and, frankly, I am a little spooked. I am driving east on Highway 46 from Paso Robles toward the junction with Highway 41—all for the sole purpose of visiting the site of James Dean's fatal car accident.

My mind keeps flashing back to ghoulish black-and-white photos of twisted metal on the roadside, images of Dean's demise easily download-able these days and sure to stay in your mind's eye.

It doesn't ease anxieties that this stretch of 46 is a narrow road that seems fraught with hazards that I fear might lead to my own demise—only without the attendant fame and public outpouring of affection that a '50s movie star commands. Me? I'd be just another statistic.

Call me wimpy, but every roadside signs seem portentous:

Daylight Headlights Section

Help Promote WRECKless Driving

Loose gravel

Please Drive Safely

Report Drunken Driving

Of course, these signs can be seen—and, let's be honest, ignored—on any number of remote California highways. But this time, I am paying heed. Unnerving skid marks mar the asphalt at several intersections on the snaking path. A severed side mirror on the soft shoulder gets my attention. All around me lie only beige hillocks, not a gas station in sight.

For the first time in recorded history, I am driving below the speed limit—50 in a 55-mph zone—and, in doing so, ticking off a conga line of drivers behind me. I pull into a rest area about 5 miles from my destination to splash water on my face and keep the shakes at bay.

What I see shakes my confidence even more. A poster board history reads, ominously, "Miles below your feet, two huge chunks of the earth's crust, tectonic plates, are grinding slowly past each other. Just east of Cholame, the highway crosses (the San Andreas) fault line where the two plates meet."

I also learn the earth here moves 2 inches a year and, every 22 years or so, there's a 6.0 temblor.

Great. Wonderful. Just my luck. I temporarily forget about the irony of dying in a car accident on the way to a memorial for a car accident victim and start envisioning the company hybrid car being swallowed in the gaping maw of a riven fault line.

At last, I pull myself together and drive the last few miles toward Dean's demise with no further freak-outs.

The James Dean memorial, erected in 1983 by a Japanese businessman who was just wild about the star of *Rebel Without a Cause*, *East of Eden* and *Giant*, sits smack-dab in the parking lot of the Jack Ranch Cafe, which is smack-dab in the middle of nowhere.

(For you sticklers, yes, I know that the memorial is 800 yards west of where the crash on September 30, 1955, took place. And I know that the current junction of highways 46 and 41 is not the true crash site, either. The roads were moved—and improved—in the decades since, and the actual site is now pastureland.)

As tributes go, it's tasteful and understated. It consists of a tree encircled by stainless steel and concrete with two plaques at the base. Inscribed is the benefactor's (one Seita Ohnishi) tribute to Dean: "It stands for James

Dean and other American Rebels who taught us the importance of having a cause."

A family in an SUV has pulled up and stands staring at the tree. Teenager Jeremy Pruyn of Lake Havasu, Ariz., has dad Jack snap his picture in front of it.

Afterward, I asked Jeremy if he knows who James Dean was.

"Not really," he said.

A couple then join me under the tree's natural canopy. This is Gary and Sue Giberson of Huntington Beach. They are in their late 60s and sure as heck know James Dean. They are on their way to their grandkids' graduation in Santa Cruz and just had to stop, again. This isn't their first time.

"We stopped here a long time ago," Gary said. "Now we can't remember. Did he get killed back there when he was coming off 41? It says 800 yards east of here, so . . ."

"They said," Sue adds, "that whoever ran into him was coming off a farm road, so it had to be that one up there."

The Gibersons know the history: how Dean was speeding in his brand-new Porsche 550 Spyder, how the 1950 Ford Tudor coupe, driven by a Cal Poly San Luis Obispo student, turned left into him, how Dean was instantly crushed.

To leaven the mood, the Gibersons tell a funny story that involves Dean. They were at a performance of the play *Come Back to the Five and Dime, Jimmy Dean, Jimmy Dean*, about a James Dean fan club, when at intermission the woman next to them started chatting them up.

Sue: "This old gal says, 'I didn't know Dean ever did movies. I thought all he did was make sausages.' I said, 'No, that's Jimmy Dean. This play's about James Dean.'"

They certainly know James inside the neighboring Jack Ranch Cafe. But, who knows, they might serve Jimmy's links, too. In any event, worker Ethan Gonsalves says the restaurant embraces all things Dean, as evidenced by the scores of publicity photos on the walls, a life-size cardboard cutout, and books about Dean they sell.

"A lot of people just come in because of the Dean thing," Gonsalves says. "I've met people from all over the world. Most of our locals who eat here are cowboys or farmers coming in for a steak or a drink. But the locals don't mind. It kind of gives us our 15 minutes of fame."

After 15 minutes at the Dean memorial, my morbid mood has been lightened, and I'm itching to hit the road. I've got a long way to go to reach home by sundown.

I turn left on Highway 41, headed for Interstate 5. The sign says "End Daytime Headlight Section." I'm pushing 70 now. Damn, when is that passing lane going to get here? These slow cars really tick me off.

Of Gas and Gastronomy

August 2012
City: Lee Vining
County: Mono
Population: 22
Elevation: 6,781 feet

I'm running low, low on gas, low on patience, low on blood sugar.

I need to stop after a long, arduous haul over Highway 120 and the Tioga Pass through the heart of Yosemite, usually a steep but gorgeous drive, but on this fall day, a real bitch. A freakish early storm has hit the area. Not a problem in lower altitudes—merely rain in the foothills. But once I reached the Sierra and headed toward Yosemite, snow fell. CalTrans, the czars of the roads in these parts, usually will close 120 if snow accumulates, so I was at once driving quickly but carefully to get over "the pass" before the heavy weather hit but also fearing my little hybrid sedan would slide right off the road and down some ravine. And did I mention I was low on gas and famished?

At last, I reached the intersection of highways 120 and 395, the heart of the Mono basin, where a Mobil gas station and attached mini-mart beckoned.

I am desperate at this point, so I stop. The gas was feloniously expensive ($4.98 a gallon), but so be it. It was the food I wondered about. I conjured images of 99-cent microwave bean burritos, shrink-wrapped Slim Jims sold next to the car air fresheners, greasy, bruised-purple hot dogs twirling in a rotisserie of grease.

Still, I walked toward the double glass doors under a sign reading "Tioga Gas Mart." I wended my way past the usual tourist trinkets (key chains and shot glasses, the T-shirts and sunglasses, mosquito repellent and lip balm), thinking, smugly, "Nothing special here."

Way in the back, though, just to the right of a bank of soda machines, this generic mini-mart transforms into nothing short of a four-star dining establishment cleverly disguised as a to-go counter and a few rows of booths, augmented by picnic tables al fresco.

The mural on the wall identifies it as the Whoa Nellie Deli, and it implores diners to "Sit and have a meal with us." My so-called sophisticated big-city palate reserved judgment until I looked at the menu, printed on a board right above your head. My eyes and esophagus opened wide when I looked at some of the choices:

- Lobster taquitos, with Brazilian black beans and mango salad: $15.50

- Wild buffalo meatloaf, with port au jus and garlic mashed potatoes: $18.95

- Grilled pork chops, with apricot-wild berry glaze: $19.95.

So blown away was I by the array of slow-food fare (burgers and pizza, too, for the culinary riffraff) at this fast-stop place that I didn't even absorb that there's a wine list, two types of margaritas and some trendy small-label beers on tap.

Actually, I had plenty of time to absorb this news and mull options. That's because the line was so long at dinner hour that I thought people were queuing up for SuperLotto jackpot tickets or something.

Paralyzed by the choices, I stepped out of line and tried to satiate my gnawing need to know how a high-end restaurant found such humble accommodations on a bluff overlooking Mono Lake.

I asked for the manager. I was led to a table and was greeted by Denise Molnar and her husband, Dan. They run the place for Denise's parents, owners Dennis and Jane Domaille, who opened the gas station/mini-mart/restaurant in 1997. Denise and Dan were crazy busy, what with the restaurant overflowing as well as people wanting to put $40 in Pump No. 3, but they indulged me with the full story of a family business that's gotten boffo reviews from Yelpsters and snobby restaurant critics alike.

Turns out, neither Dennis nor Jane are "foodies," per se, though they love a good meal like anyone else. What they share is a passion of quality and quirkiness, which led them to hire a former San Diego beach volleyball bum named Matt Toomey as the chef. Toomey had a new vision for "roadhouse" food, and the Domailles gave him free rein.

254

Soon, he was doing things like using sweet huckleberry barbecue sauce on entrees as simple as a grilled chicken breast, offering three kinds of soup daily and carrot, chocolate and cheese cakes for dessert.

Word got around. Locals came. Tourists flocked. The media took notice. Toomey became something of a celebrity chef, so successful that after more than a decade behind the grill at the mini-mart, he left last year to open a restaurant—sans gas station—in Mammoth Lakes. Taking over the toque at what people here just call "the Mobil" is Toomey's longtime sous chef, Ernesto Romero. The menu and most everything else stayed the same.

Check that: There were changes. The Mobil expanded its cultural hegemony in tiny Lee Vining by adding live music on the patio of Thursdays and Sundays, which has raised some eyebrows, according to Denise.

"We'll get, like, 300 people dancing, and someone random will come up and just want to take a gas and wonder what the hell is going on," Denise tells you. "It's kind of funny. We get a lot of foreign travelers who don't expect it."

Dan says, despite write-ups in *Sunset Magazine* and *The New York Times*, many weary travelers don't know what awaits them.

"We still get people who stumble upon it," he said. "But it's the same with the eastern Sierra as a whole. People go right past us on their way to and from Yosemite or headed to Vegas or Death Valley. If they stop here, they just get blown away."

And, it seemed, they become repeat customers. Take Joe Bushong, of San Diego. He discovered the restaurant a few years ago after talking with friends and now, "every time we come up here, we stop." As he sipped on a Golden Trout Pilsner, Bushong said he's so adapted to the notion of fine dining in a gas station that he's raised his expectations for the Mobil.

"Actually," he said, "my pork chops were a little overdone today. For the price, we expected a little better. You are paying for quality, you tend to be more picky."

I sensed that the locals cut the Mobil more slack. And, by locals, that means people who'll drive two hours from Yosemite National Park to the west, an hour from Mammoth to the south, a half hour from Bridgeport to the north. I sidled up to three 20-somethings in shorts and T-shirts downing some fish tacos and asked them if this was their first time dining at the Mobil.

When they stopped laughing, they explained they are seasonal employees at Yosemite.

"I come up about twice a month," Thomas Williams says. "Why? The park doesn't have fish tacos. I'd say at this point, I know half the people that work here."

Co-worker Samantha Clendenin, who worked at High Camp, said it's an hour-and-a-half drive over the Tioga Pass—but worth it.

"It's good to get out of the park occasionally," she said. "This is, you know, the big city by comparison."

Well, yes, the Mobil is believed to be the only place in Lee Vining that serves ahi sashimi—unless you count the bait shops.

To be fair, Lee Vining has at least three other sit-down restaurants. And you're sure they serve fine fare. But you have come for the novelty factor, to be able to gauge the surprise on friends' faces when you tell them you ate dinner at the gas station.

I got back in line and ordered. I opted for the lobster taquitos, which Denise said is a customer favorite. Spicy, moist and crunchy all at the same time, the entree was sublime. Of course, I probably could have found some spicy Doritos, crunchy pork rinds and moist snack cakes across the way in the mini-mart's snack-food aisle to stave off hunger while on the road. But I could've gotten that at any gas station. This one's special.

Banana Museum in the Desert? Sure, Why Not?

April 2013
City: Mecca
County: Riverside
Population: 8,577
Elevation: –187 feet

Confession: I'm just the kind of weird, wanderlust-imbued traveler Fred Garbutt is counting on. The way Fred see things, if he could just get the word out, curious roadside-attraction aficionados would flock to the palace of potassium that is the International Banana Museum.

Count me in. There I was in Palm Springs, relaxing, and the only thought I'd given to bananas lounging by the pool was whether I should imbibe a banana daiquiri. But then I flicked through one of those slick brochures they put in racks at cheap motels, telling you all about the nearby "sights" to see, and my eye caught a blurb about the International Banana Museum on the North Shore of the Salton Sea.

I decamped forthwith for the hour-long trek on a lonely desert road. And there it stood, 9 miles southeast from a town called Mecca on Highway 111, a bright yellow low-slung concrete building with an equally brilliant-hued Volkswagen Beetle out front and a 20-foot sign reading:

WORLD FAMOUS INTERNATIONAL BANANA MUSEUM
GUINNESS WORLD RECORD COLLECTION

Though impossible to miss amid the beige terrain and blue sparkling water of the Salton Sea, I wondered what quirk of fate and geography had led to this site being the nexus for 'nanas. The only other business around was Skip's Liquor right next door, with its tantalizing sign touting "Bait, Ice, Beer."

Why not a banana museum in India, Ecuador, Costa Rica? You know, a place that actually produces the fruit being so venerated?

Clearly, I was asking too many questions, overthinking things like always.

I soon learned that choosing the Salton Sea as a banana hub had mostly to do with commerce, not geographic concerns. It had much to do with Skip's, that liquor store on a crumbling stretch of the highway, and the owner's fervent belief that bananas would lure the curious.

Don't laugh. You must never underestimate the power of this nutrient-dense super fruit, worshipped by untold millions for its fiber-rich sweetened goodness, not to mention its perfect packaging.

Only five months after its opening in 2012, the International Banana Museum found itself featured on BBC television, hosted a documentary film crew from the Netherlands, had several cable TV shows stateside come calling, and was written up in scads of travel blogs, prompting a torrent of babble on Twitter and Facebook.

Inside what once was a rundown pub was a blinding array of yellow banana items, everything from 10-foot inflatable bananas to books, CDs and posters on the theme, to clocks and plush toys and a banana vehicle— about 21,000 items in all, including a recently acquired rare 1960s banana-shaped record player.

Yes, the museum was "international," since some items come from Russia, Peru and Denmark.

Curator Garbutt, who operated a tennis-court construction business in the Palm Springs area and whose family owns Skip's, never set out to be the Banana Man, the moniker he now gives himself. This whole enterprise began as something of a family joke, until it got serious and took on a life of its own.

In late 2009, the family matriarch, Virginia, read something online about a gentleman named Ken Bannister selling his collection of bananalia on eBay because he lost his lease at his museum in Hesperia in Riverside County. Bannister had long been the top banana, first opening his museum in the Los Angeles suburb of Altadena in the early 1970s, but apparently he wanted to pass on his fruity artifacts to a new generation—for a pretty penny, of course.

"When my mom, who I now call the Banana Nana, called me up and told me about it, I thought it might be a way to reinvent (Skip's) out here," Garbutt said. "It was really struggling. I thought turning the pub next to the liquor store (into a museum) might draw people off the highway and maybe they'd buy snacks and water at the store. It was kind of a risky concept, but I do know that people go out of their way to see the most obscure things."

In April 2010, after the banana collection failed to sell on eBay, Garbutt pounced and bought it from Bannister for an undisclosed sum in a private transaction. Let's just say it costs bundles and bundles of bananas.

Little did Garbutt know that his banana buying had just begun. It took him nearly three years to gut the bar and turn it into a presentable show-place, and during that period, he discovered that Bannister's 17,000 banana items just weren't enough to make the museum truly epic.

He purchased another 500 items himself on eBay and bought a collection of 600 pieces from a man in Mississippi. In addition, the son of a noted banana collector who was being moved to a rest home donated his dad's 3,000-banana cache.

"I wouldn't say I'm obsessed, but I am an avid banana collector," Garbutt said. "If I go into something, I go in full force. Somebody contacted me from that cable show, *Collection Obsession*, and I told them, 'I'm not one of those guys sitting there obsessed like it's some type of addiction. If I was obsessed, I'd say my home would be loused with it, too.'"

For the record, Garbutt does have one, just one, banana souvenir in his home office.

"It's a life-size heavy porcelain banana that was double-dipped in sterling silver and then gilded in 24-karat gold," he said. "I keep it on my desk."

At some point, Garbutt admitted, he came to have real affection for the fruit. He was wearing a yellow wristwatch with banana hands, a banana-print tropical shirt and a banana pendant dangling from his neck. And when people with cameras come, he changes into a full banana suit.

"I'm always trying to promote wherever I am because I'm the Banana Man," he said. "I'm not trying to be too silly, but just enough banana-y to have some fun."

Visitors seemed to enjoy themselves as well, judging by the guest book scrawled with names and little banana drawings from several continents. He said he does "decent" business selling banana-themed items such as jewelry, pens, gum and hand sanitizer. On weekends during the hotter months, Garbutt offers banana sodas, snow cones and ice-cream floats.

Alas, no banana daiquiris. Not yet, at least. Garbutt has plans for the back patio, where adults can lounge under banana fronds and a plantation mural and drink in the view of the Salton Sea while sipping on banana beer or wine.

"My goal," he said, with an arm sweep of his banana manse, "is to make this the finest beloved offbeat museum that people have ever seen."

It's either a truly noble calling or he's totally bananas.

Pop Culture That Pops in Your Mouth

January 2013
City: Burlingame
County: San Mateo
Population: 30,298
Elevation: 37 feet

Odds are, you haven't given Pez a single thought in decades. And there's really no reason to. It's that 5-inch plastic candy dispenser that shoots out pellets from a tracheotomy-scar. Wonder when they stopped making them? Oh, they still do. Cool, I guess.

Gary Doss doesn't understand my lack of excitement over Pez and probably doesn't give a whit, either.

Standing amid floor-to-ceiling dispensers at his Burlingame Museum of Pez Memorabilia, a dazzling array of pop culture touchstones—from fat Elvis to Fred Flintstone, Mary Poppins to Princess Leia—Doss smiled sheepishly and tried to make light of his 20-year curatorial curiosity. He wanted to make it clear that his love of all things Pez is equal parts entrepreneurial and endearing, not pathological and pathetic.

"Yes," he said, "it is one step from hoarding. But look around. They are neatly displayed. You don't have to step over them or anything, you know. There are a lot of people more into Pez than me."

Sensing skepticism, Doss felt the need to elaborate, to tell about the avidity (no, rabidity) of some of the Pez-heads who frequent his sugary shrine.

"Check out our Facebook page," he said. "We had a woman come in last weekend who had a life-size Pez (dispenser) tattoo on the side of her body. We got a picture of it. She had the blue letters spelling 'Pez' from her hip to her ribs, the head (of a He-Saur) on the inside of her upper arm and the Pez candy coming out of her armpit. One of the commenters said, 'That's got to hurt.'"

Wow, now that is hard-core.

Given such a dedicated following, it's no surprise that in the two decades since Doss, 58, turned his computer store on a busy downtown street into a dispensary (yes, he sells Pez dispensers) of nostalgia as well as cubed, candy-coated sugary snacks, the Pez museum has grown both in items and in stature.

Examples of every Pez dispenser ever manufactured, more than 900 in all, are represented within two small but tidy rooms, as well as Pez posters, vintage Pez-vending machines, Pez apparel and Pez literature and, of course, the candy itself.

Pez has long been an American pop-culture fascination, combining as it does two archetypal products: candy and toys. Though its heyday in this country may have been the Eisenhower-Kennedy years, Pez endures in all the fine establishments—Rite Aid, CVS, Big Lots and, of course, Walmart.

As much as a staple as Pez has been to American baby boomers, its history dates before even the Greatest Generation. The candy was conceived in Vienna in 1927 and marketed strictly as a breath mint. The name, according to the company's website, came from abbreviating the word *Pfefferminz*, German for peppermint.

The first of the iconic dispensers (originally called "Box Regulars" by company flacks) hit shelves in 1948, shaped to resemble a cigarette lighter to "encourage people to quit smoking," the website states.

By the early 1950s, Pez had a foothold in the United States as the "first interactive candy," meaning the first to have a delivery system. Soon, Popeyes and Santa Clauses and Disney characters were shooting sugary pellets into millions of mouths and helping dentists everywhere buy second homes.

While the nation has become more health conscious, Pez has continued to make profits, according to the company. Perhaps owing to the value of nostalgia, in the past year, Pez opened a visitors' center at its Orange, Conn., U.S. headquarters, replete with every dispenser the company has made.

No need to fly cross-country to have a look, though. A drive to the Bay Area will give you all the Pez you can stomach.

Maybe because it is near San Francisco International Airport, Doss' museum has attracted visitors from Europe and Asia, as well as the large domestic Pez-head population. But, while charging just $3 a head for entrance, how does Doss make ends meet in the obscenely high cost-of-living Bay Area?

"Luckily," he said, "there's this thing called the Internet. We do an awful lot of business that way. That's how I make it work. I know that Pez is silly, but we deal with serious collectors all over the world. We got into it early and that helps. Our website opened in 1995."

Doss' Web-savviness was hardly dumb luck. The Pez museum was, after all, originally the site of his early-'90s computer store. You can still see the business's name stenciled on the front door: "Computer Spectrum."

Doss, back in the day, sold "cutting-edge" Atari STs and Commodore Amigas to early computer adopters and, just for kicks, he decorated the shelves with a dozen or so Pez dispensers from his home collection.

"We got far more people coming in each month looking at Pez, then buying Pez, than we did computers after a while," Doss said. "So, it turned into this. The only credit I ever give myself is that I let it happen. I haven't sold a computer in 17 years. I don't miss it. There's a lot less customer support selling Pez."

True, even though the dispensers are seemingly made from the flimsiest of mass-produced plastic, they hold up well over time. That could be because most collectors don't actively use them to deliver candy; rather, the dispensers become objets d'art.

"No, it's not the candy," Doss said, "although it's not bad. There are a lot of new flavors to enjoy. It's the silliness of it. Pez is almost unequaled in its ability to license such a wide and diverse group of characters. I mean, from *Star Wars* to Hello Kitty to the three gentlemen from (the reality TV show) *Orange County Choppers*, that's pretty all-encompassing."

He paused over the *OC Chopper* guys, still pristine in their box.

"They came out four years ago—and they are historic," Doss said. "These are the only Pez made (portraying) living people. They hold that unique Pez honor."

Wait, what about the display in the back room of members of the rock band KISS? Gene Simmons and company are living, right?

"That's been debated," he said, smiling. "I say they are in character, that they are characters. But we can have that debate if you like."

I deferred to Doss' authority. He shrugged and claimed he's far from the grand poobah of Pez.

"I personally know 10 other collectors that have far more than I do," he said. "Most of my Pez were purchased pre-eBay. I hit a lot of garage sales and antique shows. A lot of the very rare Pez I got at Pez conventions. There are eight of them in the U.S. alone."

Head by head, Doss methodically built his collection until it became complete. With one exception, there isn't a single Pez dispenser made that this man does not own. He is justifiably proud showing off the rarities housed in special glass display cases. He points to a "bride and groom" Pez match, suitable to be placed atop a wedding cake.

"That was made for a (Pez) employee back in the '70s," he said. "This Mary Poppins over here is a very rare dispenser, too."

He herded me over to the far wall.

"This is the rarest of all," Doss continued. "It was made in 1972. It is called 'Make a Face,' kind of like a Mr. Potato Head. It was quickly rushed off store shelves because they got very concerned about the little plastic parts and kids swallowing them along with the candy."

So, Pez's loss was collectors' gain.

Doss says "Make a Face" makes big dough among Pez collectors, as does the rare fruit-series. Decades ago, at Pez headquarters in Traun, Austria, prototypes were made of dispensers shaped like a pear, orange, pineapple and lemon. They never were released, perhaps because Pez executives realized kids wouldn't go for such a healthy and nutritious dispenser. In any event, collectors slavered over the few prototypes to be had.

Doss has a pineapple, orange and pear.

A lemon head remains elusive.

"There's just one," he said. "And it's owned by a woman on the East Coast by the name of Dora. She'll probably die with it in her hand. I know somebody who'd give her $5,000 for it on the spot."

For a piece of plastic that cost 20 cents to make?

"Probably not even that much," he said.

Stamp of Approval

November 2012
City: Fort Bragg
County: Mendocino
Population: 7,250
Elevation: 85 feet

So my first heinous breach of tattoo etiquette may have gone unnoticed, or politely ignored. I believe I mistakenly called Madame Chinchilla, grand dame of the Triangle Tattoo Studio and Museum along with loyal partner Mr. G., Madame Chowchilla.

Let the record hereby show that Madame C. is not named after the grungy Central Valley town, rather after a crepuscular rodent with velvety fur. Not that she's at all hirsute, I'm quick to add, as evidenced by the Technicolor body art up and down Madame C.'s arms and torso that was obscured by nary a smidgen of unsightly body hair.

But it was my second tattoo faux pas that drew a sharp, frosty rebuke from Madame C.

In an effort to express how wowed I was at the joint's vast collection of tattoo memorabilia spanning centuries and many cultures, I gushed about the array of tattoo guns lining one wall.

"Actually, they are not guns," she said. "They are called tattoo machines. Only in prison are they called guns."

Chastened, I tried to make light of my insensitive remark but only added to the awkwardness.

"Sorry," I said, smiling. "I swear I've never been in prison."

"I can tell by your arms," she said, giving me the once-over. "Or, at least, you weren't in prison very long."

True, my middle-aged body is inkless, virginally inkless. Even in these days when every suburban mom flaunts a tasteful butterfly on the shoulder and bank CEOs sport barbed-wire tats on biceps, I do not have a single tattoo piercing my epidermis. No tramp stamp for me, not even a heart tattoo inscribed to dear old mom.

Who am I, then, to be assessing perhaps the most elaborate shrine to an ancient art form, one in which the body is the canvas and one's means of expression?

"It's OK," Madame Chinchilla demurred. "It's very mainstream now. We're open to all people. We fill up our guest books really fast. We love having people look around. Tattoos tell a story."

Stories abound at this funky, well-preserved two-story Victorian in the heart of this former lumber town. And Madame Chinchilla, veteran tattoo artist and author, was nice enough even to stop work on a floral design on a woman's right shoulder to show me around.

There is something, really, for people of all interests.

Are you a patriotic American?

There's an entire wall devoted to flag-waving U.S. of A. depictions, dating from World War I to the Afghanistan conflict to the fight against ISIS.

Are you an amateur cultural anthropologist?

There's a multimedia display—video, pictorial, text—about the ancient Maori culture in New Zealand and its body marking.

Are you curious about tattoo culture's permanent mark on circus life?

There's an impressive display of circus art, including a shrine to sideshow legend Captain Don Leslie. (Madame C., by the way, is the late Leslie's biographer; purchase her book at the museum.) The highlight of the Captain Don wing is a "Sword Swallowing Anatomy Guide," spanning the sublingual gland down to the small intestines. This blown-up text could serve as Captain Don's epitaph: "Q: How do you swallow a sword? A: Very carefully. —Cpt. Don."

And lest you think the tattoo arts remain a macho, misogynistic culture, check out the "Women's Wall" in Madame C.'s studio in the back.

"These are tattooed women from all over the world, different eras and contemporary," she said. "I've designed it so the contemporary is next to the historical, because history repeats itself, you know."

It seems that tattoo artists don't like to repeat themselves. At least that's the impression one gets from looking at all the different designs. Under an exhibit dubbed "Classics," originals by lauded artist Norman "Sailor Jerry" Collins (pictured champing on a cigar) include the iconic eagle and talons, anchor, skull-rose-and-heart combo.

Another curiosity is the enduring popularity of a "Twin Screw Propellers" design, worn by superstitious mariners who believed the props would prevent drowning by "propelling them back to shore." One provocative photo shows "proud wearer" Monty Montgomery with propellers inked on each cheek (uh, the lower ones). On the left cheek, it reads, "Twin Screws"; on the right, "Stay Clear."

Mr. G. says many of their museum's pieces have been donated by the tattoo community, but he and Madame C. have also bought a lot in the past 27 years. He said some artifacts came from legendary San Francisco tattoo artist Lyle Tuttle, whose museum was damaged in the 1989 Loma Prieta earthquake.

Many of Madame C. and Mr. G.'s maritime pieces have been shown all over the country in a touring exhibition, *Skin & Bones—Tattoos in the Life of the American Sailor*, which debuted at the Philadelphia Independence Seaport Museum in 2009.

Madame C. and Mr. G., however, are humble curators.

"Ours is one of the older (museums)," Mr. G. said. "But it's the people with the most money who have the most stuff in their tattoo museums. There's always somebody bigger and better."

Five rooms, plus a long staircase of memorabilia certainly proved impressive enough to museum visitors Kate, of Prescott, Ariz., and Clyde, of Spokane, Wash.

"Isn't this crazy?" Kate exclaimed.

"This is something else," Clyde added, "all the old guns and stuff."

Uh, oh. Did he call them guns?

Breakfast in Samoa

May 2012
City: Samoa
County: Humboldt
Population: 258
Elevation: 39 feet

God, I was hungry. A lumberjack type of hunger. A morning spent among the big, ancient sequoias and redwoods in the forests of Humboldt County, the famous Avenue of the Giants, will do that to a guy. My appetite was Bunyanesque.

Then again, this is marijuana-loving Humboldt County, where the munchies are said to be an endemic affliction.

So, on the trip into this spit of land 7 miles west of Eureka, once home to the country's largest logging operation, the invitation to literally eat like a lumberjack is too tempting to pass up.

The Samoa Cookhouse, 119 years old and virtually unchanged since that pungent mill made this a happening place, provides road-weary travelers a chance to roll up their sleeves, loosen a notch or two from their belts and dine at a place saturated in history and gravy in equal measure.

Judging from the packed parking lot, others had the same idea to strap on the ol' feedbag and indulge in caloric, sclerotic offerings delivered family-style in bowls and platters to customers at long wooden tables.

Family-style? Must be the 19-child Duggar family, such were the Brobdingnagian portions.

But then, lumberjacks worked long, hard days burning carbs and building sinew, so they needed to bulk up.

We modern Americans? Uh, not so much.

Still, if you find yourself anywhere near the Arcata-Eureka metroplex, dig in. This is eating-as-entertainment. As history, too. You can make up for it by eating cottage cheese and celery the rest of the week.

On a fall Sunday morning, despite the crowded lot, the place was not even half full. That's because the Cookhouse is a massive structure, built for 500 flannel-shirted, sawdust-begrimed men who worked for modest wages, a cot in the bunkhouse and three squares a day. Serving them were single women who toiled 11 hours a day and then were locked upstairs in a dormitory, safe from the lascivious looks and covetous advances of the loggers.

Today, waitress Pam Angelo—who lives in a yellow, former company-owned house visible from the Cookhouse front window—sits diners down and gives them silverware from the old coffee cans on the table. But no menu. Here, you eat what they give ya, pal, and you like it, OK?

In no time, a big, white bowl of scrambled eggs is set down, along with a platter of French toast and sausage links, biscuits and gravy, a pitcher of orange juice and pot of coffee.

This is no haute cuisine. But it is hot. And plentiful. Lunch and dinner are no different—literally a meat-and-potatoes diet.

Remember, you aren't here to excite your palate. Take a look around at the remnants of the town's logging past, put yourself in the place of the saw-wielding strongmen or the aproned women who lived in that time.

Pamphlets and plaques on the walls make it seem a hard life, bereft of succor. But as Angelo tells it, romance did bloom.

"There was a woodbox built in the back here where the girls used to sneak in and out," she said. "They were all single then and maybe they were coming to look for a mate. But (the owners) tried to lock the women in at night and lock the men out."

As a mating ritual, perhaps, the lumberjacks used to jokingly untie the waitresses' apron strings or furtively hook gravy ladles to their backs. The men were not big on manners, according to local historian Evelyn McCormick quoted in a pamphlet. They often brawled over the best spots to sit and, McCormick noted, "ate ravenously, as if the food might disappear before their very eyes."

Looking around on this Sunday morning, diners appeared more civilized. The Cookhouse is not a place for the asocial or those seeking a private conversation as they dine. It's communal. *Hey, pass the eggs, will ya, bub?*

The great thing is, you overhear some pointed conversations, such as the jocular banter about cars among three old friends from the Humbugs VW Club in Eureka, Manny Pabalate, Bill Taylor and Phillip Hooker. The men eat here often.

"Pretty much the same menu every day," Taylor said.

"Yeah," said Pabalate. "Eat and eat and keep eating until you can't do it anymore."

"When I discovered this place," Hooker, a portly man, said, "I was 6-foot-2, 120 pounds. Look at me now."

Soon, the group is joined by manager Jeff Brustman, who over his 13 years at the helm has the lore of the Cookhouse down pat.

"Everything here was for practicality in 1893," he said. "Instead of mopping the floor, there are eight holes drilled down directly below with a grate and they'd squeegee the water and let it drain down. At one point, there was a teepee burner (pre-smokestack days) at the far end of the building. It would catch the building on fire sometimes. Remember, it was a gigantic burner going 24 hours a day.

"Instead of moving the teepee or moving the cookhouse, which would've been monumental, they just installed sprinklers on the roof, and when the winds would kick up out of the south and there'd be a fire potential, they'd turn on the sprinklers and soak the thing."

Sated by this surfeit of victuals, I waddled out just as another wave of hungry folks flowed in. It's a ritual going on 120 years now. Here's hoping the Cookhouse lasts as long as those big trees off Highway 101.

7

Small World, Big Pain

Disneyland exists in order to hide that it is the "real" country, all of "real" America that is Disneyland (a bit like prisons are there to hide that it is the social in its entirety, in its banal omnipresence, that is carceral).
—Jean Baudrillard, *Simulacra and Simulation*

If Disneyland was indeed the Happiest Place on Earth, you'd either keep it a secret or the price of admission would be free and not equivalent to the yearly per capita income of a small sub-Saharan African nation like Detroit.
—Paul Beatty, *The Sellout*

Confessions of a Disney Agnostic

May 2015
City: Anaheim
County: Orange
Population: 336,265
Elevation: 157 feet

Disneyland overlords, all about branding and stealth marketing, apparently have an in-house name for the likes of me: "Nonfamily Guest."

Hey, I've been called worse.

It's nothing derisive—derision and mockery, after all, is verboten at "The Happiest Place on Earth"—but I cannot help but feel the term connotes something vaguely sad and pathetic, a sense of displacement, as if you're that odd-man-out guest at a Thanksgiving dinner, welcome but not quite accepted, superfluous even, the answer to the old children's book game of what's-wrong-with-this-picture.

But that's just me, long a sufferer of intense, sometimes crippling, self-consciousness. I had been assured and reassured before making my first pilgrimage to the park since I was a snot-nosed 11-year-old in 1971—somehow, I avoided accompanying my own brood here during their child-hoods—that Disneyland is crawling with adults, sans kids, all looking to have a good time.

Wait, that sounds creepy. Let me rephrase: Disneyland, I am told, can be just as enjoyable, just as infused with wide-eyed wonderment, for those with crow's feet and middle-aged spread as for those whose cheeks are spackled with cotton candy or topographical maps of acne. It's a nostalgia trip, veteran "nonfamily guests" say, a chance to relive misty watercolor memories and, for a few hours, forget that your 401(k) is tapped out, and you'll probably be working until you shuffle off this mortal coil.

By now, you've probably inferred that I am not the ideal NFG. Much of my misspent youth occurred in the Orange County 'burb of Placentia—not a place of uterine-like placidity, despite its name—located not 10 miles (as the drone flies) from Disneyland, such proximity meaning the place held little mystique, no sense of a Magic Kingdom visit being an epoch-making childhood event. Leftover E-tickets (yeah, I'm dating myself) were strewn about the house like detritus.

To understand the viselike hold Disneyland has on some grownups, and to quell my anxiety for my first visit inside its gates in 44 years, I contacted a Sacramento woman, Kelly Shinar-Reed, 56, who is just wild about the place, a NFG par excellence.

She only visited the park a few times as a child but, as an adult, has been back, with equally smitten friends, at least once a year for a dozen years. She assured me that, of course, the lines for Space Mountain would be dotted with men graying at the temples and women in thick pince-nez bifocals who aren't just ushering around their grandkids; that childless couples in their early 30s roam the grounds, especially over at the California Adventure annex, where alcohol is served; that you'll find many couples not thinking twice about squeezing into so-called kiddie attractions like Mr. Toad's Wild Ride and the Submarine Voyage.

"Only now they call it the Finding Nemo Voyage," Shinar-Reed said. "That's a good one to do. Try that."

Really? Doesn't she feel slightly silly standing in line for rides where you're not fretting about the height limit but hoping beyond hope they don't have an upper weight limit?

"I'm not self-conscious at all," she said, laughing. "I just push the kids out of the way and go."

She was kidding, I think.

"I'm a big kid at heart, totally," she added.

Me? I'm a curmudgeon at heart, my mom once claiming to a concerned elementary school principal that I was "6 going on 60," sadly born without the whimsy gene.

Yet, I would heed Shinar-Reed's advice. I wouldn't, as she does, subject myself to three days of Disney delirium, which assuredly would result in hospitalization and a 72-hour hold, but I would go with an open mind and wallet (the park is much more expensive than in 1971; a one-day "park-hopper" pass is $155). I would stand in long lines next to squalling blobs of infectious protoplasm held by their uptight anti-vaxxer parents, but I draw the line at the Snow White ride. I don't do Snow White. I would attend the *Frozen* sing-along but vowed not to "let it go" and give voice. I would not don mouse ears—that much degradation is absolutely death-dealing—but I would kindly chat up adults wearing same. I would not ingest corn dogs, cotton candy or ice cream—doctor's orders, not mine—but search for the reasonably healthful concessions Shinar-Reed swore are in abundance.

"Any final bits of advice?" I asked her.

"It gets pretty crowded at night, so I usually like to get there first thing in the morning," she said. "But if it gets busy in one section, just keep moving. And have fun."

Half past 8 a.m., and the swarm already has descended. The park opens at 8, but apparently you can pay extra and get early admission. Already, I feel I've been outsmarted by these smug extended families at the head of the line for Space Mountain. I take Shinar-Reed's advice and try to use the Fast Pass machine, an ATM-like device in which you insert your ticket and out spits a card with a one-hour "window of time" when your place in line will be reserved. My window would've been 10:30–11:30. I really don't want to make a commitment, at least not this early.

Besides, I'm here, in large part, to do that man-on-the-street thing and scan for NFGs. But all I'm seeing are parents steering strollers, sporting thousand-yard stares, hell-bent on exiting Tomorrowland and careening,

271

double time, hut-hut, over to Mickey's Toontown. Traffic slows by the ubiquitous stroller parking lots, overseen by gimlet-eyed valet attendants. Some of these tricked-out conveyances look so elaborate, sporting whitewall tires and multiple cup holders, pouches, zippered panniers and UV-shielding sunroofs, that they might cost more than an automobile.

At last, I find my way back to the roundabout on Main Street, the park's geographic center. A crowd has formed around the bronzed, life-size statue of Walt Disney, one arm pointing into the firmament, the other clasping that adorable scamp, Mickey Mouse. From a distance—and maybe it's just my middle-aged myopia—Uncle Walt looks uncannily like the statue of Saddam Hussein that U.S. troops lassoed and tore down in 2003.

Here, I meet a couple holding hands, the balding man wearing a backpack and the woman holding a clutch purse. There's no stroller nearby, no toddlers orbiting their legs. Might they be the elusive "nonfamily guests"?

"You are never too old for Disneyland," says Alana Barron, 25, of Edmonton, Canada.

Her partner, Steve Kane, 30, confirms it. They are vacationing and came to Disneyland for themselves.

"When I was a kid, we couldn't afford to go as a family," Kane says. "As soon as I could afford it on my own, I'm here. I mean, as a kid, this is the place you want to go. There's literally no other place you want to go as a child, particularly if you're from out of town."

Over at the entrance to Fantasyland, I make another NFG spotting. A young couple is posing before the castle facade, a selfie-stick with pink smartphone attached extended from the arm of the woman sporting Mickey Mouse ears and a bright red bow.

They are Ashneel and Ivania Nand, from the Northern California suburb of Pittsburg. Ashneel looks a little abashed when I approach. Maybe it's because I caught them in mid-selfie, maybe just a reaction to the whole Disneyland-as-an-adult gestalt.

"I was just telling her, it's kind of weird we're here because Disneyland is for families, people with kids, you know," he says. "But sometimes you just gotta forget about it. I just got off Space Mountain. I still love it. Some of those turns, I was like, this is crazy."

"We don't feel too out of place at all," Ivania adds. "It's awesome."

Must just be me. Time to have some fun. I take the plunge and get a Fast Pass for Space Mountain, a two-hour wait.

A sign says the wait for the venerable Pirates of the Caribbean ride is 20 minutes, so I queue up, taking deep breaths to quell my agoraphobic inclinations. As the line shuffles through switchbacks denoted by metal railings, I check out people exiting the ride. I notice some wringing out their T-shirts.

Soaked in nostalgia?

No, just soaked.

I try to make people think I'm part of the extended family ahead of me, lest I be branded as that most pathetic of outcasts—the solo NFG. I sort of glom on to them. But once we're inside and darkness descends, I back off a little. The toddler in her father's arms is scared and shaking, her face a rictus of fear, her eyes red-rimmed. The happy, smiling attendant filling the boats tries to keep families together. When she gets to me, she says, a tad patronizingly, "You by yourself? OK. Go to (row) number six."

The back of the boat for me.

From childhood, I remember Pirates of the Caribbean being scarier. But the animatronic pirates shooting at each other over the tour boats is just how I recall it. The tame, though still stomach-churning, dives we take in the boat come as a surprise, but that hologram of Jack Sparrow cackling out of the mists wasn't on the original ride, was it? I do remember, and unfortunately can't forget, the "Yo Ho" song in my head.

I retreat to the Jolly Holiday Bakery Café to regroup over a ridiculous $2.50 bottle of water and strike up a conversation with honeymooners Teresa and Chad Day, both 36, from Kent, Wash. I mention my slight disappointment with Pirates, and Chad nods. He's experiencing the downside of nostalgia, the feeling that not everything is as before.

"Little things have changed," he says. "The fireworks thing at night: They used to have a Tinkerbell that would come down at the end of the parade, on the zip line, you know? That was part of the attraction of fireworks. Not anymore."

But the couple is otherwise effusive with praise. There's no other place they'd rather spend their honeymoon. Disney functionaries have given them buttons advertising their "just-married" status and, says Teresa, "They are so attentive. From 20 feet away, they'll recognize that and make a fuss over us."

I probe, with the gravitas of a Megyn Kelly, "Do the buttons enable you to cut in line?"

Alas, no.

"The lines are about the same as when I was a kid, really long at Splash Mountain," Chad says. "You know, when I was little, I actually got to see the movie the ride is based on (*Song of the South*, 1946) in a movie theater. Kids don't know anything about the movie."

As Disney, apparently, would like it. You won't find *Song of the South* on sale in stores in Critter Country, or anywhere else. Seems the film was based on the old Uncle Remus stories—with the racially insensitive character Tar Baby—so it's not deemed suitable for today's audiences.

"Great ride, though," Chad says.

Here is just one of the indignities NFGs of a certain age must endure, a sign at the entrance to Splash Mountain (and other extreme rides):

WARNING!

For safety you should be in good health and free from high blood pressure, heart, back or neck problems, motion sickness or other conditions that could be aggravated by this adventure . . .

High blood pressure? Check.

Back problems? Check.

Motion sickness? Check.

Other conditions? Check and check.

Still, if these two kids in front of me can handle Splash Mountain, with its 52.5-foot drop on a 45-degree angle, then so can this NFG. Though I must admit, as we made our way to the six-seat logs that would hurtle us about, both the little girl, no older than 6, and I were visibly fretting. The girl's mother, directly in front of me, kept reassuring the girl that "you'll have fun," while her older brother, probably 9, made faces at her. Dad, up front, was oblivious.

Turns out, I share a log with the family. The smiley-faced attendant put me ("alone, sir?") in the back. As we ascend, the water rushing past us, the girl starts sobbing, the mom trying to distract her by bopping to the plucky banjo music.

Once we level off, the brother turns and says to the sobbing sister, "It's over. Good job," knowing full well what awaits. Mom, slightly shrill: "We're having fun!"

After several stomach-flipping descents, including the 52.5-foot plunge, the partially soaked but fully traumatized girl is inconsolable. Mom leans forward, rubs the girl's shoulders, says, "You did it, honey!" Brother: "No, we're not done."

More tears.

Even with a Fast Pass, the wait is long at the Indiana Jones Adventure Ride. To kill time in Adventureland, I wait in another line—for lunch. The Bengal Barbecue, specializing in kabobs, looks to be the most healthful option. I need protein to gird myself for Indiana Jones, so I opt for the $4.99 Chieftain Chicken Skewers, glazed with Polynesian sauce. What arrives a minute later are three tiny chicken cubes impaled on a stick, swimming in red syrup. It's a three-bite lunch.

Dinner, several hours later, is at the fancy Blue Bayou, reservations mandatory. I snag a table in the corner, though, sans reservation. Strangely, there are no other "parties of one." Shinar-Reed had raved about the ambiance of the Blue Bayou, and it's nice, truly it is, dimly lit, right on the water as the boats carrying Pirates of the Caribbean riders float by. I fear, however, that the riders will spy me all by my lonesome, tucking into a $40 salmon fillet the size of a Taco Bell taquito, and think, "Loser." I eat fast and leave.

Curmudgeonly NFG though I am, even I must admit that the Indiana Jones ride is . . . fun. The bladder-jangling jeep ride and special effects, culminating in the hologram of the giant stone rolling toward you, is worth the wait.

As I stagger off, I notice I'm not the only 50-plus rider. Jackson Wong, 63, and his wife, who wants nothing to do with a soaked, gaping guy like me, are longtime NFGs. They live in San Francisco—he's a retired engineer— and were in Orange County for a wedding.

"Every time we happen to be down here, we stop by," he says. "Nice place to hang out for a day."

Wong first came to Disneyland for his high school graduation decades ago, and I ask how the place has changed.

"That's one of the nice things about it—it doesn't," he says. "They refine it. They improve it. They add to it, but everything that's existing is the same."

Tracy Kalvin, age 39: "Kids? Oh, crap, honey. Where are the kids?"

Graham Handford, 28: "Oh, they'll come back—eventually."

This couple, from Vancouver, Canada, is easy to spot in Frontierland. They lurk at the Shootin' Exposition, having just blown away several animals (not real, of course) and loving every second of it, when yours truly notices Kalvin's elaborate tattoo sleeves and pegs the two as NFGs.

They only feign parenthood for a few seconds. This is Kalvin's first time at Disneyland (Handford came in fifth grade) and they seem happy not to be pushing a stroller.

Handford: "We plan to catch some rides, have a drink or two. That's my idea of a good day."

I inform them that Disneyland is a "dry" park—no adult libations, that is—and the two are crestfallen and slightly panicked. I tell them the alcohol is on the other side.

"What other side?" Kalvin asks. "You mean there's more?"

I fill them in on California Adventure, its wine-tasting room, its craft beer garden, the margaritas at the *Frozen* exhibits. Kalvin is stoked. A careening little boy with light-up shoes almost runs her down, and she smiles. I mention something about Disneyland being a form of birth control, and she shakes her head.

"After being here, I want kids now," she says. "Well, not right now. But it looks like it'd be way more fun with kids."

When making the crossover to California Adventure, I expect a higher ratio of NFGs. Wrong. Kids gravitate toward the *Frozen* attractions in Hollywood Land and rides at Cars Land. Never underestimate the power of movies as an indoctrinating medium.

To gain entrance to a late-afternoon *Frozen* sing-along, I had to hustle over in the morning for a Fast Pass. Just before curtain, I am the only adult waiting in the lobby without a child in tow. This is awkward. I even creep myself out. For the first time in forever, I consider a profession where I just sit at a desk crunching numbers, a job with no human interaction. But I am not allowed to leave the theater early, though I'm scanning the exits and avoiding eye contact with pursed-lips moms no doubt trying to memorize my facial features to later give to the police sketch artist.

Confession: I have never seen *Frozen*. But the movie excerpts prove entertaining, as does the tyke three rows up who stands and acts out every scene in which Queen Elsa appears, her mom positively beaming.

Afterward, I need a drink.

But no alcohol. I'm working, after all, and it just doesn't seem right to get buzzed at Disneyland, or California Adventure. It is jarring to see adults walking around with cups of beer and fluted plastic wine glasses.

California Adventure has my drug of choice in the form of a Starbucks. Once revived, I have no trouble tracking down NFGs. One obvious place is the bar, formally known as the Carthay Circle Lounge, next to the white-tablecloth Carthay Circle Restaurant (in a reproduction of the theater where *Snow White and the Seven Dwarfs* premiered in 1937).

There, I find three 20-something friends, Rebecca Talsky, Dhae Jones and Britney Hewitt, enjoying cocktails. Jones says she's there for the rides, but Hewitt is bluntly honest. "If there's lines for rides, I just like to drink," she says. "That sounds bad, but it's true."

Newlyweds Antony Lowbridge-Ellis and David Lowbridge-Ellis, both 32, of Birmingham, England, have just finished a wine tasting and are feeling quite happy in "The Happiest Place on Earth." The two have visited all the Disney theme parks in Europe and North America and, Antony says, will hit Asia next. They make no apologies for being adults having Disney fun.

"Some of our friends think it's all a 'It's a small world' kind of twee thing, but, actually it's great," David says. "I'm a cynical person, but I find my cynicism evaporates as soon as I walk in through the gates."

I, too, feel my skepticism drying up like the vast Mojave.

I, too, regain that childlike sense of wonder I thought had been snuffed out decades ago by my mannered, pretentious California smugness.

In an epiphanic flash as vivid as the Main Street Electrical Parade, it strikes me: Right here on Disneyland's Main Street, U.S.A., this exact spot is the elusive center of California I had sought for five years while driving the state's interstate freeway system, bucolic backroads and steel-belted-radial-busting gravel roads.

I waited for someone to embrace me and say, "Welcome home." But people just whizzed on by, a stroller wheel rolling over my foot only adding to the indignity, and a resting-bitch-face mom in a ball cap shooting me a wary look when I yelped in pain.

Yeah, this is the California I know and love.

Acknowledgements

I'd like to thank my family—Beth, Casey, Cormac and Maggie—for understanding why I needed to spend so much time driving around California for a living. Thanks to Kent Sorsky and Craven Street Books for their support. Thanks, too, to my *Sacramento Bee* editors for their guidance—especially Tamma Adamek, Janet Vitt, Tim Swanson, Scott Lebar. Kathy Morrison, Rita Blomster, Reed Parsell, Tom Sellers ,and Ken Campbell. I'd also like to thank all the subjects profiled in this book for opening their homes, businesses, roadside attractions and personal lives to my sometimes intrusive questions. I'd also be remiss not to thank the Starbucks off Highway 99 in Turlock and the Starbucks off Interstate 5 near Santa Nella for keeping me caffeinated and awake as I made way-too-many north-south trips across the spine of the state.

Index

About the Author

SAM MCMANIS is a former columnist and feature writer for the *Sacramento Bee*. He is a four-time winner of the Society of Features Journalism awards and three-time Best of the West honoree. He also has been a staff writer and editor at the *San Francisco Chronicle* and a sportswriter for the *Los Angeles Times*. His profiles and essays have appeared in the *New York Times*, *Wall Street Journal* and elsewhere. He lives and writes in Washington state.

CPSIA information can be obtained
at www.ICGtesting.com
Printed in the USA
FSOW02n1228110118
43030FS